A Grammar and Dictionary of the Timucua Language

A Grammar and Dictionary *of the* Timucua Language

Third Edition

Julian Granberry

The University of Alabama Press

Tuscaloosa

To the memory
of
Fr. Francisco Pareja,
John R. Swanton
and
the now-vanished Timucua people

The University of Alabama Press
Tuscaloosa, Alabama 35487–0380

Manufactured in the United States of America

∞

The paper on which this book is printed meets the minimum requirements of American Standard for Information Science-Permanence of Paper for Printed Library Materials, ANSI Z39.48-1984.

Library of Congress Cataloging-in-Publication Data

Granberry Julian.
A grammar and dictionary of the Timucua language / Julian Granberry. —
3rd ed.
p. cm.
Includes bibliographical references.
ISBN 0-8173-0704-4 (alk. paper)
1. Timucua language—Dictionaries—English. 2. English language—
Dictionaries—Timucua. 3. Timucua language—Grammar. I. Title.
PM2451.Z5G73 1993
497'.5—dc20

British Library Cataloguing-in-Publication Data available

CONTENTS

TABLES

FIGURES

PREFACE

Third Edition

In 1929 the late John R. Swanton of the Smithsonian Institution's Bureau of American Ethnology began work on a lexicon of the Timucua language of Florida (*47th Annual Report of the Bureau of American Ethnology* 1932:2). During that year and in 1930, with the help of Miss Mae W. Tucker of the Bureau, Swanton worked through five of the primary sources of Frs. Francisco Pareja and Gregorio de Movilla, the two major researchers of the language in the early 1600's, to produce a vocabulary master-file and separate Timucua-English and English-Timucua indexes. These are now housed as part of the National Anthropological Archives at the Smithsonian (NAA Cat. Nos. 2446-b and 2446-d respectively).

For reasons all too familiar to anyone in research Swanton was unable to complete this monumental task, and when my 1956 paper 'Timucua I: Prosodics and Phonemics of the Mocama Dialect' appeared in the *International Journal of American Linguistics* (vol. 22, no. 2:97-105) he wrote me asking if I would be interested in completing his Timucua work. I of course responded positively to this unusually generous offer, particularly inasmuch as I had begun the same task independently in 1952. Through the assistance of Matthew W. Stirling, then Chief of the Bureau, Swanton's photocopies of the original texts (NAA MS's 2401A-E), his notes (NAA Cat. Nos. 2446-c, 2446-g), translations of the original sources (NAA Cat.

No. 2446-e), and the above-mentioned card files, were shipped to me (November 20, 1956) at the Laboratory of Anthropology at the University of Florida, where I then worked.

From late 1956 through 1967, at the University of Florida and later at the Central Florida Museum in Orlando and the Department of Anthropology at Florida Atlantic University in Boca Raton, I worked as time permitted at checking each of the entries listed by Swanton and Miss Tucker against the original sources, updating the files where necessary and correcting, in my own copy only, the small number of errors which had crept into the original files. I also added lexical data from Pareja's two other volumes in Timucua.

From 1967 through early 1970, with the aid of a modest but very helpful grant from the Penrose Fund (No. 4633) of the American Philosophical Society, the final files were completed and work was begun on the dictionary itself.

My initial reason in 1952 for wanting to compile a dictionary of Timucua was that such an organized listing of lexical forms would be of considerable help in clarifying both the genetic affiliations of the language and, through an examination of borrowings, the movements of the Timucua peoples from some putative non-Floridian homeland to the Georgia-Florida region they occupied at the time of European discovery. I was well aware that quite a variety of opinion existed on this topic, and it seemed reasonable to suggest that nothing approaching a final statement could be made until the lexical and grammatical content of the language had been described in some detail.

In the early stages of the work I was not fully aware of the extreme complexity of the matter. As the dictionary began to take shape in 1970-71, however, it soon became apparent that any such document would be little more than a lexical list. Comparative work, form-by-form, was called for to turn a Timucua-English vocabulary into something approaching the dictionary both Swanton and I had in mind.

In the same manner that the dictionary will need constant updating, the grammatical sketch included in this work is not intended as exhaustive. It is not *the* grammar of Timucua. There are many points which need more investigation than I have given them here. The most important is a complete examination of all textually attested verbal structures — a thorough classification of Timucua verbs from the point of view of their morphemic, lexemic, syntactic, semological, and semantic characteristics. This is urgently called for. I have not yet completed that classification. A precise examination of the stylistic variants of syntax and semology is also lacking. Without this fine-toothed view of the attested data it will be impossible to say precisely why one morpheme variant rather than another occurs in the same semological slot. While there is no universal 'rule' negating the possibility of exact morphemic synonymity, literal free-variation is always suspect. These problems must ultimately be elucidated through careful examination of the texts and must, regrettably, wait for other papers and, likely, other investigators.

The grammatical coverage, in other words, represents *a* grammar of Timucua, and that from a particular theoretical/methodological viewpoint. My view of language and languages represents a personal blending of George L. Trager's and Henry Lee Smith, Jr.'s *aspectual analysis* (Trager 1963, Smith 1967), Sydney Lamb's *stratificational analysis* (Lamb 1966), and the significant insights into things-linguistic of Charles F. Hockett (cf. especially Hockett 1947, 1958, 1961). The premises of this analytical frame are *strictly* empirical — that is, they insist that only quantifiable data be used in describing language phenomena. In such theory and method one *must*, therefore, begin the examination of language with phonological data, even if this is seen, as in the case of Timucua, solely in orthographic representation. The top-down, 'semantic net' methods so popular and appealing to many today, are not acceptable in this frame, for they allow the investigator to inject as many personal, unique — and therefore non-empirical — premises into his description as he wishes. The framework of my analysis necessitates the derivation of morphological, semological, semantic descriptions and their tactical statements from phonological description. I am fully aware that this framework is considered dated by some, but I find it the sole repository of what remains of empirical method in linguistics today. I do not have reason to espouse the currently popular, naïve evolutionary assumption that the present is 'better' than the past, that current theories are somehow, *a priori*, more 'intelligent' than those of the past, or that 'progress' flows from some dense ill-formed past through a bright and organized present toward an enlightened, 'correct' future. I consequently make no apologies for my hard-bitten Missouri Show-Me empirical stance. Experience tells me that empiricism is both technically more elegant and pragmatically more valuable than the current universalist trends. My readers, of course, have the right to disagree.

Some readers also seem to find my terminology forbidding, convoluted, or naïve. The objections lie largely in the realm of verbal suffix labels and the fact that I have not placed them in a 'time-line' matrix, indicating more clearly how the Timucua 'divided the flow of time'. Since there is no Timucua 'time-line', and time does not 'flow' in Timucua, I can only point out that the terminology used reflects *Timucua* grammatical categories and has come after many years of painstaking examination of the data. Optional terms are in some cases of course possible. My personal feeling is that the present terminology is adequate for the purpose, for it assumes no grandiose world-scheme of minute (and therefore culture-bound) language 'universals' nor categories that 'must' be there. It accounts solely for the quantifiable data in terms of itself, and that in as parsimonious a manner as possible. Where traditional grammatical terms do not clarify a category adequately, I have not hesitated to coin a new term in ordinary, common English, always carefully defined for the reader. While this may let one see only half a 'real' Timucua fleetingly and through shadows, I would personally rather see that than a full, crisp image of my own invention, constricted by Standard Average European grammatical conventions.

Timucua archaeological data in the first and second editions of the present volume were drawn largely from the published materials available in the early to mid-1980's, mirroring primarily the seminal work of John M. Goggin and the contemporaneous and later work of David S. Brose, Adelaide and Ripley P. Bullen, Dave D. Davis, Kathleen A. Deagan, Charles A. Fairbanks, James A. Ford, John W. Griffin, Jerald T. Milanich, William H. Sears, and Gordon R. Willey. Having completed the bulk of my graduate level archaeological training through work on Central and North Florida Timucua-area sites under the guidance of John Goggin in the 1950's, I felt competent to handle the data from that time, revising it as a result of the later work of Brose, Bullen, Davis, Deagan, Fairbanks, Ford, Griffin, Milanich, and Sears in the succeeding two decades. Since the early 1980's, however — most particularly during the past four to five years — an increasing number of well-trained younger archaeologists, in most cases students of the above, have interested themselves in the archaeology of the North and North-Central Florida regions. Some genuinely significant work has appeared as a result of their efforts.

I have consequently revised the *Archaeological Correlates* section of Chapter 1 to take much of this new data into consideration. By and large, however, I find that such new information does not alter my hypothesis that the Timucua language, culture, and people were intrusive to Florida, and that all three represented not the massive 'invasion' of a new, replacing people to the peninsula, but, rather, a slow and gradual hybridization of the indigenous non-Timucuan peoples and lifeways with the blood-lines and lifeways of small numbers of non-native intruders who eventually became culturally dominant. Such a creolization process clearly ocurred earliest and with greatest impact in the St. Johns River Valley and on the Alachua Prairies, to judge from both archaeological and ethnohistoric data, and those regions became the heartland of Timucua settlement.

The steady, incontestible cultural continuity from at least Archaic times on into historic times in the Timucua area as clearly lets us know that the newcomers were few in number, at least at the the start, and that their new customs, artifactual conventions, and language only gradually became the norm — in much the same way, it seems to me, that Indo-European customs, language, and artifacts introduced by minority Aryan intruders, eventually became the norm in Europe in the 3rd and 2nd millenia B.C.

The distribution of such widely spread anomalous Southeastern archaeological traits as ceramic wares — specifically fiber-tempered wares — in otherwise variant cultural matrices throughout the region, points, I think, toward the few-in-number newcomers not as invaders and conquerors but, rather, more likely as riverine traders, in keeping with the traditions of their putative Amazonian-Colombian homeland. There, as the *Mindala*, they fulfilled the same function. In spite of the arrival and presence of the Timucua, we still see an essentially Muskogean Southeast in the centuries from the late Archaic through Spanish Colonial times. The Timucua-Muskogean commonalities are not difficult to explain; it is the Timucua anomalies which need further elucidation — from whence did they come and how (and why) did they intertwine in various degrees with the numerous segments of the Muskogean world to which they were introduced. Only considerably more controlled excavation and comparison of archaeological complexes and traditions will clarify the Timucua-Muskogean relationship and, eventually, verify or refute the elements of my hypothesis of Timucua origins and spread. Current archaeological work in the Timucua area by younger archaeologists such as Glen Doran, John H. Hann, Kenneth W. Johnson, Rochelle Marrinan, Michael Russo, Rebecca Saunders, John F. Scarry, Richard H. Vernon, Brent R. Weisman, John E. Worth and many others, may ultimately further define this still obscure picture. For the moment, the data they have added and the comparisons they have drawn simply add more flesh to the picture and render the hypothesis I am presenting both more convincing and provocative.

Through the long period during which the present analysis was being prepared I have owed much to a small group of colleagues, most importantly, of course, to John R. Swanton during the last few years of his life. The volume is certainly as much his as mine, though I do not know what his reaction would have been to my treatment of the data. My most constant help and encouragement came from the late John M. Goggin, the late Clifford Evans, his wife Betty Meggers, William H. Sears, Mary R. Haas, and, in recent years, Mary Ritchie Key. All afforded various kinds of help over periods in some cases of many, many years. All have been good friends and colleagues, and I doubt that the task would have been completed without their genuine and constant encouragement.

I would also like to acknowledge the interest of Mr. Dudley Griner of Tallahassee and Cross City, the Hon. Everett Kelley of Tavares and Tallahassee (State of Florida House of Representatives), the Hon. Marian Lewis of North Palm Beach and Tallahassee (State of Florida House of Representatives), and of Mr. Elling Eide of Sarasota, all providers of greatly appreciated support in the later years of my work on this volume. Mr. Eide in particular gently prodded me more than most to get the writing to completion. His continuing interest and a grant through him from the Castro Foundation of Ocala, Florida, to help offset publication costs of the first edition are both tremendously appreciated.

Sixty-some years after its inception Swanton's Timucua dictionary is at last something of a reality. It will need continual improvement, but it is hoped that it will serve in its present state both as the data-source and ethnographic research tool Dr. Swanton envisioned as well as a tool in comparative linguistics, a dimension I felt should be added. I am at least *sure* that my 'South American Connection' will be a bone of contention to both linguist and archaeologist for many years to come. I hope, in any case, that this will be so, for it will only be through much more archaeological and linguistic work — field, laboratory, and comparative — that my hypothesis concerning the nature, origins and spread of the Timucua language, people, and culture will be corroborated, refined, or, perhaps, replaced.

The first edition of the volume was issued in November 1987 and a second, corrected, edition in September 1989. The University of Alabama Press has kindly made it possible to issue this third edition, and I would like to express my thanks to

PREFACE

Malcolm MacDonald, Director, and, particularly, to Judith Knight, Editor, for their many kindnesses and support. Dr. T. Dale Nicklas of Kansas City generously acted as a critical reader on the linguistic aspects of my work for the Press and provided helpful suggestions, comments, and assistance with Muskogean linguistic forms. I am in equal debt to the Press's anonymous archaeology reader, whose perceptive and constructive remarks were also much to the point. I have also received a number of helpful suggestions and citations of misprints and errors from other users of the volume. So far as I have been able, I have cleared up all of these points in the present edition.

Julian Granberry
Horseshoe Beach, Florida
November 1992

USER'S GUIDE

THE SOURCES

While there are only nine surviving primary sources in the Timucua language, all early 17th century, seven are of considerable length. They give us more than adequate documentation on which to base grammatical and lexical statements. Without these sources, in fact, we would be in total ignorance of the nature of the Timucua language. Some of these sources have considerable ethnographic value (see Milanich and Sturtevant 1972). Other occurrences of single lexical items in contemporary Spanish, French, and English sources are of only limited, largely phonological value. While Florida was known to the Spanish from the very early 1500's, it was not until Juan Ponce de León's first voyage in 1513 that the area and its inhabitants began to attract notice. Even then it was not until Hernando de Soto's epochal expedition of May 1539 - September 1543 that intimate contact was made with any of the Timucua-speaking peoples. We have some helpful ethnographic information in the interesting narrative of the de Soto expedition left by the Gentleman of Elvas (Robertson 1933), but we have to wait until the arrival of Jean Ribault and the French in 1562 and his successor René de Laudonnière in 1564 before we have any substantive ethnographic data (Lorant 1946), supplemented by the famous drawings of Jacques Le Moyne, the artist who accompanied the expedition (Lorant 1946, Le Moyne 1875).

The bulk of our information on all the native peoples of

Florida and their languages stems from the work of priests of the Jesuit and Franciscan Orders (see Zubillaga 1941, 1946; Geiger 1937, 1940). Most important of these beyond question was Fr. Francisco Pareja, a Franciscan missionary, who arrived in St. Augustine in 1595 to begin service among the Timucua, a position he filled with distinction for thirty-one years (Archivo General de Indias, *Petition to the Spanish Crown, September 1, 1621* [Legajo 53, Estante 2, Cajón 11]). For most of this time he was stationed at the mission of San Juan del Puerto, founded in 1587 on Ft. George Island, near the mouth of the St. Johns River. Sometime after 1626 he left Florida for Mexico, where, we are relatively certain, he died on June 25, 1628 (Smith 1858).

This highly intelligent, literate, and compassionate man quickly became the leading, and for a time only, scholar of the Timucua language. He wrote four catechisms in parallel Timucua-Spanish (Pareja 1612*a*, 1612*b*, 1613, 1627) and an extremely well-done, though-be-it Latin Model, grammar (Pareja 1614, reprinted as Adam and Vinson 1886). There is also mention of two other texts and a *Vocabulario* (Pareja 1613: 1ff), but they were either never published, have not survived, or have so far escaped discovery. Pareja's five extant works constitute over 2,000 pages of Timucua text.

There are two additional catechisms in parallel Timucua-Spanish by Fr. Gregorio de Movilla, another Franciscan missionary in the Floridian religious province of Santa Elena (Movilla 1635*a*, 1635*b*).

The final two known Timucua documents are letters from Timucua leaders to the Spanish Crown. One, dated 1688, has been published (Smith 1860*a*, Gatschet 1880, Vinson 1883). It comes from Potano province. The other, dated 9 December 1651, has not been published (Archivo General de Indias, Escribanía de Cámara, Legajo 155, folios 380-383). It occurs with a Spanish translation signed by Fr. Alonso Escudero, and a copy is in the National Anthropological Archives as NAA Cat. No. 2446-f. This letter was written by Manuel, chief of the Yustaga mission town of San Miguel de Asile, and we know that its translator, Fr. Escudero, was associated with the Yustaga mission of Santa Cruz de Tari(hica). Since the Potano dialect was spoken in Potano, Yustaga, and Ocale provinces, one may say with a high degree of reliability that both letters were written in the Potano dialect. The internal linguistic evidence of the two letters would substaniate this assumption. All other original sources are in the Mocama dialect.

It is quite probable that additional unnoticed petitions and documents in Timucua survive in the Archivo General de Indias in Seville and in Spain's many other public and ducal archives. The nine extant sources make Timucua one of the best-attested extinct native American languages. It is from this invaluable data that the present description of Timucua comes. The five extant works of Fr. Pareja are:

> 1. *Cathecismo, en Lengua Castellana, y Timuquana.* En el qual se contiene lo que se les puede enseñar a los adultos que an de ser baptizados. Compvesto por el P.F. Francisco Pareja, religioso de la Orden del seraphico P.S. Francisco, Guardian del conuento de la purissima Cōcepcion de N. Señora de S. Augustin, y Padre de la Custodia de sancta Elena de la Florida. En Mexico. En la Imprēta de la Viuda de Pedro Balli. Por C. Adriano Cesar. M.DC.XII.

This volume, in photostat form, is NAA MS. 2401C. This copy was made from the only known extant original, at the New York Historical Society, donated by Buckingham Smith in the late 1880's.

> 2. *Catechismo y Breve Exposicion de la Doctrina Christiana,* Muy vtil y necessaria, asi para los Españoles, como para los Naturales, en Lengua Castellana, y Timuquana en modo de preguntas, y respuestas. Cōpuesto por el P.F. Francisco Pareja de la Orden de N. Seraphico P.S. Frāncisco, Padre de la Custodia de S. Elena de la Florida. Con Licencia de los Svperiores, en Mexico, en casa de la viuda de Pedro Balli. Año de 1612. Por C.A. Cesar.

This volume, also in photostat form, is NAA MS. 2401A. The sole known original, bound with the first volume described above, is the property of the New York Historical Society, a gift from

Buckingham Smith.

3. *Confessionario en Lengua Castellana, Y Timuquana con Algunos Consejos para Animar al Penitente.* Y assi mismo van declarados algunos effectos y prerrogariuas [*sic*] deste sancto sacramento de la Confession. Todo muy vtil y prouechoso, assi para que los padres confessores sepan instruyr al penitente como para que ellos aprendan à saberse confessar. Ordenado por el Padre Fr. Francisco Pareja, Padre de la Custodia de santa Elena de la Florida. Religioso de la Orden de nuestro Seraphico Padre San Francisco, Impresso con licencia en Mexico, en la Emprenta de la Viuda de Diego Lopez Daualos. Año de 1613.

This volume, in photostat form, is NAA MS. 2401B. The original, also a gift of Buckingham Smith, is at the New York Historical Society.

4. *Arte y Pronunciacion de la Lengua Timvquana, y Castellana,* Compvesto y de nuevo sacado à luz, por el Padre Fray Francisco Pareja, Diffinidor, y Padre perpetuo de la Prouincia de Santa Elena de la Florida, Religioso de la Orden de nuestro Seraphico Padre S. Francisco: y natural de la Villa de Auñon, del Arçobispado de Toledo. Impresso Con licencia en Mexico. En la Emprenta de Ioan Ruyz. Año de 1614.

This volume has been published by Lucien Adam and Julien Vinson as t. 11 in the series *Bibliothèque Linguistique Américaine* (Paris, 1886). The editors used the only known original, at that time in the possession of José Fernando Ramírez.

5. *Cathecismo, y Examen para los que Comvlgan en Lengua Castellana, y Timuquana.* En el qual se cõtiene el respecto que se deue tener à los templos, con algunos Similes del santissimo Sacramento, y sus effectos; y la preparaciõ para la cõmunion actual y espiritual; y para quãdo se dà à los enfermos. Las gracias que despues de la cõmunion se deuen dar à Dios, que se recibe en ella. Y algunos milagros deste santissimo Sacramento. Y dischos de Santos, y de personas doctas, que aconsejan y exortan à su frequencia. Aora en Esta II. Impression Corregido, y enmedado, y algo necessario añadido Por el Padre Fr. Francisco Pareja, Religioso de la Orden de N. Seraphico P.S. Francisco, y Padre de la Provincia

de Santa Elena de la Florida, Natural de Auñon, Diocesi del Arçobispado de Toledo. Con Privilegio En Mexico, en la Imprenta de Iuan Ruyz. Año de 1627.

An original of this volume, purchased in 1846 from Asher's, is in the Department of Printed Books, the British Museum, London (No. 3505.d.f30). A microfilm of this volume was used for the present analysis.

In addition to the surviving works of Fr. Pareja, the two works of Fr. Gregorio de Movilla were also used in the preparation of this volume. Fr. de Movilla's works are:

1. *Forma Breve de Administrar los Sacramentos a los Indios, y Españoles que Viuen entre Ellos*. Approbado por Avtoridad Apostolica, y sacado del Manual Mexicano, que se vsa en toda la nueua España y Pirù, mutandis, esto es, lo q̄ estaua en lēgua Mexicana traducido en lengua Floridana. Para vso de los Religiosos de nro Padre S. Francisco, que son los ministros de las Prouincias de la Florida. Por el Padre Fr. Gregorio de Mouilla. Con licencia del señor Don Lope Altamirano Comissario general de la santa Cruzada. Impresso en Mexico. Por Iuan Ruyz. Año de 1635.

This volume, in photostat form, is NAA MS. 2401E, from the original in the New York Historical Society Library.

2. *Explicacion de la Doctrina qve Compvso el Cardenal Belarmino, por Mandad del Señor Papa Clemente 8*. Tradvcida en Lengva Floridana: por el Padre Fr. Gregorio de Mouilla, Diffinidor de la Prouincia de santa Elena, de la Orden de S. Francisco, natural de la Villa de Carrion de los Condes, hijo de la Prouincia de la Concepcion, y del Conuento recolecto de nra Señora de Calahorra. Corregida, enmendada y añadida en esta segunda impression, por el mesmo Autor. En Mexico. Impressa con Licencia en la Imprenta de Iuan Ruyz. Año de 1635.

This volume, also in photostat form, is NAA MS. 2401D and comes from the original at the New York Historical Society, bound together with the Movilla work listed above as No. 1.

USER'S GUIDE

Including the present volume, there are 28 secondary sources on Timucua as of January 1993: Adam and Vinson 1886; Crawford 1979; Gatschet 1877*a*, 1877*b*, 1878, 1880, 1881, n.d.; Gatschet and Grasserie 1889; Granberry 1956, 1971, 1987, 1989, 1990, 1991, 1993 (this volume); Grasserie 1888*a*, 1888*b*, 1889, 1892; Noble 1965*b*; Smith 1858, 1860*a*, 1860*b*, 1860*c*; Swanton 1929, n.d.; Vinson 1883.

The often used and oft-quoted studies of Gatschet, which represent considerable scholarly effort and worth, should be used with some caution for purposes of grammatical analysis, for Gatschet has normalized the orthography of many of his textual quotations without so indicating. This should not be viewed as poor scholarship or less than candid treatment of the data. Normalization was, during the mid-to-late 1800's, a frequent and usual method of handling the somewhat irregular orthographies of no longer extant exotic languages, particularly those of the Americas. Adam and Vinson do precisely the same in the introduction to their reprint of Pareja's *Arte* (Adam and Vinson 1886:i-xxxi, particularly xxi-xxvii).

TREATMENT OF THE SOURCES

Swanton's card files for the two Movilla volumes, the two Timucua letters, and the first three Pareja volumes listed above formed a single alphabetical arrangement of the Timucua words from those sources. Each entry included the word itself and a notation of its occurrences in the sources by folio or page number. This constituted the NAA 2446-b file. I made a photocopy of this file and added the vocabulary of the last two Pareja volumes given above to my own copy of the file. As indicated above, Swanton and Miss Tucker also prepared separate alphabetical card files for Timucua-English and English-Timucua lexicons (NAA 2446-d). These files did not include source folio/pages for any of the items. Again, I added items from the two additional Pareja volumes to my own copy of these files. All entries in both 2446-b and 2446-d were then checked against each other as well as against the original sources.

In the final Timucua-English and English-Timucua lists original source spellings were rigorously kept, even if they seemed only to mirror the rather randomly applied spelling conventions of 16th and 17th century Spanish — the use of *v* for *u* or *j* for *i*, for instance.

It was to the data thus derived that the procedures discussed in the following sections were applied.

CANONICAL FORMS AND PHONEMICIZATION

The canonical form of each entry in the dictionary section of the volume represents a standardized spelling. It is canonical in the sense that it represents the statistically most frequent spelling in the primary sources. It is based on all attestations of the form in those sources and takes into consideration both the phonological and morphological norms of the language. Aberrant spellings, if they can be called that, are also listed for most forms, or recurrent aberrant spelling conventions are described at the beginning of each letter section of the dictionary. Cross-references from such spellings to the canonical form are made.

In the dictionary canonical forms for all entries are given in bold-face. In the phonemicization non-root morphemes in an entry are separated from the root form and from each other by hyphens. In instances in which vowel alteration takes place, described in detail under *Phonological Processes* in the grammar section of the volume, the specific alteration type is indicated by number/letter in parentheses immediately after the entry form.

Each entry is also given in what has here been called a phonemicization. It should be realized that these reconstituted sound units cannot be called 'phonemes' in the strict sense of that term, for they are reconstructions. It is helpful that Pareja, however, discusses the differences between Timucua and Spanish sounds at some length (Adam and Vinson 1886:2-8). It is largely this discussion which makes it possible to suggest putative phonemicizations of the orthogaphic representations in the original sources. Additional spellings of isolated items in other Spanish, French, and English sources have occasionally helped in making such reconstructions. For a fuller discussion of the problems attendant upon such reconstitution of extinct phonemic systems consult Broadbent (1957).

The following table indicates the relationship between such reconstituted phonemic units, source spellings, and the canonical spelling used throughout this volume.

TABLE 1

ORTHOGRAPHY & RECONSTITUTED PHONEMES

*PHONEME	SOURCE	CANONICAL
/a/	a	*a*
/e/	e	*e*
/i/	i, y + consonant,*i*	
	j + consonant	*f*
/o/	o	*o*
/u/	u, v + consonant*u*	
/p/	p	*p*
/t/: [t] ~ [d]	t, (n)d ~ (n)t	*t*
/k/	c (a, o, u);	*c (a, o, u)*
	q (e,i)	*q (e, i)*
/k^{w}/	qu, cu	*qu*
/č/	ch	*ch*
/f/ (= [φ] ?)	f, h + vowel, b	*f*
/b/ (= [β] ?)	b, bu, g (a, o, u),*b* gu (a, o, u), (h)u + vowel, v + vowel, vowel + u + vowel	
/s/	s, c (e, i), ç	*s*
/h/	h, j, g (e, i)	*h*
/m/	m	*m*
/n/	n	*n*

/l/	l (never doubled)	*l*
/r/	r (never doubled)	*r*
/y/	y, vowel + i + vowel	*y*

There are a few Spanish loans which use /*g*/, as orthographic <*g*>, before *a* or *u* (<*gato*> = 'cat', for example), but this phoneme does not occur in native Timucua forms. The only voiced allophone of a stop is [*d*] of /*t*/ after /*n*/, clearly described by Pareja (Adam and Vinson 1886:3); it is occasionally spelled with an orthographic <*d*>.

Because the phonemes of Timucua are, and must always remain, unattested, conjectural phonological units, Timucua forms in this volume are written in italicized canonical orthography. This has been done both to keep the reader constantly reminded that he is *not* dealing with a genuine phonemic notation and to provide an orthography essentially identical with Pareja's source spellings. In instances in which a particular aberrant source spelling is cited it will be given in orthographic braces < > along with the italicized canonical spelling. In instances in which a phonemic reconstitution may offer problems or alternate solutions, the reconstituted form is enclosed in phonemic slant-lines / /. The reconstituted phonemic orthography, it may be noted, differs only minimally from the source and canonical orthographies: <*ca, o, u*> = /*ka, o, u*/, <*qe, i*> = /*ke, i*/, <*qu*> = /k^w/, <*ch*> = /*č*/.

It should be pointed out that Pareja's and Movilla's works show numerous examples of typographical errors, attributable, I would think, to the fact that the Mexican type-setters were dealing with a language totally unfamiliar to them and were, of course, setting type from handwritten manuscript. Similar problems still occur today in the few Timucua text republications (*cf*. Milanich and Sturtevant 1972:49 (folio 124, Line 3), where <*chulufi*> — 'bird' — in the original is misprinted as <*chulusi*>). In most instances these problems can be readily resolved by one familiar with the language and the texts.

A more serious problem is the orthographic representation

of polymorphemic lexemes, usually verbal forms. Pareja's writing of Future and Potential forms, for example, gives the main verb and following auxiliary verb as a single graphic unit, implying normal phonological transition between the two verb forms and, consequently, mono-lexemic status (Adam and Vinson 1886:66*ff*, 86*ff*) for the total form. There are, however, textual examples of such structures in which the auxiliary verb is written with orthographic space between it and the preceding main verb. The same orthographic ambivalence occurs with verbal suffix strings attached to a main verb — they are normally written as an orthographic unit, implying mono-lexemic status, but such forms occasionally occur with some suffixes separated from the main verb by orthographic space. The suffixes involved and their place of graphic separation seem quite random and arbitrary. I have handled all such problems in this volume from the point of view of Pareja's *Arte* (Adam and Vinson 1886), where separation rarely occurs, with the full realization that a careful study of the texts is called for before a definitive statement can be made — mono-lexemic or polylexemic. It may, in fact be an unresolvable problem, since we have so little to go on in reconstructing phonological transitions, crucial to all matters lexemic and syntactic in any language.

ENTRY OF FORMS

Entries in the dictionary are in alphabetical order and are given for all spellings in the original sources, both canonical and aberrant. Reconstituted phonemicizations are not, however, listed as main entries.

Full definition of a form is given only under the canonical spelling, with cross-references from statistically less frequent spellings. Such cross-references contain only two parts: the entry itself in ordinary print followed by a 'see' statement and the canonical form in bold-face. Canonical spelling entries take the following form:

word (Alteration Type) [Other spellings] (phonemicization) *part of speech* 1. Main source meaning. 2. Second source meaning, etc. A. IDIOMATIC FORMS: Usage. B. DERIVED FORMS: Usage. [Comparative forms in other languages]

Needless to say, not all spaces are necessarily filled for all entries.

The meanings of forms are, as nearly as possible, given in decreasing order of their frequency in the original sources, realizing of course that those sources are of a blatantly proselytizing nature, even for the 17th century, and that normal frequencies are therefore undoubtedly skewed to a certain extent. This failing is somewhat mitigated by Pareja's overt statement in the *Arte* that when he lists more than one form for a given meaning he first gives *los mas politicos,* the others being *como serranos* (Adam and Vinson 1886:8). We can be fairly sure that the forms Pareja uses are 'proper' Timucua of the Mocama dialect, with which he was most conversant and which was the dominant dialect of the language in Eastern Timucua territory.

The English-Timucua index should be viewed solely as a finder-list — Timucua forms are simply listed in decreasing order of frequency where possible, otherwise alphabetically, in their canonical forms. To obtain additional information the user must consult the Timucua-English dictionary section of the volume itself. I do not apologize for the presence of such words as 'flagellation' and 'choir' and the absence of more everyday words such as 'frog' The choice was a given from the sources and represents neither a free nor a complete vocabulary selection. While regrettable, the resulting Timucua lexicon is sizable enough to be of considerable value from any point of view.

Non-Timucua language forms cited in the grammar and dictionary sections of the volume have been given at the end of the volume. Two lists of such forms are given — one in strictly alphabetical order, regardless of the language of origin, a second in which the non-Timucua forms are arranged alphabetically by their individual language of origin, both native American as well as European.

As pointed out earlier, it is likely that the present

dictionary does not contain all attested Timucua lexemes. There may well be additional forms in documents from the Archivo de Indias and other sources which have been overlooked. Future researchers will, it is hoped, add such additional forms as they find them. It is also possible that the meanings assigned to specific forms will have to be revised as researchers working with the original sources view the contexts of individual forms.

Lastly, it should be pointed out that while the arrangement of the entries in the first and second editions of the dictionary included all meanings, no matter how variant, for a single morpheme or lexeme under one entry, many users have suggested that it would be easier to use the listings if, as in most modern language dictionaries, distinctly separate semological/semantic functions of a single phonological form were placed in separate entries — otherwise it smacked to some of including 'meet' with meat' or 'to' with 'two' with 'too'. That is, Timucua, like most human languages, had what are traditionally called homophonous morphemes and lexemes, forms with identical phonological shape but different, unrelated morphemic, syntactic, and/or semological and semantic function. I have accordingly separated such single entries into multiple entries in the present edition.

1 THE TIMUCUA LANGUAGE

1 THE TIMUCUA LANGUAGE

LOCATION & BRIEF HISTORY

The Timucua language was spoken from an indeterminate position on the Georgia coast — at least as far north as the Altamaha River — south through north and central Florida to the Daytona Beach region. Southeastern Georgia as far inland as the Okefenokee Swamp, all of interior north Florida from the Aucilla River in the west to the Atlantic in the east, and all of central Florida from the Withlacoochee River east to Cape Canaveral was Timucua territory (Granberry 1987:15-19, Deagan 1978:89-90, Milanich 1978:60-61). The Florida Gulf coast lowlands west of the Aucilla and the Withlacoochee were not part of the Timucua realm. They were, rather, populated by tribal groups of Muskogean affiliation, stretching from the Apalachee homelands down the entire Gulf coast periphery to, and probably including, the Calusa country of far south Florida. South and west of a line from the sources of the Withlacoochee through southern Orange County to Lake Harney, just inland and slightly north of Cape Canaveral, there seems to have been sparse, if any, Timucua settlement. The Florida east coast peoples from the Cape south to the Keys were also most probably Muskogean-speaking.

Inland and to the west of this heartland region the Timucua-speaking Oconi and Tawasa were situated along the river systems of otherwise solidly Muskogean-speaking central Georgia and Alabama (Swanton 1946:165, 190-191), possibly occupying this riverine niche as far north as the Tennessee-North Carolina-Georgia-Alabama border and perhaps sporadically as far west as the Fourche Maline River in southeastern Oklahoma, to judge from archaeological evidence (Ford 1969:176, 188). The possibility of this latter extension is reinforced by a significant number of Timucua lexical forms probably borrowed from Choctaw (8 items) and the western languages of Eastern Muskogean (Apalachee, Koasati, and Alabama, with 21) as well as at least one form of possible Natchez origin — Tim. *iyola* : Nat. */ula/* 'snake' (Granberry 1987:43). The Oconi were found as far west and south as the confluence of the Flint, Chattahoochee, and Apalachicola Rivers in the mid-1600's, and in the 1700's they settled on the Alachua Prairies of north-central Florida, retrenching as all the remnant Timucua tribes did toward Spanish protection in St. Augustine against increasing Muskogean and Anglo-American pressures from the north. The earliest reference to the Tawasa stems from the de Soto expedition of 1540, when they were located on the Tallapoosa or upper Alabama River (Swanton 1929). One hundred and seventy years later they were still located in the region between Montgomery, Alabama, and the Chattahoochee-Apalachicola confluence with extensions as far west and south as the Mobile area.

Timucua was the primary native language in this large area at the time of the arrival of the Spanish and French in the late 1500's. If linguistic and archaeological correlations are accurate, it may have been spoken in this region from approximately 2,000 B.C. (Meggers and Evans 1978:297; Granberry, 1991). It remained so until the end of the First Spanish Period in 1763, when the remnant Timucua speakers, heavily Christianized and acculturated to European lifeways, were moved to Cuba. There they were settled in the town of San Agustín Nueva near Habana, familiarly called then as now by the Timucua name Ceibamocha, 'Speaking Place by the Ceiba Tree' — *mo* + *cha* = 'speaking place' (personal communication, Michael Gannon, November 1989). This represents a typical manner of naming primary Timucua towns, as in Utinamocha(ra) 'Speaking Place of the Lord of the Land', the name of one of the primary Timucua towns of Utina Province. Ultimately these refugees merged with the general population (Granberry 1987:19). Some Tawasa speakers survived until the early 1700's — we have a short Tawasa vocabulary from 1707 — but they, too, soon disappeared as a separate entity, absorbed into the Muskogean-speaking Alabama, by whom they were still remembered by name as late as 1914 (Swanton 1929:446).

While we have no information on the organization of either the Oconi or the Tawasa at the time of initial French and Spanish colonization, the Timucua of southeast Georgia and Florida were organized into tribal-political units, some apparently very loose-jointed, others with a considerable degree of formalization. The approximate geographical boundaries of these entities are shown on the map in Fig.1. These tribal units have been ably defined and discussed by Milanich (1978) and Deagan (1978) and can be summarized as follows:

TABLE 2

TRIBAL UNITS, STATUS, AND LOCATION

UNIT	STATUS	LOCATION
YUSTAGA	Independent	E. of the Aucilla & W. of the Suwannee (Madison & Taylor Counties).
UTINA	Independent	N. of the Santa Fe into S. Georgia & from the E. bank of the Suwannee to the W. bank of the St. Johns.
POTANO	Independent?	Alachua County.
OCALE	Independent?	Marion County, NE of the Withlacoochee E. to the Ocala Nat. Forest & S. to the Central Florida lakes.
ICAFUI/ CASCANGUE	Independent?	Georgia opposite Jekyll Island W. to the Satilla River.

YUI	Independent	W. of the Satilla & St. Mary's on W. to the Okefenokee.
YUFERA	Independent	Between the Satilla & the N. bank of the St. Mary's opposite Cumberland Is.
TACATACURU	Independent	Cumberland Island.
SATURIWA	Independent	From the Atlantic W. to the E. banks of the St. Mary's & St. Johns, from the S. bank of the St. Mary's in the N. to S. of St. Augustine in the S.
AGUA DULCE	Independent ?	From the Atlantic W. to the E. bank of the St. Johns from just S. of St. Augustine in the N. to the vicinity of Lake Harney in the S.
ACUERA	Independent ?	Between the Oklawaha & St. Johns, from the Ocala Nat. Forest in the N. to just S. of Orlando in the S.

In addition to the above tribal-political entities Pareja (1627:f.37) refers to the Tucururu, presumably somewhere in southeastern Georgia. This, however, is the sole mention, so far as I am aware, of this Timucua-speaking group, and we cannot even make an intelligent guess regarding its identity or affiliations.

Laudonnière and Le Moyne (Lorant 1946) refer to the Onatheaqua, located immediately to the east of the Aucilla River on the East/West Florida boundary, but there is no other mention of this group in the literature of the times. Onatheaqua does not have a Timucua ring to it. It is possibly Muskogean (<*th*> = [*t*] ?).

The Tocobaga, Oçita (=Pohoy?), and Mococo, encountered by the de Soto expedition in the Tampa Bay region and mistakenly considered by Swanton (1946:193) to be Timucua, were most probably not Timucuan, judging from the archaeological and the

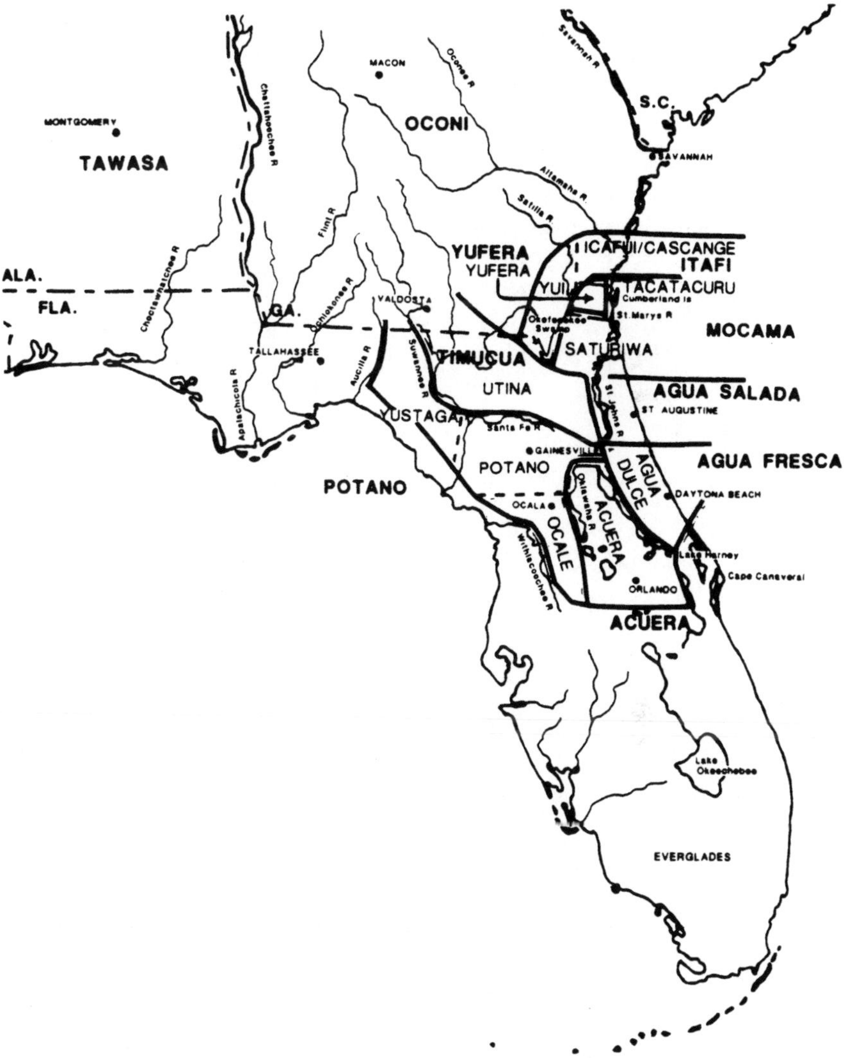

FIG. 1
Timucua Political & Dialect Boundaries ca. 1600 A.D.
(**TIMUCUA** = Dialect area, UTINA = Political region)

ethnographic evidence. Rather the affiliations seem to be with the clearly Muskogean peoples of northwest Florida and/or the probably Muskogean Calusa to the south (Bullen 1978).

Lastly, two bogus terms, Yust*e*ga and Mocam*o*, have inadvertently crept into the literature on Florida archaeology since the 1960's. Neither spelling occurs in any original source, or, for that matter, secondary source, from the late 16th century through the mid 20th century. Mocamo, in fact, is morphologically impossible in Timucua, and these mistakes should be corrected back to Yust*a*ga and Mocam*a*, as they uniformly occur in the sources of the times.

DIALECTS

While dialect differences within Timucua seem to have been slight, it is neverthless the case that dialect boundaries, as indicated by Pareja, seem to have coincided very closely with tribal-political boundaries. This is probably just another way of saying that tribal-political entities were defined largely along dialect lines. The only dialect we are unable to correlate with a political entity is the Tucururu dialect, which, as indicated above, is only mentioned once.

We know that there were eleven Timucua dialects: *Timucua* proper, *Potano*, *Itafi*, *Yufera*, *Mocama*, *Tucururu*, *Agua Fresca*, *Agua Salada*, *Acuera*, *Oconi*, and *Tawasa* (Pareja 1627:36-37; Adam and Vinson 1886:xxi, 47, 88, 119, 121; Granberry 1987:19-20; Swanton 1929). The term *Agua Salada* (Salt Water) has often been taken as a descriptive phrase referring to the Mocama dialect and the two conflated as a single dialect, usually referred to as Agua Salada (Milanich and Sturtevant 1972:1). The latter, however, is a distinct and different dialect, spoken on undefined sections of the Florida Atlantic coast in the Eastern Timucua region. Judging from lexical forms explicitly cited by Pareja, Agua Salada is more closely aligned to the western dialects — Potano and Timucua — than to Mocama (Adam and Vinson 1886:88, 121). Other than a short Tawasa word-list and isolated words in other dialects in Pareja's *Arte* the surviving texts represent the Mocama and Potano dialects exclusively.

The present study deals with the Mocama dialect only, inasmuch as this was the dialect with which Pareja and Movilla were intimately familiar and in which they wrote their religious tracts. This dialect, spoken all along the Atlantic coast of Florida from Cumberland Island in the north to the area of St. Augustine in the south and as far west as the east banks of the St. Johns River, was the dominant dialect of the Eastern Timucua (Deagan 1978:92). The Timucua dialect proper was the dominant dialect of the Western Timucua, to the west of the St. Johns (Milanich 1978:62). Pareja's division reflects our current archaeological definition of Eastern vs. Western Timucua sub-cultural differences (Milanich 1978, Deagan 1978).

Dialects and tribal-political entities may be correlated as follows:

TABLE 3

DIALECTS & TRIBAL/POLITICAL UNITS

DIALECT	UNIT
Acuera	Acuera
Agua Salada	Coastal Saturiwa
Agua Fresca	Agua Dulce
Itafi	Icafui/Cascange, Yui (Ibi)
Mocama	Tacatacuru, Saturiwa
Oconi	Oconi (not a unit)
Potano	Yustaga, Potano, Ocale ?
Tawasa	Tawasa (not a unit)
Timucua	Utina
Tucururu	Tucururu
Yufera	Yufera

My earlier statements on Timucua dialects (Granberry 1956:99) were incomplete and should not be followed.

The only dialect other than Mocama and Potano for which we have any substantive data is Tawasa. For that dialect we have a 60-word lexicon from 1707 given by a native speaker named Lamhatty (Swanton 1929:447-449). For the other non-dominant dialects we must rely on the occasional citation of forms in Pareja's *Arte*.

From Lamhatty's vocabulary it is clear that Tawasa speakers had been in close contact with the Muskogean Alabama for a considerable period of time. A blend of both Timucua and Alabama lexical stems and grammatical affixes occurs even in that short word-list. So, for example, the Muskogean same-subject suffix *-t* occurs often in Lamhatty's forms, as does the Timucua proximate time verbal suffix *-la*. One cannot help but wonder whether the Tawasa speech of the early 1700's had not undergone the same kind of creolization that we see in the neighboring Mobilian 'jargon' (Haas 1975, Crawford 1978).

We do know that there was a close relationship between the Alabama and the Tawasa, for the *Toasi* are mentioned by the de Soto chroniclers as early as 1540 on the lower Tallapoosa or upper Alabama River in the vicinity of present-day Montgomery (Swanton 1946:190).

In the dictionary section of this volume lexical items from a specific Timucua dialect other than Mocama are so labeled. Forms without a dialect label are Mocama and in all likelihood also common Timucua. For ready reference Lamhatty's vocabulary and the non-Mocama lexical forms given in Pareja's *Arte* (1614, Adam and Vinson 1886) are also given in the following table. The Potano vocabulary of the two Timucua letters discussed earlier has not been thoroughly analyzed yet and is, therefore, not included in the following list. All forms are given in the source spelling (Tawasa forms are from Swanton 1929:447-449). In the Tawasa forms, on the basis of English graph-phoneme correspondences, orthographic *<à(h)>* is interpreted as */a/*; *<è(h)>* as */e/*; *<e>*, *<é>*, *<eé>*, *<ée>*, *<ie>*, *<ié>*, and *<ea>* as */i/*; *<o>*, *<ò>*,*<ough>*, and *<óo>* as */o/*; *<oo>*, *<oó>*, *<oò>*, *<ou>*, and *<oú>* as */u/*; and *<ú>* as */u/* or */b/* depending on the orthographic context.

TABLE 4
DIALECT FORMS

DIALECT FORM	MOCAMA	ENGLISH
OCONI		
unanâ	*unan*	Future
unenâ	*unan*	Future
TIMUCUA		
hachoncoleqe	*hachaqueniqe*	Why isn't
ponati	*ponati*	he coming?
naquenechusto	*naquenechuancu*	Why is it so?
quenechusto	*quenechuteo*	Why is it so?
unano	*unan*	Future
unateo	*unana*	Future
unale	*unale*	Future
chi	*che*	to call from afar
homitaniacu	*homitala*	I am going
homila	*homitala*	I am going
caquenenco	*quene*	it is so
naquenenco	*naquene*	It is so?
chebala	*chebatela*	he needs
chebetamala	*chebatama*	they need
nemnemomacoco	*nemoque habasi*	speak to him in secret
nemomacocoqua	*nemoque habasi*	speak to him in secret
YUFERA		
cafa	*yuque*	port
noyuqye	*yuque*	port
cumen	*unana*	Future
unale	*unale*	Future
hocamintemico	*homitala*	I am going
taymala	*chebatela*	he needs
taymotamala	*chebatama*	they need
POTANO		
chaqueneti	*choco*	not to know
chi	*che*	to call from afar
homitaniacu	*homitala*	I am going
homila	*homitala*	I am going
taymala	*chebatela*	he needs
taymotomala	*chebatama*	they need

THE TIMUCUA LANGUAGE

AGUA SALADA

yaca	*choco*	not to know
unale	*unale*	Future

TAWASA

effalàh	*efa + la* (= 'it is')	dog
pisso	*pesolo*	bread
soúa	*soba*	meat
pítchot (*-t* = subject)	*picho*	knife
ocoòt (*-t* = subject)	*ucu*	drink
Necóa	?	potato
Chesapà (Ala. *časi*)	*tapola*	corn
heăt (Eng. *cat*)	*hiyaraba*	cat
yáukfah (*yánkfa ?*)	*yaha*	1
Eúksah	*yucha*	2
Hóp-ho	*hapu*	3
Checúttah	*cheqeta*	4
Márouah	*marua*	5
Mareékah	*mareca*	6
pekétchah	*piqicha*	7
pekénnahough	*piqinaho*	8
peétchcuttah	*peqecheqeta*	9
toómah	*tuma*	10
toomayaúkfa	(*tuma*)*yucha*	11
tomoeúcha	*tumayucha*	20
tomo-eucha-Hop-ho-Coláh	*tumayucha hapu*	23
tomo-eucha-Maréekah	*tumayucha mareca*	26
fóóley	*hue + le* (= 'it is')	hand
Secah	?	leg
secútchenou	?	stocking
'scùt	?	pipe
hewéenou	*hinino*	tobacco
ocut-soúa	*ucuchua*	door
I-hewanna	?	chair
Hássey (Ala. *haši*)	*ela*	sun
I'nny (Ala. *nihta*)	*equela*	day
Miltéwah	*ilaqe*	night
A'ssick (Ala. *nila haši*)	*acu*	moon
A'ssick hóomah	*Acu homa* (= 'finish')	full moon
oū	*ho*	I
hé	*he*	you
chénah, chénoh (Nat. *ičina*)	*oqe*	he
Uēkqūah	*ca*	here
Uēkheth	*heqe*	there
Hūekquah	?	. . . ay (?)

so macu	*isaco*	go
hĕmèh	*hime*	come
héwah	*hiba*	sit down
Tútcah (Cr. *tóʼtka)*	*taca*	fire
Tútcah hemèh	*taca hime*	come to the fire
Loókqŭy	*(a)ruqui*	boy
Néăh	*nia*	woman
Wiedōō	*biro*	man
Colúte	*colo*	bow
Piékcutt (Span. *pico)* (*-t* = subject)	*atulu*	arrow
loúchat (Span. *lucha)* (*-t* = subject)	*ica*	fight
Cŏckqūit	*pile*	tied
Wiéott (*-t* = subject)	*ibi*	water
Wiéott opùt (*-t* = subject)	*ibi* + *api* (= 'salt')	salt water
Àssick-toúquah	*ela* + *toco* (= 'rise')	east
Àssick-Eachah	*ela* + *echa* (= 'set')	west
Oū bāp (Choc. *bok)*	*aye* + *ibi*	mountain water
yōw,e	*yayu*	great
Chicky, Chiéky	*chiri, qichi*	litle
sōquàh	*chuca*	how many

ARCHAEOLOGICAL CORRELATES

The late John Goggin made the first attempt to correlate the then known linguistic, ethnographic, and archaeological data on the Timucua (Goggin 1953). His insights still hold together remarkably well after a period of almost forty years of increasingly intensive archaeological work in the Timucua region.

The most recent summaries of archaeological correlates of Timucua tribal/linguistic units are those of Milanich (1978) for the Western Timucua and Deagan (1978) for the Eastern Timucua. Both are careful, well-written accounts which build on Goggin's earlier base. The primary alteration of Goggin's data is the elimination of his Southern Timucua group (Tocobaga, Oçita, Mocoço), largely on the basis of data acquired since the time Goggin wrote, which would suggest that these Tampa Bay tribes were likely Muskogean in language and wider cultural affiliation (Bullen 1978).

Both Kathleen Deagan and Jerald Milanich have continued their work in the Timucua area, and, since the late-1980's, a wide range of excavation, associated laboratory analysis, and comparative archaeological, ethnozoological, and ethnohistoric research has been undertaken in various parts of the Timucua-speaking areas by an unusually talented group of younger scholars, the third generation of Timucua-region archaeologists. Among those particularly active in the area are: Stanley C. Bond, Jr., Amy Bushnell, Ann S. Cordell, Glen H. Doran, David J. Hally, John H. Hann, Kenneth W. Johnson, Richard E. Johnson, Timothy Kohler, Chung H. Lee, Lana J. Loucks, Rochelle Marrinan, Bruce C. Nelson, Lee Newsom, Irvy R. Quitmyer, William H. Radisch, Elizabeth J. Reitz, Donna L. Ruhl, Michael Russo, Rebecca Saunders, John F. and C. Margaret Scarry, Brenda J. Sigler-Lavelle, David H. Thomas, Richard H. Vernon, Brent R. Weisman, and John E. Worth. The work of these professionals has added considerable refinement both to our picture of Timucua society — particularly in Utina (Timucua), Potano, Icafui, and Saturiwa Provinces — and to definition of the movements of Timucua and Muskogean peoples within northern Florida and southern Georgia during the late prehistoric and early historic, Mission, periods (cf. Deagan 1985, 1987; Weisman 1992).

The Eastern Timucua (Yui, Icafui/Cascange, Yufera, Tacatacuru, Saturiwa, Agua Dulce, and Acuera) are represented archaeologically by the long St. Johns Tradition in Florida and this tradition together with the Wilmington-Savannah on the Georgia coast, the latter showing a blend of what seem to be native Timucua with indigenous Muskogean-Guale artifactual traits. The Western Timucua (Yustaga, Utina, Potano, Ocale) participate in two sub-traditions of the Alachua Tradition — exemplified by the Alachua and Suwannee Valley ceramic series in North-Central Florida and North Florida respectively, and, somewhat later, by the Fort Walton/Leon-Jefferson Traditions. The picture in the western region is considerably more complex than that in the eastern region inasmuch as the north-central and northwestern parts of Florida were from earliest times a mixing-ground for peoples (?) and traits, both indigenous and foreign, from the west, east, and, particularly, the north.

In both the eastern and western regions there is clear cultural continuity from at least a thousand years before the historic period to that time-marker (Milanich 1978:61). In the eastern region, in fact, there is definite archaeologically-indicated continuity from Mt. Taylor times (ca. 4,000-2,000 B.C.) through St. Johns IIc times (1513-1565 A.D.). Such continuity of material culture traits, while implying a considerable degree of continuity in non-material traits and possible *in situ* population, does not necessarily also imply that the Timucua language was indigenous to the eastern (especially) or western Timucua regions. We will look at the latter statement in considerable detail later.

It may be pointed out, as Gatschet first noted in 1880 (p. 465), that the lexical base of the Timucua language is not genetically related to any language 'spoken in the neighborhood of its native soil.' A thorough examination of the vocabularies of not only neighboring languages but also of all documented North American languages, stocks, and phyla shows no convincing relationship nor even large-scale borrowing of lexical forms. There is, as would be expected, a small number of Muskogean borrowings, some from probable Proto-Muskogean times (ca. 2,000-1,000 B.C.), most from later times. There is no convincing broader Gulf, Algonquian, Siouan, Iroquoian, Coahuiltecan, or other affiliation, either lexically or grammatically. From a native North American point of view Timucua is a linguistic anomaly.

It is of some interest to note that there is also a very important archaeological anomaly at approximately the 2,500-1,500 B.C. time level in what Goggin, Milanich, and Deagan have called the Eastern Timucua region. This is the rather sudden appearance of ceramic wares in a Late Archaic context in the St. Johns and Savannah River regions. The wares, the earliest known in North America, while showing some similarity in shape and function to earlier steatite wares, show, as the late James Ford

(1969) has pointed out, difficult-to-explain detailed trait similarities and near-identities to wares from the northwestern Caribbean coast of Colombia. As Ford indicates, it is hard to rationalize the independent invention of such a complex artifactual system on the Archaic base of the Southeastern United States, particularly since no gradual developmental sequence from that base to the subsequent ceramic base has so far been discovered. It may not appear completely 'full-blown', but the archaeological impression is close to that.

I am, obviously, implying that the two anomalous systems — the Timucua language and the archaeologically-defined Orange and Stallings Island cultures — may have more in common than meets the eye. Radiocarbon dates and the time of arrival of Timucua speech in North America as indicated by the few Proto-Muskogean words in the language both point to the 2,500-2,000 B.C. time-line. Such problems of origin have been studiously avoided in all recent summaries and detailed statements on Florida archaeology almost as though they were not problems (Milanich and Fairbanks 1980, for example). While fully agreeing that origin problems are always difficult of solution, it is nonetheless now possible to form an intelligent, testable hypothesis in the light of our current linguistic and archaeological data. Such an hypothesis is suggested later in this volume.

LINGUISTIC COMPONENTS OF TIMUCUA AND THEIR ORIGINS

BACKGROUND

Crawford (1979) has summarized the history of the linguistic investigation of Timucua from Brinton (1858) to the time of his writing. As he points out, attempts have been made to connect Timucua genetically to a wide range of North and South American languages, all to no avail.

Even a cursory examination of Timucua language data

makes it abundantly clear that one is dealing with an unusual system. Lexically an isolate, it nonetheless contains a fairly large number of lexical items stemming from several quite readily discernible sources. Grammatically it also fits a well-known areal model in a single part of the Americas and conforms especially well to one segment of that model still in existence today. Yet no one source can explain the totality of the system. There is no known dominant contributor.

The language has all the expectations of what anthropologists and linguists refer to as a *creolized system*, and it is probably for this reason that attempts to find THE linguistic source of Timucua have been fruitless. The lack of success in assigning Timucua to a single genetic source is, in fact, a piece of positive data in itself. The language has no single provenience, in either space or time. Its sources are clearly multiple, as we shall see, and one must, rather, talk of the process of linguistic, and possibly ethnic, *formation*, not provenience. Our problem is to identify the sources and estimate the frequency and importance of each to the overall system. We may then be able to arrange the components in some kind of logical temporal and spatial framework.

If we have difficulty in finding a dominant lexical contributor to Timucua, we have, as suggested above, less trouble in finding a primary grammatical contributor. The basic patterns of Timucua grammar conform rather closely to Macro-Chibchan. The nearest similarities are, on the one hand, to the Warao isolate of the Orinoco Delta in far eastern Venezuela, tentatively assigned by Greenberg to the Paezan stock within Macro-Chibchan (Greenberg 1960), and, on the other hand, to Cuna, a member of the Chibchan stock proper within the macro-phylum. Specific similarities are examined later in this chapter.

There are also individual morphemes and lexemes with striking resemblance to modern Warao as well as an even larger number of lexemes with equally striking resemblance to languages of the Vaupés-Caquetá-Inírida-Guaviare branch of Northern Maipuran Arawakan. The number and close correspondence of nominal and verbal prefix and suffix morphemes with those of Warao is noteworthy — 44% of Warao noun suffixes and 17% of Warao verb suffixes have Timucua parallels or identities.

Floyd Lounsbury (Rouse 1986:121) has suggested that the similarities, particularly to Warao, 'are neither numerous nor strong enough to eliminate independent invention or the transmission of linguistic norms from one local population through another through trade or other means of intercommunication.' While it is certainly the case that the number of resemblances is small, certain peculiarities of the morphemic structure and semological usage would, in my opinion, mitigate against Lounsbury's suggestion of independent invention. The peculiarities are shared only by 17th century Timucua and modern Warao; they do not occur in other neighboring languages in either the Southeast or Venezuela, nor, for that matter, in any other native South or North American language. To attribute such a situation to independent invention would, I think, be greatly stretching a point. On the other hand, to attribute such similarities to borrowing as a result of various kinds of intercommunication, particularly if the common elements are not dominant in one of the languages, is not only feasible but quite likely.

The picture is not a simple one, but the multiple sources of Timucua lexicon and grammar point to a long process of creolization. Such a process can, of course, take many forms. When one culture and language is politically dominant one usually sees large-scale relexification, as in the case of Anglo-Saxon after the Norman Conquest of 1066. If total military subjugation and fragmentation of the non-dominant population is involved, as was the case in the Atlantic slave trade, almost total relexification and large-scale grammatical restructuring of the non-dominant language(s) usually occurs, the Caribbean Creoles serving as the classic case. If contact between cultures is largely economic, without extensive military or political domination on the part of one of the participants, and the economic adventurers are relatively few in number, as in the case of the development of Swahili, the basic lexicon of the less dominant language tends to remain largely intact but with lexical, morphemic, and syntactic borrowings from the more dominant participant.

Timucua would seem to be an example of the last sort — peaceable economic contact over a long period of time leading to incorporation of lexical and grammatical structures from non-native sources. While the non-native source for the Bantu peoples of East Africa was largely unitary — the Omani dialect of southern Arabia, with its many Persian borrowings — the contact sources for Timucua seem to have been multiple — at least one or more Waraoid languages, Northwestern Chibchan, Northern Maipuran Arawakan, and Muskogean, the latter through a 3,000-year time period.

The uniqueness of Timucua is that no single dominant source for the language can be identified. A primary lexical source of unknown origin, clearly not Waroid, is countered by a primarily Waroid grammatical source. None of the lexical contributors can be considered dominant in any sense. The only similar case of which I am aware is that of the Mbugu language of northern Tanzania (Goodman 1971). Mbugu, too, has a primary lexical source of unknown origin, though its grammar is essentially Bantu. There are additional contributing lexical and grammatical elements from both Sudanic and Hamitic languages, neither of them dominant.

The Timucua case is perhaps more amenable to solution than that of Mbugu, however, for we have considerable archaeological data with which to work both in the Southeastern United States and in the Amazonia-Northwestern South America regions, some of it quite enlightening with regard to the possible formation of the Timucua language.

STRUCTURE

The most striking accord between Timucua and Warao is that found in the morphemic structure of nouns. In both languages a lexeme has nominal usage syntactically and semologically if the root morpheme, usually a free-form, is capable of taking the noun-pluralizing suffix Tim. *-tooma* : War.

-tuma (Osborn 1967*b*:254). There are six additional affixes which either designate a lexeme as a noun or derive a noun of some particular type from another noun or other part of speech (Osborn 1967*b*:254):

TABLE 5

NOMINAL SUFFIXES: TIMUCUA/WARAO

TIMUCUA		WARAO	
na-	nominalizer	*-na*	nominalizer
-si[1]	reflexive goal-marker	*-si*	goal-marker
-ma[2]	definite goal-marker	*-ma*	goal-marker
-co	augmentative	*-ka*	diminutive
-siba	quantitative	*-sebe*	quantitative
-ma[3]	plural agent	*-mo*	plural agent

This list exhausts the noun-designating and noun-deriving machinery of Timucua and represents 6 from a total of 17 such affixes for Warao (see Osborn 1967*b*:254). There is one additional member of this group of affixes which shows a similarity between the two languages. 'Long' occurs in Warao as the noun-deriving suffix *-wari* (Osborn 1967*b*:254). In Timucua 'long' is indicated by the bi-morphemic lexeme *ihi-riba*. Metathesis might explain War. *-wari* : Tim. *-riba*. That is, 8 (44%) of Warao noun-designating, noun-deriving affixes are mirrored by similar or identical forms in Timucua, accounting for 100% of the noun-designating, noun-deriving machinery in that language.

The possessive affixes of both languages are also similar (Osborn 1967*b*:254):

TABLE 6

POSSESSIVE AFFIXES: TIMUCUA/WARAO

	TIMUCUA	WARAO
1S	*-na*	*ma-*
2S	*-ya* ~ *-ye*	*hia-* ~ *hi-*
3P	*-Ø* ~ *-ma*[1] (+ *-ma*[2] > *-mima*)	*Ø-* ~ *a-*
1P	*-na* + *-ca* > *-nica*	*ka-*
2P	*-ya* + *-ca* ~ *-qe* > *-yaca* ~ *-yaqe*	*yatu-*
3P	*-ma*[1] + *-ca* + *-re* (+ *-ma*[2]) > *-micare(ma)*	—

Timucua 3S optionally but with high frequency adds the goal-deriving suffix *-ma*^{2}, essentially a definite article. Homophonous *-ma*^{1} and *-ma*^{2}, a single morpheme by form, behave according to different rules of phonological alteration and are therefore considered separate morphotactic entities, indicated by the superscript notation. Both Timucua *-ma*^{1} and Warao *a-* indicate 3S unless otherwise specified, but they may be used with any specified person, as in Timucua *heca pahama* 'our house' (*heca* = 'we'), Warao *oko amõhõ* 'our hand(s)' (Osborn 1967*b*:258). They are both markers of general possession, regardless of the person of the possessor. As Osborn points out (his N = noun) 'unless the person is otherwise specified *a-* + N may be glossed *the-N* or *third-person's N*' (Osborn 1967*b*:258), indicating an identical semological function for Timucua *-ma*^{1} (+/- *-ma*^{2}) and Warao *a -*.

The *-ca* pluralizer of Timucua is also frequently used as a general noun pluralizer. When it is so used it is normally followed by lexeme-final suffix *-re*, which has no counterpart in Warao. A *-rV* suffix, however, does occur widely in Arawakan languages to indicate a possessed noun, a noun in 'combining form', or a stative when affixed to nouns (Matteson 1972:164, Payne 1990:81). In Timucua *-re* is used as a noun-combining form with both singular and plural possessive affixes on plural nouns only, as in *pahana* 'my house', *pahanicare* 'my houses' (*-na* + *-ca* > *-nica*), *pahaye* 'your (sg.) house', *pahayecare* 'your (sg.) houses', *pahama* or *pahamima* 'his house', *pahamicare* 'his houses' (*-ma*^{1} + *-ca* > *-mica*). With plural possessive affixes the same principle occurs: *pahanica* 'our house', *pahanicacare* 'our houses', *pahayaqe* 'your (pl.) house', *pahayaqecare* 'your (pl.) houses', *pahamicarema* 'their house', *pahamicaremacare* 'their houses'. In actual practice, however, special stative verbal structures are more usually used to identify a plural possessive plural noun: *heca pahamilecare* 'our houses' (= '3P pronoun + they are possessed houses'), *pahamitilacare* 'their houses' (= 'they are 3P-possessed houses'). Morpheme *-re* is rarely used to indicate morpheme combination except with nouns, always in the plural, the sole noted exception being its use in the 3P pronominal affix group *-micarema* 'their'.

The structure of lexical verbs in Timucua and Warao is also strikingly similar. Of a total of 59 Warao designative and derivational verbal affixes 10 (17%) occur in identical or very similar form and semological function in Timucua. In both languages the verb is structurally defined by the presence or potential presence of the verb-pluralizing suffix Timucua *-bo* : Warao *-bu* (Osborn 1968:46). Other forms showing similarity are:

TABLE 7

VERBAL AFFIXES: TIMUCUA/WARAO

TIMUCUA		WARAO	
-hero	optative	*-mehere*	desire
-he	potential	*-buhu*	potential
-cu	subjunctive	*-ku ~ -kuna*	subjunctive
-qe	optative	*-ko*	optative
-ta/-te	durative	*-ta*	occurrence-momentaneous
		-ti	durative
-no	infinitive	*-ne*	gerundive
-co	conditional	*-kore*	conditional, simultaneous
ya	negative	*-yana*	negative
-o	intensive	*-u*	intensive

As in the case of the nominal affixes, the verbal affixes and their semological descriptions have been taken from Osborn (1968:46-47, 62).

The Tim. *-si*[1] : War. *-si* nominal suffix, a goal-marker in both languages, also occurs with lexemic verbs in both languages to indicate 'reflexive' or 'reciprocal'.

Of a total of 32 verb-designative, verb-deriving affixes in Timucua 11, including *-si*[1], are similar to Warao forms — 35% of the Timucua total.

In addition to the morphemic similarities between 17th-century Timucua and 20th-century Warao there are striking resemblances in patterns of phonological vowel harmony. The concept itself is totally alien to the native languages of the

American Southeast, but it is very prevalent in Amazonian languages, regardless of phylum affiliation. The specific patterns seen in both Timucua and Warao are so similar to one another and to those generally found in most Macro-Chibchan languages that they cannot be ignored. I hasten to add that it is of course realized that phonological processes may be similar or even identical in widely divergent languages without the slightest implication of genetic relatedness, and it is also recognized that we are here comparing two languages four hundred years apart in time. The resemblances are still striking.

In both Timucua and modern Warao the process of vowel harmony is morpheme-specific. In Warao it affects directional prefixes of */CV-/* shape when they occur immediately before a base. In Timucua it affects a finite number of bases, usually kin-terms, when they occur with immediately following pronominal suffixes and also with pronominal suffixes when they are followed by any other suffix. The kin-term pattern is itself not reminiscent of Warao, but, as will be discussed later in this section, has an exact parallel in Proto-Maipuran Arawak (*cf.* Payne 1990:80-82). In both languages the change is regressive, affecting the first morpheme in the set only. In both languages it is only the last vowel of the first morpheme which changes. The change is conditioned by the nature of the first vowel in the second morpheme of the set, whether or not consonants intervene. These regressive substitutions may be summarized by saying that in the circumstances just described a low vowel as the last vowel of the first morpheme may not occur before a low vowel as the first (or frequently only) vowel of the second morpheme.

Both Timucua and Warao have five-vowel systems, but the arrangement differs in the two languages. In both languages */i/*, */a/*, and */u/* are high-front, low-central, and high-back vowels respectively. Vowels */e/* and */o/* in Warao are phonetically [*ε*] and [*o*]~[ɔ], [*o*] predominating statistically (Osborn 1967*a*:111). In Timucua the patterns of vowel harmony suggest that */e/* was [*ε*] or [*æ*] and */o/* was [ɔ] or [*ω*]. The latter allophonic structure of */e/* and */o/* is typical of many Chibchan languages, such as Cuna (cf. Holmer 1946:185).

In both languages morpheme-final /e/ in the first of such a morpheme-set is raised to /i/, with the exception that in Timucua /e/ before /e/ > /a/, as in *itaye* 'your father' (*ite* 'father' > *ita* + -*ye* 'your (sg.)'). In Warao this rule means that /Ce-/ directional prefixes become /Ci-/ before bases with /a/ as their first vowel, as in *sewiri* 'to arrive by canoe' (*se-* + *wiri* 'to paddle'), *sinaka*/ 'to fall down' (*se-* > *si-* + *naka* 'to fall'), *temoi* 'to blow on' (*te-* + *moi* 'to blow'), and *tiahi* 'to cut on' (*te-* > *ti-* + *ahi* 'to cut') (Osborn 1967*a*:118). In Timucua the process affects only base + pronominal suffix sets, since there are no pronominal suffixes except variant *-ye* of *-ya* 'your (sg.)' which contain /e/ before /e/, /a/, or /o/; for example, *itina* 'my father' (*ite* > *iti* + *-na* 'my'). The latter may be contrasted with a non-kin base such as *paha* 'house', as in *pahana* 'my house'. In the sole instance in which the /e/-/e/ combination occurs in Timucua, *itaye* 'your father' (*ite* > *ita* + *-ye* 'your (sg.)'), /e/ > /a/, as indicated earlier.

In Timucua low vowel /a/ is also replaced by /i/ before another low vowel, as in *itimile* 'it is his father' (*ite* > *iti* + *-ma²* > *-mi* 'his, the' + *-le* 'it is'), *pahanicare* 'my houses' (*paha* + *-na* > *-ni* 'my' + *-ca* 'plural' + *-re* 'noun combining-form'), and *pahamino* 'it is his house' (*paha* + *-ma²* > *-mi* 'his, the' + *-no* 'it is').

There are no other kin-term bases nor pronominal suffixes which end in /o/, so it is impossible to say what /o/-/e/, /o/-/a/, or /o/-/o/ would have become in Timucua.

It is, for both languages, tempting to postulate an earlier period in which specific kinds of morpheme-sets containing a low vowel as the last vowel of the first member of such sets altered before any second morpheme which also contained a low vowel as its initial vowel, regardless of whether there were intervening consonants. The normal substitution was to raise the initial morpheme's final low vowel to /i/ except in combinations of /e/-/e/, where in Timucua, at least, the first /e/ becomes /a/. The suggestion is unarguably circular in that Timucua vowels /e/:[ɛ]~[æ], /o/:[ɔ]~[ω] have been defined to accommodate the system. Nevertheless, such an accommodation yields regular predictions and also has precedent in Cuna and other

Chibchan languages (*cf.* Holmer 1946:185).

There are also structural similarities between Timucua and non-Waroid Macro-Chibchan languages. By far the greatest degree of similarity is with Cuna, a Chibchan language of Panama.

Noun and verb-pluralizing suffixes containing a bilabial stop, nasal, spirant, or seminvowel — */p/*, */b/*, */m/*, */φ/* , */β/*, or */w/* — followed by a central */a/* or back */o/* or */u/* are quite frequent in Chibchan and Paezan languages (Wheeler 1972). Cuna, for example, uses */-(r)pa(a)/*, */-ma/* (with the verbal suffix */-la/*), and */-pi(i)/* to indicate plurality in both verbs and nouns, as in *uce* 'hot' and *ucepa(a)* 'much heat', *uamala* 'there are many fish' (*ua* 'fish' + *-ma* + *-la* 'there are'), *sanpi(i)* 'all meat', *penamala* 'you all are going' (*pe-* 'you' + *-na-* 'go' + *-ma* + *-la* 'verbalizer') (Holmer 1946:185ff). This usage is quite congruent with Timucua *-bo* and *-ma³* verb pluralizers, described earlier.

Timucua has a lexeme *puqua* (morphemically *pu-* + *-qua* 'intensifier') indicating 'much, many', similar in usage to the Cuna *-(r)pa(a)* morpheme. Both languages, like Warao, have a *-ka* plural. In Timucua this is normally combined with *-re*, in Cuna with *-na*, as in Cuna *niiskana* 'stars' (Holmer 1946:186), Timucua *chubobocare* 'stars'.

Cuna uses *-la* with nouns to indicate the result of a verbal action and *-le* with verbs to indicate a passive participle. Timucua uses both suffixes with nouns to indicate verbalization, as in *itinile* 'he is my father' (*ite* > *iti* 'father' + *-na* > *-ni* 'my' + *-le* 'it is'). With verbs Timucua *-la~-le* indicates 'proximate time', as in *hontala* 'I am' (*ho-* 'I' + *-ini-* > *-n-* 'be' + *-ta* 'durative' + *-la* 'proximate time'), paralleling Cuna *uamala* 'there are many fish' and *penamala* 'you all are going' (Holmer 1946:186).

The *-ma* morpheme, as indicated earlier, fills three separate tactical slots: *-ma¹* '3S', *-ma²* definite goal-marker 'the', and *-ma³* '3P verbal subject'. The semological functions of *-ma¹* and *-ma²* are shared with Warao; the semological function of *-ma³* is shared with Cuna.

Cuna *-ti* derives verbs from nouns, as in *soko* 'to say', *soketi* 'the act of saying'. A suffix *-tae* indicates 'habitual action'

(Holmer 1946). Timucua uses *-ta* to derive nouns from verbs, as in *heba* 'speak', *hebata* 'the act of speaking'. It uses *-ta ~ -te* as an indicator of 'durative action' with verbs, as in the example *hontala* 'I am' used above. Perfect action in Cuna is indicated by *-ca*, in Timucua by *-chu* (Holmer 1946). Present time is indicated in Cuna with *-na*, *-la*, or *-ya*; Timucua uses the *-la~-le* suffix, as pointed out earlier, to indicate 'proximate time'.

In addition to the phonological similarity in the allophonic definition of the /*e*/ and /*o*/ phonemes in Timucua and Cuna it is also of interest to note that Cuna form-initial, post-junctural vowels are pre-aspirated (Holmer 1946:187). Pareja's orthography for Timucua shows many pairs of lexeme variants in which an intial /*h*/ sometimes is used and sometimes is not, as in *eca* or *heca* 'wind', *hiba* or *iba* 'rain'.

There are several structural similarities between Timucua and the Misumaplan Chibchan languages of Central America. Twahka (Paya) uses pluralizing suffixes /*-rau*/ and /*-pak*/, for example, both meaning 'abundance' (Conzemius 1929:79). Timucua uses independent lexemes *ara* and *puqua* with the same meaning. In Twahka the morphemes in question are used largely with bases designating plants, while in Timucua *ara* and *puqua* are generally used only with bases designating plants or animals (but not humans).

Timucua has some structural resemblances to the Panoan languages. Greenberg (1960) assigned these languages to a Gê-Panoan-Cariban phylum, unrealted to Macro-Chibchan or Andean-Equatorial, but no regular sound correspondences link them to either Gê or Cariban (Rodrigues 1985:397) and Key (1968) has shown a definite genetic relationship between Panoan and Tacana. Though largely limited to two regions — the Andean foothills and an area in northwestern Bolivia — with Brazilian Yanomama as a possible northeastern extension (Migliazza 1978, 1985:29), the Panoan tribes, while often far-ranging traders (the Shipibo, for example), seem not to have had any great migratory tendencies at any time in their history (Lathrap 1970:81). They seem to have occupied their present areas throughout the past, the discontinuities between the two major Panoan-speaking regions representing Arawak migratory intrusions into the Pre-Andine area of far western Amazonia.

The system of grammatical affixation of Chacobo shows the following similarities with Timucua: Tim. *-bo* '1P/2P verb subject' : Ch. */-bo/* 'noun, plural'; Tim. *-beta* 'for, with' : Ch.*/-bïta/* 'with' ; Tim. *ocho* 'behind' : Ch. */-čo/* 'behind'; Tim. *ca* 'here' : Ch. */-ka(ya)/* 'here'; Tim. *-qe* 'optative' : Ch. */-ki/* 'conditional'; Tim. -*na²* 'durative' : Ch. */-na-/* 'to become'; Tim. *-no¹* 'active' : Ch. */-no? o/* 'locative intransitive'; Tim. *-no* + *-so* 'active transitive' : Ch. /-*no?so/* 'locative transitive'; Tim. *-so* : Ch. */-so/* 'transitive'. The base morpheme glossed as 'black' in both languages is also similar — Tim. *chucu* : Ch. */čïkï/*. Chacobo data are from Prost (1962:108-115).

There are three Timucua affixes with structural parallels in Northern Maipuran Arawakan. All are monosyllabic affixes, and the similarities may therefore be fortuitous. They are: Tim. *ha* 'be in the future' : Goajiro */-he/* 'future time'; Tim. *na-* 'V > N' : Island Carib */n-~-na/* '1st person'; and the form cited earlier, Tim. *-re* 'noun, combining-form'. We have already noted that Timucua *na-* 'V > N' is paralleled by Warao */-na/* with the same semological function. It is also possible that Timucua *ha>* 'be in the future' is paralleled by Warao */ha-/* 'must, have to, will' with the same function as the Timucua form (Osborn 1968:54). That is, the similarities reflect broadly generalized pan-Amazonian/pan-Chibchan patterns rather than specific Arawakan sources.

There is, however, an interesting, almost exact parallel between certain possessive devices posited for Proto-Maipuran Arawakan and similar devices in Timucua. David L. Payne has recently demonstrated that Proto-Maipuran Arawakan had five structurally demarcated noun classes (1987:66, 1990:80-82). Proto-Maipuran would have been a linguistic entity in the Rio Negro region of Amazonia around 3,000 B.C. (Noble 1965*a*:110-112). Each of the five classes utilized a class-specific device for indicating the noun in possessed state — a suffix (3 classes), an alteration of the stem-final vowel (1 class), or a Ø morpheme suffix (1 class). Nouns in the possessed state also contain a person/number-indicating possessive prefix. Of these class-specific possessive devices, two, discussed earlier, are paralleled in 17th century Timucua — the use of a *-re* suffix, and the use of a change of the stem-final vowel of a select group of morphemes.

Unlike Proto-Maipuran, Timucua frequently utilizes both devices with the same morpheme, though certain remnants of a possible structurally-defined noun class system may be discerned. Payne points out that 'in many Maipuran languages, either zero or final stem vowel change is characteristic of the noun class including inalienably possessed item. These are most frequently body parts and, in some languages, kinship terms' (Payne 1990:81). Alteration of morpheme-final vowel, as we have already seen, is characteristic of possessed kin-terms in Timucua — *ite* 'father', *itina* 'my father', *itaye* 'your father'. In Proto-Maipuran the morpheme-final vowel most usually changed to *-e*, while in Timucua it adjusted its shape according to vowel harmony rules typical of Macro-Chibchan. Payne also points out that nouns belonging to the *-re* noun class in Proto-Maipuran seem to have arbitrary semantic-semological signals — or at least it has not yet been possible to find an underlying commonality of meaning or function which links them with what would seem to us any consistent logic (Payne 1990:82). The use of *-re* in Timucua seems equally arbitrary, occurring with the possessed form of almost all nominal lexemes.

There is, finally, only one structural similarity between Timucua and any of the Muskogean languages — Timucua *ha* 'be in the future' and Choctaw *-he* 'future time'. The monosyllabicity of the form, however, renders comparison rather meaningless in and of itself.

VOCABULARY

Contrasting with this overwhelmingly Macro-Chibchan/Waroid grammar is the non-Waroid, non-Chibchan basic vocabulary, only a small percentage of which can be traced unambiguously to any source.

Numbers and pronouns are often taken as indicators of the

extent of outside influence on a language, since these systems, in common with all cultural sub-systems showing extreme high frequency of use, are normally very resistant to change. Both systems tend to maintain an overall patterning inherited from genetic forebears, and intrusive borrowings are generally quite obvious, as in the case of English independent pronoun borrowings from Scandinavian. A determination, therefore, of resemblances between the number or pronominal systems of several languages is likely to tell us something about genetic relatedness and borrowing.

The number system of Timucua is particularly informative in this regard. Timucua cardinal numbers are: *yaha~yaucfa* '1', *yucha~yucsa* '2', *hapu* '3', *cheqeta* '4', *marua* '5', *mareca* '6', *piqicha* '7', *piqinahu* '8', *peqecheqeta* '9', *tuma* '10', *chupi* '100'. *Chupi* is certainly a borrowing from Muskogean */čokpi-/* '100' (Alabama, Koasati, Creek), related to */čõ˙pi/* 'large'. *Tuma* '10' is related to the pluralizing morpheme *-tooma*, used also as a free lexeme with the meaning 'all, total, complete'. *Hapu* '3' is similar to Pre-Andine Maipuran */hepü/* '2' (Canamarí), though */pa/* occurs as a component of many numbers in a large range of Arawakan languages. *Cheqeta* '4' bears a resemblance to Muskogean */osta˙ka/* '4' (Alabama, Koasati). 'Five' *marua* is similar to Paezan Chocó */mare/* '5' in */kwĩ mare/* '4' (= '1 from 5'), though the */mare/* form itself is not presently used for '5' in Chocó (Loewen 1963:366). A possible etymology for Timucua *marua* is **-mir-* 'all, complete' as in *amiro, mirica* 'all' plus *hue~be* 'hand' > *mir-hue* > *marua* 'complete hand = 5'.

The same *-mir-* > *mar-* element is found in *mareca* '6', which might be taken to mean 'all + 1'. If this is the case, then one would expect that '7' should be 'all + 2', something like *marucha* or *marucsa*, neither of which, however, occur. *Piqicha*, the form for '7', though, does have the final syllable *-cha*, which could well be the *-cha* of *yucha* '2'. The possible morpheme *piqi-~peqe-* in that case needs explanation. It is presumably the same *piqi-* which occurs in *piqinahu* '8' and *peqecheqeta* '9'. *Peqecheqeta* certainly contains *peqe-* plus *cheqeta* '4', leading one to assume that *piqi-~peqe-* means '5' or 'hand' or some similar concept.

Piqinahu, then, should mean '5 + 3' or 'hand + 3', *-nahu* a possible aberrant variant of *hapu* '3'. *Piqicha* '7' should mean '5 + 2', which, as suggested earlier, is indeed possible. This somewhat circuitous etymologizing would lead us to assume a meaning of '5' or 'hand' for the putative morpheme *piqi- ~ peqe-*, occurring as a bound form only in these three numerals.

The overall pattern of the Timucua cardinal number system is one in which there are separate morphemes for 1-4, a term for 5 meaning 'complete hand' or something similar, and, for numbers 6-9, words meaning 'hand + 1, 2, 3, 4'. 'Ten' in such systems is often, as in Timucua, a term meaning 'total'. The *HAND + system* is not used in Arawakan nor, in quite the same manner, in the native languages of the Southeastern United States. It does, however, occur with frequency in the Chibchan and Paezan languages, particularly those of the Colombia-Panama border region. The Cuna cardinal numerals, for example, are: */kwena/* '1', */po(o)/* '2', */pa(a)/* '3', */pakke/* '4', */attale/* '5', */nerkwa/* (*/lel/* > */ner/* 'head' + */kwa/* '1' = 'head + 1') '6', */kukle/* '7', */paapakka/* '8', */pakkepakka/* '9', */ampeki/* '10'. Ordinals are formed by adding */-kwa/* '1' to the cardinals, as in */paakwa/* 'third' (Holmer 1946:185*ff*).

The Cuna term for '5', */attale/*, means 'hand on head' — */atta/* 'hand' + */le(l)/* 'head' - a typical Chibchan '5'-term, found also in the Misumalpan languages of Central America, as in Mískito */matalal/~/matasip/* '5' — */mata/* 'hand' + */lal/* 'head' or */sip/* 'complete'. In Ulua */tin/* 'hand' = '5' (Conzemius 1929:57*ff*). In the Cuna instance '6' is 'head + 1', as indicated above. */Kukle/* '7', is */kuk-/* (an alternate form of '2') +*/le/* '2 + head'. In '8' and '9', however, we see exactly the system used in Timucua — '8' = '3 + */pakka/*', '9' = '4 + */pakka/*'. Just as in Timucua the ordinary form for '5', *marua,* is not used to compound higher numbers, so in Cuna */attale/* is not used for that purpose. Instead a morpheme with obscure meaning, */pakka/*, is used in such compounds. Just as we hypothesized a relic morpheme *piqi-~peqe-* '5/hand' in Timucua, so we can hypothesize a relic morpheme */pakka/* '5/hand' in Cuna. In the Cuna system '8' = '3 + 5/hand' and '9' = '4 + 5/hand'. 'Ten', */ampeki/*, means 'both hands', */pakka/* here assuming a form */-peki/*, almost identical to the Timucua equivalent.

While, in short, the phonological form and content of the Timucua cardinal numbers 1-4 shows no lexical similarity to any other native language of North or South America, the overall system shows remarkable similarities to that of Colombian-Panamanian Chibchan and Paezan, with extensions of that system well into Central America. The two Timucua '5' bases, *mar-* and *piqi-~peqe-*, show close phonological correspondence as well as identical semological function and syntactic usage to Paezan Chocó */mare/* '5' and Chibchan Cuna */pakka/~/-peki/* respectively.

This intriguing similarity is also mirrored, and, consequently, the probable accuracy of the present suggestion reinforced, by data from Cavineña and Reyesano, both Tacanan languages of the Andean foothills of northwestern Bolivia, and from Shipibo-Canibo, a Panoan language of the Andean foothills of the middle reaches of the Ucayali River in Peru. Unlike Chocó and Cuna, neither of these language groups is part of Macro-Chibchan, no matter how liberally defined. Mary Ritchie Key (1968), however, has amply demonstrated the relationship between Tacanan and Panoan. Her data indicate that '5' is */pišika/* in Tacanan Cavineña and Reyesano and */pičika/* in Panoan Shipibo-Canibo (Key 1968:80, 93, 104).

We are perhaps in the presence of one of those unbiquitous pan-Amazonian forms, in this case itself probably borrowed from Quechua '5', *pička* — all Tacanan-Panoan numerals above '3' seem to have come from that source (Key 1968). The fact, however, that a putative **/pVk~č~š(V)-/* morpheme meaning '5' or 'hand' seems almost pan-Panoan and pan-Tacanan, while it is clearly a relic morpheme in both Cuna and Timucua, used only in number compounds above the level of '5' rather than for '5' itself, would lead one to suspect the form came from a Pano-Tacanan or even Quechua source to Chibchan-Paezan rather than *vice versa*. What, specifically, this means for Timucua is difficult to say. The form might have been borrowed into Timucua directly from a Quechua or Pano-Tacanan source.

Given the fact that the central consonant is stop */k/* in Timucua */piki-~peke-/*, as in Cuna */pakka-/*, rather than a spirant or affricate, */š/* or */č/*, as in Tacanan */piši-ka/*, Panoan */piči-ka/*, or Quechua */pič-ka/*, however, a borrowing from Chibchan-Paezan is suggested — after those languages had themselves taken the morpheme, for whatever reasons, from Pano-Tacanan or Quechua. The possibilities are many, but whatever the direction and nature of the loan, it seems rather certain that the Chibchan-Paezan languages and Timucua at some point in their histories took the **/pVk~č~š(V)-/* morpheme into their lexical stock. A thorough comparative study of the characteristics of the Chibchan-Paezan and Pano-Tacanan number systems is called for to unravel this interesting problem.

Unlike the Timucua number system, Timucua independent personal pronouns show no similarity to any other specific language or language group except for the infrequently used 3S form *oqe*, which is reminiscent of Arawakan, as in Campa */oka/* 'this', and the 2P form *yaqe*, which is similar to modern Warao */yatu/* with the same meaning. For comparative purposes both the independent pronouns and the verbal pronoun affixes of Timucua are given in the following table:

TABLE 8

TIMUCUA PRONOUNS

INDEPENDENT		VERBAL PRONOUNS
1S	*ho-ni-he*	*ho-, ni-*
2S	*ho-chi-e*	*chi-*
3S	*Ø, oqe*	*Ø-*
1P	*he-ca, ni-he-ca*	*ni-* + STEM + *-bo*
2P	*yaqe, chi-he-ca*	*chi-* + STEM + *-bo*
3P	*Ø, oqe-ca-re*	*Ø-* + STEM + *-ma*[3]

The remainder of the Timucua lexicon shows forms similar to: Warao (or some earlier Warao-related language), Chibchan-Paezan, Tucanoan, Gê, Arawakan, Panoan, and the Muskogean languages. In a total surviving lexicon of approximately 1,500 roots only 189 are sufficiently similar to be tentatively considered borrowings. Ninety-two percent of the Timucua lexicon, that is, shows no convincing relationship to any other native American language at the present stage of research. Each of these possible connections will be discussed in turn.

It is difficult to assess the resemblances between Timucua and modern Warao inasmuch as we are comparing forms from languages almost 400 years apart. We are as yet unfortunately unable to reconstruct an earlier stage of Warao, even from internal evidence, and the equivalences suggested here are open to criticism. We do know, however, from toponymic data that Warao-like languages, such as the Guayquerí of Margarita Island, were at one time spoken from an indeterminate position on the Caribbean coast of Colombia-Venezuela between Lake Maracaibo and the Magdalena east through the Orinoco Delta (Wilbert 1957:11-18, McCorkle 1952:64). Speakers of these languages occupied the northern segment of South America as far south as the Amazonian rain forest and the confluence of the Rio Vaupés and the Rio Negro. From ethnographic evidence it is also clear that the origin of the present-day Warao lay far to the west of the Orinoco Delta, quite likely as far west as the Maracaibo region itself or even lower Central America to judge from modern Warao myths and cosmology (Wilbert 1973:40*ff*). It is, of course, clear that Timucua did not borrow directly from Warao or its immediate ancestors to judge from the lack of regular phonological correspondences. Nonetheless the similarities seem close enough to warrant discussion.

The following Timucua/Warao resemblances are particularly noteworthy. They are given with the Timucua first. Warao data are from Osborn (1967*a*:108*ff*, 1967*b*:253*ff*, 1968:46*ff*) and Barral (1957):

TABLE 9

TIMUCUA - WARAO LEXICAL PARALLELS

(1) *itori* : *ruru-ruru [duru-duru]* 'alligator'
(2) *yurico* : *oriki* 'anger'
(3) *atulu* : *atabu* 'arrow'
(4) *utasi* : *ataihase* 'attack'
(5) *aruqui* : *araka* 'child : younger brother'
(6) *na-* : *nao-* 'come'
(7) *cuque* : *kuku-* 'cover'
(8) *hio* : *hoa* 'curse'
(9) *miso* : *misi-* 'devil'
(10) *ipa(ru)* : *hobi* 'drink'
(11) *uti* : *hota* 'earth : high land/mountain'
(12) *ho* : *ho-* 'eat'
(13) *eca* : *eku* 'enter/in'
(14) *eca* : *mon-uka* 'equal'
(15) *asu-rupa* : *so* 'excrement'
(16) *mucu* : *mu* 'eye'
(17) *amara* : *emoera* 'fat : to be soft'
(18) *bara* : *yiwara* 'finish'
(19) *taca* : *rokia [dokia]* 'fire : flame'
(20) *yabi* : *yaba-* 'fishhook : to fish'
(21) *habe* : *ohia* 'fox'
(22) *abara* : *ari-* 'harvest' (see also #18 'finish')
(23) *ha-* : *ha-* 'have'
(24) *ocoto* : *noko* 'hear'
(25) *cume* : *kobe* 'heart/breast'
(26) *hono* : *nõhõ* 'hunger'
(27) *ho-ni-he* : *ina* 'I'
(28) *nihi* : *na-* 'kill'
(29) *nahiabo* : *nahobo* 'know/understand'
(30) *caro* : *o-kera* 'light'
(31) *hani* : *hahinai* 'lose'
(32) *hoba/huba* : *obo-* 'love'
(33) *biro* : *arao* 'man : people'
(34) *soba* : *toma* 'meat'
(35) *acu* : *waniku* 'moon'
(36) *nariba* : *nibora* 'old man : man'
(37) *abi* : *aba* 'put on : put'
(38) *hono-sta* : *hunu* 'shellfish : shrimp'
(39) *heba* : *ehewere* 'sing: sing/cradle song'
(40) *beni* : *abani* 'slow'
(41) *yoroba* : *ni-hara-baka* 'snake : cayman'
(42) *hani* : *ha-* 'stop'
(43) *tari* : *taera* 'strong'
(44) *aca/haca* : *haka 'wind'*
(45) *acuera* : *ak^{w}eru* 'name of the southernmost Timucua border province : border, coast'

There are also lexical resemblances with Chibchan and Paezan languages. Chocó data is from Loewen (1963:357*ff*), Cuna data from Holmer (1946:185*ff*), Chibcha and Cuica data from Wheeler (1972:93*ff*), Misumalpan (Sumu, Cacaopera, Matagalpa) from Conzemius (1929:57*ff*) and Campbell (1979:944*ff*), Arawakan (Manare) data from Noble (1965*a*) and

Matteson (1972:160*ff*), and Brunca, Yaruro, and Esmeralda data from Loukotka (1968:234, 236):

TABLE 10

TIMUCUA - CHIBCHAN LEXICAL PARALLELS

(1) *itori* : Chocó *kore* 'alligator'
(2) *chulufi* : Cuica *ču* 'bird'
(3) *marua* : Chocó *mare* 'five'
(4) *na(ta)* : Cuna *naa- (< na-)* 'go'
(5) *hue/be* : Chocó *hua* 'hand'
(6) *ta-pola* : Chocó *pe*, Chibcha *aba*, Manare *epa* 'maize'
(7) *biro* : Yanomama *waro/waru* 'man'
(8) *acu* : Chocó *(h)edexo*, Sumu *waiku*, Cacaopera *aiku*, Matagalpa *aiko* 'moon' (also Chocó Saixa dialect *axo-nihino* 'sun' : Timucua *acu nihino* 'fiery moon')
(9) *nipita* : Chocó *itae* 'mouth'
(10) *hiba* : Cuna *iya* 'rain'
(11) *chu-bo(bo)* : Yaruro *boé* 'star'
(12) *ituqua* : Sumu, Ulua *tuke*, Brunca *-kʷa*, Cuna *wa-*, Chibcha *p-kʷa*, Manare *kʷa* 'tongue'
(13) *ibi(ne)* : Yaruro *wi*, Esmeralda *wivi* 'water'

There are six interesting free-base parallels between Timucua and Proto-Tucanoan as reconstructed by Waltz and Wheeler (1972:119-148). Tucanoan languages are neither Macro-Chibchan nor Andean-Equatorial in Greenberg's classification. They were and are centered in the Rio Vaupés-Rio Negro confluence region of Venezuela, Colombia, and Brazil. The forms in question are:

TABLE 11

TIMUCUA - TUCANOAN LEXICAL PARALLELS

(1) *itori* : **iSo(-ri)* *(S = /s/ ~/h/~/y/~/d/)* 'alligator/cayman' (*-ri* is a frequent Amazonian noun-designating affix)
(2) *isi* : **zie* 'blood'
(3) *ucu* : **ũkũ* 'drink'
(4) *napona* : **poa* 'hair'
(5) *hue/be* : **wã* 'hand'
(6) *qechela* :**kasero/katsero* 'skin/bark'

THE TIMUCUA LANGUAGE

There is a single Timucua form — *yaraha/hiyaraba* 'panther' — which has possible parallels in the Gê languages. In Remokamekran 'jaguar' is *oróbo*, in Aponegikran *orópa*, in Kayapó *róp* (Loukotka 1968:82). Eastern Gê (Xavante) uses an alternate stem *hu~ru* (Loukotka 1968:83). One is tempted to postulate a Timucua form utilizing both stems, **hu-orop/ba* > **(hi)yarah/ba*. The very ingenuity of the etymology, however, gives one reason to pause. There is also a Pre-Andine Maipuran **hi-yVra-ta* form meaning 'kill', which is interestingly similar (Matteson 1972:179), and the Tupinambá form *yawar* 'jaguar' (Rodrigues 1985:391). We are perhaps dealing with one of those pan-Amazonian lexemes, which occur so frequently across both languages and stocks, particularly with flora and fauna forms which are widely distributed in the region.

Resemblances between Timucua and Arawakan have been noticed for many years. Swadesh (1964:548) has presented a tentative listing of such forms, though unfortunately his data were both inadequate and inaccurate, for he presents a fair number of erroneous forms for both Timucua and the Arawakan languages. Nonetheless his insight was correct, as the following list of resemblances indicates. It may be noted that there are three primary Arawakan sub-groups to which Timucua lexemes show resemblance: (1) Non-Maipuran (Culino, Paumarí, Yamamadí, Apolista), (2) Pre-Andine Maipuran (Canamarí, Chamicuro, Ipuriná, Piro, Campa), and (3) Northern Maipuran (especially Baré, Piapoco, Baniva-Yavitero, Achagua, Carútana, and Tariana — the Vaupés-Inírida-Guaviare branch of Northern Maipuran). The implications of this will be examined in greater detail later in this chapter. Arawakan forms in the following list are taken from Matteson (1972:160*ff*), Loukotka (1968:125-149) and my own field notes:

TABLE 12
TIMUCUA - ARAWAKAN LEXICAL PARALLELS

(1) *cume* : Proto-Pre-Andine **tsomi*, Canamarí *tsuma ('back')*, Culino *tsuhuri* 'breast/chest/heart'
(2) *chocolo* : Chamicuro *tulu*, Lokono *óloa* 'heart'
(3) *iqe* : Culino *tsiki* 'earth'
(4) *paha* : Apolista *pi-*, Yamamadí *ube*, general Eastern Maipuran *pa-*, Goajiro *pe-*, Guahibo *po-*, Lokono *báhɨ-* 'house'
(5) *neqero* : Culino *ikibuti* 'kneel'
(6) *biro* : Taino *-eri*, Piapoco *-ali* 'man'
(7) *pira* : Paumarí *puru* 'red : black (?)'
(8) *chocori* : Culino *kara-* 'strong'
(9) *aye* : Culino *awa*, Lokono *ada* 'tree'
(10) *yuba* : Canamarí *tsuma* (see also #1 'breast /chest/heart') 'back'
(11) *ichicosa* : general Pre-Andine Maipuran *kači-* 'cold'
(12) *ucu* : general Pre-Andine Maipuran *-ika* 'drink : eat'
(13) *taca* : general Pre-Andine Maipuran *titi, tak* ('sun'), general Eastern Maipuran *tike* 'fire'
(14) *hue/be* : Ipuriná, Apolista *wa-*, Piro *we-*, Lokono *we-*, Baré *wa-*, Achagua *-he* 'hand'
(15) *ilaqi* : Piro *ilačinu* 'night'
(16) *-ti* : Campa *-te* 'not'
(17) *ca/oca* : Campa *oka* 'this'
(18) *ora* : Campa *ora* 'that'
(19) *hapu* : Canamarí *hepü* 'three'
(20) *itori* : Proto-Arawakan **(iy)akare* 'alligator/cayman'
(21) *ichico* : Baré *nika* 'bite : 'eat'
(22) *isi* : Catapolitani *iti*, Marawa *isa* 'blood'
(23) *yabi* : Baré *nabi*, Achagua *yahe*, Piapoco *api* 'bone'
(24) *tiqi* : Manao *teki*, Lokono *-dike* 'ear'
(25) *uti* : Baré *rati* 'earth'
(26) *iqe* : Baniva, Piapoco *(h)ipe* 'earth'
(27) *he* : Waliperi *he*, Achagua *iha* 'eat'
(28) *ho* : Island Carib *háu* 'eat'
(29) *mucu* : Manao *uku-* 'eye'
(30) *ite* : Lokono *itʰi* 'father'
(31) *cuyu* : Achagua *ku-* 'fish'
(32) *isa* : general Northern Maipuran *isa* 'good'
(33) *penani* : general Northern Maipuran *-p/bi* 'with the hands : hand'
(34) *cuna* : Manao */küuna/* 'head'
(35) *chito* : Piapoco,

Catapolítani *iwita* 'head'
(36) *nu-* : Baré *nu-* 'know'
(37) *chofa* : Carútana *čupana* 'liver'
(38) *tapola* : Guaná *tsoporo,* Terena *soporo* 'maize'
(39) *ano* : general Northern Maipuran *ena-* 'man'
(40) *acu* : Baré *ki, Yavitero ke,* Lokono *kači,* Yamamadí *maxi* ('sun') 'moon'
(41) *bali* : Baniva *tali,* Layaná *bahalo/* 'mouth'
(42) *hiba* : Baré *hi'ya,* Goajiro *huyá* 'rain'
(43) *ene* : Machiguenga *nea* 'see'
(44) *yoroba* : Lokono *óri* 'snake'
(45) *chobobo* : Piapoco, Baniva *-wi-* 'star'
(46) *yobo* : Achagua, Goajiro, Piapoco *iba,* Manao *ipa,* Baré *tiba* 'stone'
(47) *ela* : Achagua *eri,* Tariana, Piapoco *-eri ('*moon'*),* Amarizana *eri-* ('fire'), Arekena *ale,* Goajiro *-ali* 'sun/day'
(48) *api* : Tariana, Arekena, Carútana, Baré *-ip/bi* 'tail'
(49) *ibi(ne)* : Baré *uni,* Baniva, Yavitero, Maipuré *weni* 'water'
(50) *nia* : Baré, Tariana, Piapoco, Achagua, Baniva *ina-* 'woman'
(51) *hinino* : Taíno *hynino* 'tobacco'

Of the 151 Timucua forms showing resemblances to northern South American forms 15 show what may be called multiple-resemblance. That is, these forms show similarity to more than one stock or phylum. The greatest degree of similarity is with the Arawakan languages. Inasmuch, however, as all the Amazonian languages, regardless of stock or phylum affiliation, borrowed very heavily from one another beginning in very early times, it is difficult to assign a clear-cut origin to such putative loans into Timucua. The intense riverine trade of the entire Amazon region since time immemorial has tended to blur many language differences, grammatical as well as lexical, within and between phyla (Migliazza 1985:20), and it is accordingly near-impossible to define with any degree of reliability the exact origin of most of the pan-Amazonian lexemes. In the list here the Arawakan forms are from Noble (1965*a*), Matteson (1972), or Taylor (1977); Proto-Tucanoan forms are taken from Waltz and

TABLE 13

MULTIPLE-RESEMBLANCE FORMS

GLOSS	TIMUCUA	ARAWAK	TUCANO	WARAO	OTHER
1. Alligator	itori	*(iy)akare	*iSo(-ri)	[duru-]	yakare (Tupí)
2. Blood	isi	iti/isi	*zie		
3. Drink	ucu	-ika ('eat')	*ũkũ		
4. Earth	uti	-atu		hota	
5. Eat	ho	hau		ho-	
	he	he/ha			
6. Eye	mucu	-uka		mu	
7. Fire	taca	tak-/tik-		[dokia]	
8. Hand	hue/be	we-/wa-	*wã		hua (Chocó)
9. Heart	cume	*tsomi		kobe	
10. Maize	tapola	tsoporo			pe (Chocó)
11. Man	biro	-eri/-ali		arao	oi (Yaruro)
					waro (Yanom)
12. Moon	acu	-axi		waniku	axo (Chocó)
13. Snake	yoroba	óri		-hara-	
14. Star	chubobo	-wi-			boé (Yaruro)
15. Water	ibi(ne)	weni/uni			wi (Yaruro)

Wheeler (1972); Warao forms are from Osborn (1967a, 1967b, 1968), Barral (1957), de Goeje (1930), and Williams (1928, 1929). Other forms, largely Macro-Chibchan, are from Loukotka (1968), Rodrigues (1985), and my own field notes.

It may be noted that Timucua resemblances to Arawakan, unlike those to Warao and the Macro-Chibchan languages, seem to cover two fairly specific semantic domains: (1) natural phenomena and animal forms, (2) body parts.

One of the most obvious and striking characteristics of lexemes in the Arawakan languages and in many other Amazonian language groups is what Matteson (1972:164) refers to as a 'clutter of grammatical markers,' lexemes consisting of long strings of predominantly mono-syllabic morphemes, many of which do not naturally occur alone as free-forms with any clear denotative semantic content but which have clear semological connotative meaning (that is, a broad semantic 'freight' and consistent grammatical function). Some of the most difficult to analyze of these bound-bases occur at the beginning of lexemes and, as Noble (1965*a*:27-35) pointed out quite accurately, usually have the phonological shape */t(a)-/*, */k-/*, */c-/*, */m-/*, */n-/*, */x-/* (=*/h/*), */a-/*, */i/y-/*, or */u-/*.

Noble unfortunately referred to these putative morphemes as '*class prefixes*', calling to mind a situation similar to that in the Bantu languages and others in which genuine class prefixes are a dominant grammatical feature. The case in Arawakan, however, one quickly finds, is not so clear cut. David L. Payne (1987:66, 1990:80-82) has demonstrated that Proto-Maipuran did, indeed, have five noun classes, but the semological and semantic criteria for membership in a given class are nebulous at the least, and class membership is shown not by prefixation but, rather, by the use of class-specific possessive devices, four of which involve suffixation — three classes using phonologically expressed forms, one a Ø suffix — and the fifth device a stem-final vowel change.

In some instances Noble's 'prefixes' simply do not seem to be independent separable morphemes at all but, rather, initial integral phonological components of free-base morphemes. Even in cases in which we clearly are dealing with separable, prefix-like morphemes they do not, in any instance of which I am aware, define clear-cut or even broad semantic or semological classes, as in the Bantu languages. It seems more realistic, as Taylor and Hoff (1966:305) have pointed out, to consider such morphemes 'petrified affix' components of frozen compounds in which the first element has become a non-productive morpheme in the language.

This phenomenon is not as strange as it may appear on first consideration. It occurs in many languages, and is reminiscent of the lexeme-initial 'relic morpheme' *sl-* in English, as in the words *slither*, *slippery*, *slide*, *slush*, *slurp*, *slobber*, etc., in which there is, to the native speaker, a vaguely defined underlying connotative 'meaning' of 'wetness', 'mushiness', and 'untidiness' associated with such forms, regardless of their otherwise various and unrelated denotations. A native speaker of English would likewise not associate this _sl-_ with the lexeme-initial _sl-_ of _slow_, _slumber_, or _slap_ — there _is_, that is, _something_ underlying the _sl-_ of the first group which does not underlie the latter words. Its original form and meaning, however, lies so far in the linguistic past as to be unrecoverable.

Such 'petrified affixes', furthermore, are not always lexeme-initial, as Noble implies, but also occur, in complete agreement with the norms of Arawakan lexemic structure, in varying lexeme-internal positions, as morpheme _/ha/_ 'liquid' in */_yi_-**ha**-_ki_-l^y_e/_ 'eye', */_ka_-**ha**-_re/_ 'lake', */_ha-po-e-ni_-**ha**/ 'river', */_ka-si_-**ha**/ 'sap', */_w/hinɨ/i_-**ha**/ 'water', */_pa-ka_-**hã**-_ka/_ 'wet', */po-piri-**ha**-ri/ 'dry' (Matteson 1972:163, 176-185). In my view this in no way invalidates Noble's painstaking work; it simply means that much more careful phonological, grammatical, and comparative work is needed before we will be able to iron out the problems of lexeme-initial 'petrified' bound-morpheme definition vs. ordinary lexeme-initial regular phonological correspondences.

Certainly the wide use of morphemes such as _/pi/_ 'rod-shaped object' in words such as 'vine', 'finger'; of _/-pi/_ in words for furry, fuzzy objects such as 'bat', 'bird', 'body hair', 'feather'; of _/tsa/_ 'cord' in words for 'rope', 'vine', 'hair'; of _/ke~ki/_ 'pole or stick-like objects' in words for 'crocodile', 'fish', 'leg', 'neck', 'spine', 'stick' (Matteson 1972:163-164) does seem to point to a former system of word-class definition. As Taylor and Hoff point out (1966:304) 'in some cases, at least, Noble is undoubtedly right as to the one-time morphemic status of some synchronically immovable segments.' To decide which are and which are not 'petrified affixes' and then to determine which, if any, are indeed class-designating is the unresolved problem.

In any event such lexeme-initial entities also occur in Timucua, but only in those lexical items which show a similarity to one branch or another of Arawakan, such as Timucua _ta-pola_ 'maize', Arawakan (Guaná) _/tso-poro/_ 'maize', Arawakan (Terena) _/so-poro/_ 'maize', quite possibly containing the Arawakan _/tsa/_ 'cord' morpheme, widely used in words for 'hair' and other objects with long or twisted fibers (such as corn-silk?).

THE TIMUCUA LANGUAGE

The fact that there is a widely recurring */pe/* 'maize' morpheme in many languages of Amazonia and the neighboring regions (Chocó */pe/* 'maize', for example), perhaps related to or identical with the Arawakan */pi/* 'rod-shaped object', reinforces the suggestion. The Timucua lexeme-final *-la* is either the 'proximate time' indicator *-la* or a derivative of Arawakan */rV/* 'noun combining-form'.

Timucua also shows a small number of lexical similarities to the Muskogean languages of the Southeastern United States. These can clearly be called 'loans' and can be derived from one of two sources: (A) Proto-Muskogean, as reconstructed by Mary Haas (1940, 1941, 1945, 1946, 1947, 1948, 1949, 1950, 1956, 1960), or (B) the historically known later Muskogean languages, particularly those of the western section of Eastern Muskogean — Apalachee, Alabama, and Koasati.

TABLE 14

TIMUCUA - MUSKOGEAN LEXICAL PARALLELS

(A) PROTO-MUSKOGEAN:

(1) *cocho* : **kač-* 'cut'
(2) *puen-/pon-* : **(xwu/hu)pun-* 'go/come : go'
(3) *iqui* : **abi* 'kill'
(4) *uqua* : **ik- . . . -a* 'not'
(5) *(h)uque* : **umk*^{w}*a* 'rain'
(6) *neca* : **nuči-* 'sleep'
(7) *ibi* : **ak*^{w}*i* 'water'

(B) LATER MUSKOGEAN:

(1) *chulufi* : Koasati *kulu·si* 'bird'
(2) *caya* : Alabama *aka·ka* 'chicken'
(3) *laca* : Alabama, Koasati *loča* 'black/dirty'
(4) *efa* : Koasati *ifa* 'dog' (*cf.* also Proto-Arawakan **/ife-/* 'capybara')
(5) *ucuchua* : Alabama, Koasati *okhiča* 'door'
(6) *ipa(ru)* : Koasati *ipá* 'eat'
(7) *mucu* : Choctaw *muču(li)* 'eye : to wink'
(8) *neha* : Koasati *niha* 'fat'
(9) *taca* : Alabama, Koasati *tikba,* Creek *tó·tka* 'fire'
(10) *cheqeta* : Alabama, Koasati *ošta·ka* 'four'
(11) *oqe/oca* : Alabama *ak-* 'this/that'
(12) *chupi* : Koasati, Hitchiti, Creek *čokpi* '100'; Apalachee *čoba* , Koasati *čobá,* Mikasuki *čó·b-î* 'great, large'
(13) *isa* : Koasati *iškí* 'mother'
(14) *tola* : Creek *tola* 'laurel, sweet-bay'
(15) *utasi* : Apalachee *atasa*

'attack : war-club'
(16) *-ti* : Alabama, Koasati, Mikasuki *-ti* 'not'
(17) *huri* : Creek *hó·li* 'to liberate : war'
(18) *api* : Alabama, Koasati, Choctaw *hapi* 'salt'
(19) *uba* : Alabama, Koasati *opahk-* 'swim'
(20) *aye* : Hitchiti *ahi* 'tree'
(21) *aliho-* : Koasati *čayahli* 'walk'
(22) *nali-sono* : Alabama, Koasati *la·na,* Creek *lá·n-ĭ* 'yellow'
(23) *ho-chi-e* : Choctaw *či-* 'you'
(24) *iniha* : Creek *híniha* 'councilman'
(25) *holata* : Apalachee *holahta* 'chief'
(26) *bihi* : Choctaw *bihi* 'mulberry'

It should be noted that the Timucua form *ilaqe* 'night', already compared with Pre-Andine Piro *ilačinu* 'night', bears a strong resemblance to Proto-Muskogean */niNaki/* 'night' (**N* = Western Muskogean /*n*/, Eastern Muskogean /*ł*/).

Finally, there are three Timucua items with resemblance to lexical forms in non-Muskogean languages of the Southeastern United States: (1) *miqe* : Atakapa *mo·k* 'go', (2) *iyola* : Natchez *ula* 'snake', and (3) *paracusi* : Yuchi *pá'län ku-siä*^{n} 'village chief' : 'very small chief'.

The resemblances discussed in this section, it should be borne in mind, account for only 8% of the surviving Timucua lexicon. The remaining 92% still resists any effort of comparative treatment.

INTERPRETATION OF THE DATA

Structural and lexical data, then, indicate that Timucua probably originated as a native language of northwestern Amazonia. While it does not seem in a lexical sense genetically related to any of the languages of Greenberg's Andean-Equatorial or Macro-Chibchan phyla, its grammar is quite clearly Waroid-based. We know from toponymic data that both Warao-proper as well as Warao-related languages were spoken from an indeterminate time in the past until at least the time of Spanish intervention all along the Caribbean littoral of northern South America from somewhere to the west of Lake Maracaibo east to and including the Orinoco Delta (Wilbert 1957:11-18, McCorkle 1952). Waroid toponyms occur with some frequency as far south in Colombia as the Meta, Caquetá, Vaupés region, and as far south in Venezuela as the northern banks of the Orinoco. The toponymic evidence pointing to a western origin for the Warao is reinforced by the nature of their cult practices, with startling Central and Meso-American parallels, and by their own oral traditions of such an origin (Wilbert 1972:113, 1973:43-47).

The presence in Timucua of Cuna-like noun- and verb-designating and deriving morphemes would argue toward Timucua contact with these Chibchan peoples somewhere in the area of northwestern Colombia or the Colombia-Panama border region. The small number of root morphemes showing resemblance to both Cuna and Chocó on the one hand and Yaruro on the other would stretch the possible contact region from the Colombia-Panama border southeastward to Yaruro lands in south-central Venzuela.

The presence of even the small number of resemblances to non-Maipuran Arawakan may argue toward possible contact with pre-Maipuran Arawak speakers, perhaps as early as 3,500 B.C., if we follow Noble and Lathrap (Noble 1965*a*:111, Lathrap 1970:70-81). This would presumably have taken place somewhere along the upper reaches of the Rio Negro near its confluence with the Amazon prior to the time of development of Maipuran innovations (Lathrap 1970:70-79).

That the Timucua remained in contact with Arawakan speakers for a long period of time in the Rio Negro region is attested by the number of lexical similarities to Pre-Andine Maipuran and later developing Northern Maipuran. The time level for the split of Maipuran from general Arawakan can be tentatively placed at about 2,000-1,500 B.C., perhaps earlier (Noble 1965*a*:111). Certainly the Maipuran languages were themselves developing from Proto-Maipuran by 1,800 B.C., and Proto-Maipuran had probably developed dialect variants leading ultimately to the present-day Maipuran languages by about 1,700 B.C.

THE TIMUCUA LANGUAGE

The remainder of the Arawakan-Timucua resemblances clearly indicate Northern Maipuran contacts. Owing, however, to the imperfect phonological fit with extant Northern Maipuran it is evident that such putative Timucuan borrowings from these sources came not from the individual languages as they exist today, but from a period when Proto-Northern Maipuran was in its early developmental stages, a pre-Proto-Northern Maipuran. This would be approximately 1,9000-1,700 B.C.

That is, Timucua speakers seem to have been in relatively close and constant contact with Arawak speakers from Proto-Arawakan times (ca. 3,500 B.C.) until approximately 1,700 B.C., the time by which the different Maipuran branches had developed essentially their present characteristics. The area of contact must have been the middle Rio Negro, Vaupés, middle Japurá-Caquetá region, circled on the map in Fig. 2. The descendants of the major possible Arawak donors to the Timucua lexicon are still today located in this region, though in much altered guise after the passage of so many years. The area in question is just on the southern and eastern edge of both Macro-Chibchan speech and the earliest distribution of Waroid speech. All the essential ingredients to explain Timucua lexical and grammatical peculiarities lie within this area.

Proto-Tucanoan similarities in Timucua reinforce the Arawakan evidence. Tucano is today the *lingua franca* of the Vaupés region (Sorensen 1967, 1985), and multilingualism along the middle and lower Vaupés is the norm among native speakers of Tucanoan and Arawakan languages, particularly the Tariana, Baré, and Baniva. Most of these peoples speak their own language as well as Tucano and the Tupí *lingua gêral* Nheengatú, though the later is less frequent in some parts of the region today. The only exception are the Makú, of undetermined language affiliation (Migliazza 1985:52-54). This situation seems to have been in place since pre-European times, though its epicenter was likely the lower Vaupés in aboriginal times (Sorensen 1967).

Tribal-language exogamy is the norm in this region, and all longhouse members always grow up speaking a mother-tongue, a

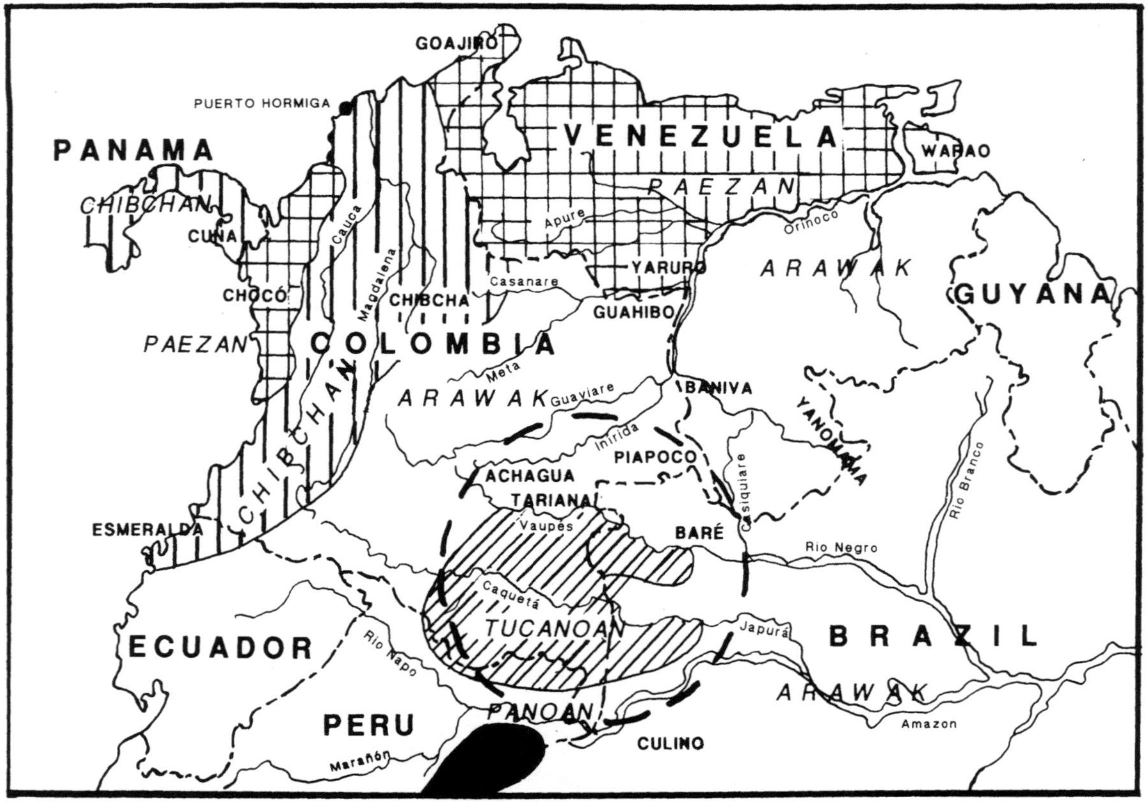

FIG. 2
Probable Epicenter of Timucua Origins ca. 2,000 B.C.

father-tongue, and two or more additional Indian languages with equal fluency. Nheengatú and/or Spanish and/or Portuguese are usually added to this list. Each language is reserved for use under specific circumstances and with specific individuals for whom the language in question is a native tongue. Ease in language-learning is a cultural trait into which each member of the society is born. Multilingual, polyglot circumstances are not viewed with the sense of awe and peculiarity they engender in Western European and Euro-American societies. Because the use of each language is carefully prescribed there is little if any lexical or grammatical mixing by the users, and there is no indication of incipient creolization in any of the languages.

Timucua resemblances to Proto-Tucanoan rather than some later form of the language indicates a Timucua presence in the critical area certainly by 2,500 B.C.

With regard to the possibility that Timucua may have developed in a region in which multilingualism has been a dominant characteristic for millenia, it is of interest to note that there are many lexical pairs or triplets in Timucua in which one variant is of native origin (that is, origin unknown), one showing Waroid, Tucanoan, or Arawakan resemblances, and another Southeastern United States origin: (1) 'snake' (a) *elatubasa* — origin unknown, (b) *yoroba*: Lokono */óri/*, (c) *iyola*: Natchez */ula/*; (2) 'strong' (a) *tari*: Warao */taera/*, (b) *chocori*: Culina */kara-/*; (3) 'eat' (a) *ho*: Warao */ho-/*, (b) *he*: Waliperi */he/*, (c) *ipa(ru)*: Koasati */ipá/*; (4) 'skin' (a) *pequa* — origin unknown, (b) *qechela*: Proto-Tucanoan **/kasero ~ katsero/*.

Multiple and variant lexical resemblances rarely occur under conditions of cultural contact in which one member is considered, for whatever reason, 'lower' and the other dominant or 'upper'. The latter situation usually results in a considerable degree of relexification of the non-dominant language, the dominant language remaining unscathed. We have in Timucua a situation closely paralleling what Morris Goodman referred to as *linguistic interpenetration* in the case of the Mbugu language of Tanzania (Goodman 1971:252). It is the same phenomenon noted by Čestmír Loukotka years ago in his classification of native

South American languages, one which he called simply *mixed languages* (Loukotka 1968:13). He found it very characteristic of South American languages in general and of Amazonian tongues in particular. Most professional linguists looked with something akin to horror on Loukotka's pedestrian term, but it is quite apt at a certain descriptive level. There is in Amazonia a very broad common lexical substratum running through all the languages of the equatorial region, regardless of family, stock, or even phylum. This is certainly the result of widespread trade, population movement (temporary or permanent), intermarriage (as in the Vaupés region's preferred language-exogamy), and other factors over an extremely long period of time. The lexical result is a very real 'mixing' in which the grammars peculiar to given languages, stocks, and phyla remain surprisingly stable and enduring.

Mixing or interpenetration, as distinct from relexification, takes place as the result of particularly intense but peaceful long-term cultural contacts in which no single party is culturally dominant. In the development of pidgins and true relexified creoles it is universally the norm that morphological complexity is drastically reduced and irregularities are regularized. This is usually not so with 'mixed' languages.

Timucua, while stemming from multiple sources, seems a case of mixing or interpenetration. The primary lexical parent(s), possibly an independent stock within Macro-Chibchan or Pano-Tacanan, perhaps not, has remained intact. If Timucua's closest genetic relatives are the Waroid languages, then its grammatical structure is also largely intact. If its grammatical structures were taken from Waroid neighbors, its own original structures must have been very close indeed to the borrowed ones — perhaps resulting from pan-areal structural similarities (cf. Migliazza 1985:20), though this does not seem to be the case. What relexification has taken place, if that is what it is, is so slight that it is questionable that the term should be used at all with regard to Timucua. A mere 8% of the surviving lexicon was affected, and many of the 'borrowings' were additions to, not replacements of, native terms.

THE TIMUCUA LANGUAGE

It is difficult to assess the exact nature of the contact between the early Timucua, Tucano, Arawak, Macro-Chibchan, and Panoan peoples which could have led to the situation we see in 17th-century Timucua. We have nothing in the way of archaeological data from the Vaupés-Caquetá-Inírida region to help us out and very little in the way of carefully-done ethnographic descriptions or ethnohistorical documentation. We are, however, fortunate in having considerable valuable ethnohistorical and archaeological data from areas to the north, west, and to a lesser extent south of the Timucua epicenter. Of particular value is the data from the archaeologically-defined *Intermediate Area*, encompassing Ecuador, Colombia from the Eastern Cordillera west and north to the Pacific and Caribbean, and most of Central America south of Guatemala.

This important cross-roads region between North and South America has recently begun to receive the archaeological attention it deserves, and specialists now realize both the critical nature of its geographic position and the highly civilized energies of its aboriginal inhabitants. Feldman and Moseley have recently pointed out that the peoples and cultures of the Intermediate Area were frequently the donors, not just the half-way-point recipients, of some extremely important cultural innovations (Feldman and Moseley 1978:139-177). It is, however, of equal importance to realize that this region did serve as the point from which Middle American innovations spread into South America and from which South American innovations spread to Middle and North America.

It is from the flanks of the Eastern Cordillera that most of the rivers of eastern Colombia and western Venezuela arise, including the Apure, Casanare, Meta, Guaviare, Inírida, Vaupés, and Caquetá-Japurá, emptying their increasing torrents ultimately into the Orinoco, Rio Negro, and the Amazon itself. The rivers served as they do today as vast networks for commerce, linking rather than separating regions in northwestern South America and leading directly to the Goajira Peninsula coast in the northwest and the Orinoco Delta in the northeast as the logical receiving-points from outside and as transporting points to that outside.

It has long been known from archaeological and ethnohistorical data that movement of peoples in the northern third of the continent has been largely by water. Accounts from early European travelers support this contention. Archaeological data certainly substantiate the notion for Arawakan speakers from the earliest times (Lathrap 1973, Rouse 1986:106-156). We know that the distances traveled for trading purposes alone were incredibly vast — Wallace noted in the late 1800's that the Vaupés region peoples regularly traveled back and forth to the Upper Amazon to sell cassava graters (Wallace 1889:336), and Schomburgk, some forty years earlier, had noted that the Waika traveled regularly to Colombia and Brazil to barter for dogs (Schomburgk 1847:198). Journeys from the Guianas to and from southeastern Colombia were not exceptional (Roth 1924:632-637).

Feldman and Moseley point out that at the time of Spanish intervention there were four major trading networks in the northern third of South America (Feldman and Moseley 1978:142). Two of these were laregly limited to the Andes region, moving goods in north-south direction. The other two, however, centered in east-west movement of goods in Ecuador, Colombia, the southern Andes, and Amazonia. The early Spanish noted these systems, stating that they were largely run and organized by a hereditary group of merchants known as the *mindala* (Salomon 1977/78:236).

In the Colombian region the *mindala* formed a group apart from the usual community, were exempt from taxation and tribute, and were of high social rank, similar to the *pochteca* of Aztec Mexico (Feldman and Moseley 1978:143). The very name *mindala* is of interest, for it readily translates into Timucua as 'The Lords' or 'The Great Ones' (*mine* 'lord, great' > *min* + *-ta* 'durative time' = [*da*] by automatic allophonic change after /*n*/ + *-la* 'proximate time' = 'Those Who Are Lords').

In Amazonia the Shipibo of Peru traveled as far as 1,600 km downstream to obtain suitable wood for blowguns (Feldman and Moseley 1978:145, Lathrap 1973:171-172). Such trade networks were not only in effect on the river systems but also involved sea voyages of considerable distances — certainly from Ecuador and Colombia as far as Peru to the south and Guatemala and Mexico to the north (Borhegyi 1959, Lathrap et al. 1975, Coe 1960, Edwards 1965). Lathrap (1973) feels that our data justify an antiquity for such sea-trading of at least 1,500 B.C., and it is not impossible that it existed as early as 3,500 B.C. (Zeidler 1977/78:26).

Trade of the nature described by the Spanish chroniclers and later European travelers, substantiated by both archaeological data and oral tradition, is often accompanied by the development of special language systems, such as Sabir (the Lingua Franca of the Mediterranean) or the many pidgins of the world. Normally such pidgins remain just that unless the contact is particularly intensive and long-lasting. In that case a creolized speech-form usually develops, building on the grammar of the less dominant language with the vocabulary of the dominant one — relexification.

If, however, long-term, intensive trade is largely in the hands of a professional trading class, such as the *pochteca* or *mindala*, and neither the language of the buyers nor the sellers is considered dominant socially or politically, then the usual result is that phenomenon we have defined as *interpenetration*, Loukotka's 'mixed languages'. The classic example is, of course, Swahili, Bantu in grammar and largely Bantu in lexicon, but with large infusions of Arabic and Perso-Arabic lexicon. Swahili has also developed grammatical peculiarities atypical of Bantu proper, largely new noun-classes resulting from the new, Arabic lexical material. While much of such new lexical material defines concepts new to the receiving culture — Swahili */kitabu/* 'book' (from Arabic), */meza/* 'table' (from Portuguese) — in many cases new, alternate lexemes for familiar concepts were added to account for use of the concept in a new social situation — Swahili */amkia/* '(to) greet' (native Bantu), */salimu/* '(to) greet' (from Arabic). This situation is familiar from Timucua, too, as we have seen.

It is suggested that late 16th- and early 17th-century

Timucua is such a creolized language. Given the lack of full-scale relexification the assumption would be that the language resulted from long-term development and use by a professional trading class such as the Perso-Arabic Omani traders of East Africa or the Aztec *pochteca.* Its original genetic base was probably Macro-Chibchan-related, stemming from southeastern Colombia or southwestern Venezuela and far northwestern Brazil. This area could readily have supplied the Waroid, Tucano, Panoan, and Arawak lexical forms seen in Timucua. That the contact was long-lasting seems indicated by Proto-Tucanoan and Proto-Arawakan/Pre-Andine Maipuran resemblances on the one hand (as early as 3,500 B.C.) and by early Northern Maipuran resemblances on the other hand (from approximately 2,000-1,800 B.C.). The long history of multilingualism in the target area would seem to substantiate the assumption. That Timucua was a trader's creole rather than what might be called a 'sedentary' creole seems indicated by the presence of lexical similarities with Chibchan Cuna and Paezan Chocó, far removed from the original putative Timucua homeland, as well as by the presence of clearly Proto-Muskogean lexical loans from southeastern North America.

If this picture is even partly valid, the trade network suggested here must have stretched from the Vaupés-Caquetá region along the river systems to the northwest, continuing up the Magdalena, Cauca, and Sinú Rivers, and culminating somewhere in or near Cuna-Chocó country. Archaeological evidence has indicated for some time now that the Caribbean coast of Colombia, centering around Barlovento and Puerto Hormiga, to the immediate west of the mouth of the Magdalena, was the focus of a trading nexus from at least 2,500 B.C. It seems not unlikely that the Timucua trade network articulated with this from early times.

The late James Ford has brought together a considerable amount of cogent evidence to support the contention that the appearance of the first ceramic wares in North America, on the Florida-Georgia Atlantic coast, was a result of direct trade from the Barlovento-Puerto Hormiga area of Colombia's Caribbean coast (Ford 1969, see also Bullen 1972). While there are many who will resist the idea, Timucua language data lend additional credence to it, for we know the Timucua ended up in Florida and Georgia, and the presence of Proto-Muskogean lexical loans in Timucua would date such an arrival, from whatever source, at approximately 2,000-1,500 B.C. This date is quite in keeping with the radiocarbon dates for fiber-tempered Stallings Island and Orange wares in Late Archaic sites in the Savannah and St. Johns River areas of the American southeast.

The fact that these North American ceramic wares occur in sites whose other artifactual content is typical of the Late Archaic is, I think, an indication that Timucua movement to North America was not the large-scale movement of a people but, rather, the result of small trading expeditions. The fact that the earliest Stallings Island radiocarbon dates are ca. 2,5215 B.C. (Rabbit Mount Site, Lab. No. GX0-345) may well indicate that the Timucua were not the first traders from the Colombian coast. The early Northern Maipuran resemblances in Timucua would preclude Timucua arrival much before 1,800 B.C. It is not impossible that the differences between Stallings Island wares and later Orange wares (ca. 1,625 B.C., Turner Site, Lab. No. G-598) are attributable to the entrance of the Timucua into this trans-Caribbean trade network. As Ford points out (1969:187) the stylistic changes in Orange ware mirror similar changes in Colombian wares, implying a continuation of such trade over a long period of time. The presence of a decidedly brachycephalic cranial type in Stallings Island sites, in contrast to the usual Southeastern Archaic dolichocephalic type, also suggests the presence of a growing number of alien people, who, though acting largely as itinerant traders, settled permanently in at least some locales (Claflin 1931:43-45).

Rouse (1986:121) erroneously attributes to me the hypothesis of 'a migration of ancestral Warao speakers northward through the West Indies from Venezuela to Florida.' This is a mistaken interpretation of my statement that 'it can be stated with at least moderate confidence that Timucua seems to show closest genetic relationship with Warao . . . what might be called a Pre-Timucua group split from the Pre-Warao of a Proto-Waroid stock ca. 3000-2000 B.C. and began to migrate to the Florida peninsula . . .' (Granberry 1971:607). While I would now, many years and considerable additional work later, modify the above, particularly the unfelicitous phrase 'closest genetic relationship', it seemed clear to me then and even clearer now that the route of such a trade network, as Ford suggests (1969:185), was through the Yucatán Channel, around western Cuba, on through the Florida Straits, and northward by way of the Gulf Stream to the St. Johns and Savannah River areas. Since there is no indication of Antillean-Timucuan interaction, linguistically or archaeologically, from any time period, a West Indian route would be quite out of the question. It should, though, be noted that there are many Waroid toponyms throughout the Greater Antilles, with the heaviest concentration in Pinar del Rio and Habana provinces in western Cuba (Granberry 1991). These, however, are attributable, it would seem from archaeological evidence, to physical Waroid population movement into the Antilles from the mainland to Trinidad and the Windward Islands at a time level at least a thousand years earler, likely associated with the Ortoiroid lithic expansion. It is not beyond possibility that the earlier familiarity with the Antilles by Macro-Chibchan speakers was what laid the groundwork for the subsequent Colombia-Florida/Georgia trade nexus.

Some of my critics feel, linguistic data notwithstanding, that my hypothesis would demand sudden cultural discontinuity throughout much of the Southeast at the late Archaic-Early Orange Period time-line, since fiber-tempered wares are widely represented in the Southeast on that early horizon and since the entire Southeast has been from time-immemorial inhabited by Muskogean speakers, whose *in situ* development is demonstrated by archaeological, ethnohistoric, and linguistic data. This criticism is, of course, logical, if — and *only* if — a Timucua presence meant the arrival of large numbers of conquest-minded migrants. This, however, as I have pointed out, is not at all the scenario I am suggesting. Cultural continuity in the Southeast —

certainly in northeast Florida — is an incontrovertible fact (*cf.* Miller 1992, Russo 1992). If one assumes on the basis of both linguistic and archaeological evidence, however, that Timucua migrations were initially the result of the accidental movement of small groups of traders, then cultural continuity in the Southeast, *with* the imposition of some artifactual traits from northwestern South America, is not at all peculiar nor to be remarked at. The spread of peoples, traits, artifacts, and languages in precisely the same manner is well-attested in Polynesia, the Greater Antilles, and in Indo-European Europe, to cite only a few of the more obvious examples..

Furthermore, a broad spectrum of cultural similarities between Late Archaic period sites on Colombia's Caribbean coast and slightly later but essentially coeval sites in the Savannah River area of Georgia's Atlantic coast and the St. Johns River area of northeast Florida is both very specific and not at all typical of those Southeastern sites of the period which we know have undeniable cultural continuity with the local past (*cf.* Waring 1968, Shannon 1986). Such parallels place a 'South American Connection' at least within the realm of possibility.

These Georgia and Florida sites — the ceramics-bearing Stallings Island and Orange Period sites — are located away from the coast proper, generally on the shores of rivers or large creeks, while the majority of Late Archaic sites are either inland or on the hammock lands of the coastal marshes. The riverine niche is, in fact, a salient characteristic of fiber-tempered ware sites and remains so until the advent of horticulture. Such an environment would, of course, have been the preferred one for the Timucua, if the hypothesis of their riverine South American origins is correct.

In Florida the pre-ceramic Mt. Taylor Late Archaic peoples also occupied such a riverine environment. It should, I would suggest, come as no surprise to find continuity from the Late Archaic into the ceramic-producing Early Formative. The river-oriented Timucua immigrant traders would naturally have gravitated to Mt. Taylor settlements. Not only are the locations of North America's first pottery-bearing sites similar to sites on the Colombian Caribbean coast, but the shapes of the physical structures are the same — in both areas they are semi-circular ring-shaped and in both areas constructed of shell (Willey 1971:268-271). Fortuitous parallels? Taken alone, possibly; taken with the accompanying ceramic near identities, the presence of a locally atypical dolicocephalic population, and the linguistic data — not likely. The parallels are simply too many, too close, and too much within the same time-frame to be dismissed as wishful imagination.

With later ceramic wares in Florida and Georgia, the Deptford in particular, we find a settlement pattern which differs markedly from that of Late Archaic, Stallings Island/Orange times (Milanich 1973). Deptford sites are located either along coastal marshes, on both the Atlantic and Gulf coasts, or, if inland, not in exclusively riverine locales. With the beginning of horticulture both coastal and riverine patterns begin to weaken, as inland settlement on better agricultural lands takes precedence. In early Deptford times, however, the then remnant fiber-tempered cultures and the Deptford cultures complement each other rather than compete within the same ecological zones (Milanich 1973:53).

The implication is that the Deptford peoples, who show cultural continuity with the succeeding Wilmington and Savannah peoples in Georgia, were likely Muskogean in both language and material culture. This seems substantiated by archaeological evidence indicating that the Guale (Apalachee <guaili> */wayli/* 'border, edge'), of known Muskogean affiliation, were the end-product of the Wilmington-Savannah tradition (Milanich 1976, Larson 1978). It seems likely that the same can be said for the Late Archaic, Early Formative peoples of the northern Florida Gulf coast. When fiber-tempered wares, generally called Norwood (Phelps 1965), appear on that coast they are distinctive from both Orange and Stallings Island wares, giving the strong impression that their presence is due to the spread of an idea and a set of artifactual techniques to an alien people, not to the movement of a new, non-local population into the area. Yet these wares date from at least as early as 2,000 on the north peninsular Gulf Coast, with a startlingly early radiocarbon date of 2,510 B.C. (4,570 +/- 110 B.P., Beta-27221, 1988) for skeletal materials in a Norwood context on Bird Island off the Dixie County coast, implying a rather rapid spread of the technique of pottery-making from the St. Johns or Georgia coast westward to the Gulf area. In spite of this early spread of putative Timucua-inspired ceramic techniques as far afield as the northern Florida Gulf Coast, however, the primary cultural ties of that region were always to the north and the south along the coastal periphery rather than to the east.

The two broadly defined linguistic-archaeological traditions, native Muskogean and intrusive Timucua, do blend in later times in Florida's geographical middle-ground, the Alachua Prairies and neighboring Columbia and Taylor counties, to produce the Alachua Tradition. The two heartlands — the St. Johns River valley and the Gulf Coast — remain Timucua and Muskogean respectively, developing into the long St. Johns Tradition in the first and the Safety Harbor/Fort Walton/Leon-Jefferson Tradition in the second.

Recent archaeological work in the Utina (Timucua) and Potano Mission Provinces of North and North-Central Florida, indicates what would seem to be considerable Timucua-Muskogean cultural mixing in the years following 700 A.D. The exact origins, nature, and causes of this process and how far it had moved toward actual creolization rather than simple culture-contact remain yet to be defined in any detail, but extensive contact is certainly indicated (*cf.* Weisman 1992).

As the result of recent work by Brent Weisman and John Worth we can make certain tentative assumptions about the Muskogean-Timucua 'mix'. Weisman and Worth have provided us with a careful revision of the ceramic typology for Utina (Timucua) and Potano provinces in North Florida from the late prehistoric period (ca. 900-1600 A.D.) through the early Mission Period (1597-1656) (Weisman 1992, Worth 1992). This revision was based on careful comparative treatment of the available ceramic collections, particularly those from the Fig Springs Site (8Co1) in Columbia County — probably the site of the mission of

San Martín de Timucua — and indicates a gradual merging of ceramic traditions of disparate origins during the time periods in question. Alongside the Alachua series it is possible to establish a closely related yet distinct Suwannee Valley series of wares, which co-exists in various overlapping ways with ceramics of the Lamar, Jefferson, and newly defined Goggin series.

Georgian origins were convincingly suggested for the Alachua Series many years ago (Milanich 1971). Such origins are also certain for Lamar Series wares (Jennings and Fairbanks 1939, Scarry 1985), and Weisman (1992:32) accurately points out that there are close similarities between the Suwannee Valley series type referred to as Fig Springs Roughed and the Chattahoochee Brushed ceramics of Georgia and Alabama, the latter certainly associated with the Muskogean-speaking Creeks of the historic period. The new Goggin series of shell-tempered wares is also Georgia-oriented, showing greatest similarity to the Dallas wares of northwestern Georgia, northeastern Alabama, and eastern Tennessee (Worth 1992: 201). At the same time Suwannee Valley series wares have enough in common with late Weeden Island ceramic types to warrant an assumption of at least partial origin from that source (Weisman 1992:31).

In brief — in spite of the fact that all the data are not in — the mixed message from North Florida between approximately 700-1656 A.D. is that this was an area of extensive, complex culture contact, contact that nonetheless did not nullify the essential Timucua character of the region.

A final problem clouding definition of Timucua-Muskogean interplay is the interesting fact that the bulk of Muskogean loans in Timucua seem to come from Apalachee, Alabama, and Koasati, the westernmost of the Eastern Muskogean languages. Though some of these lexical items have close Creek or Hitchiti cognates, the Creek and Hitchiti forms are distinct from both the Apalachee-Alabama-Koasati forms and the Timucua forms. One would expect Creek and/or Hitchiti, the more easterly of the eastern Muskogean tongues, to have been the major contributors to the Timucua lexicon. They were not. There are also a few probable Choctaw loans and two possible borrowings from

Natchez and Atakapa, futher suggesting Timucua presence as far west as the Mississippi River.

There are two possible explanations of this phenomenon. First, at the 1,800-1,000 B.C. time-level Creek and Hitchiti speakers may have been located father to the north and west than in later times, perhaps on the Georgia-Tennessee border, ancestral Alabama, Koasati, and Apalachee speakers forming a 'layer' of population to the south of them and spreading farther east than we now realize. This possibility is raised by the use of the Apalachee or Koasati name Guale (the English spelled it Wali), Apalachee */wayli/*, Koasati */waylí/* 'border, edge' (*cf.* Kimball 1988:396), to refer to the easternmost of the known Muskogean peoples on the Atlantic coast of Georgia.

Apalachee has been shown to have been most closely related to Alabama and Koasati, in the western branch of Eastern Muskogean (Haas 1949, Kimball 1987, 1988). If the unknown language of the Guale was, indeed, most closely related to Apalachee, Alabama, and Koasati, the problem would not be difficult to resolve — it would be likely that the greatest bulk of Muskogean loans in Timucua had a Guale source. A grammar of Guale is known to have been written by Fr. Domingo Augustín between 1565 and 1585, but it has vanished in the maw of Spanish colonial bureaucratic records, either in the Consejo de Indias or perhaps the records of the Jesuit Order (Swanton 1946:135).

Secondly, if we should find that Guale belonged in the eastern branch of Eastern Muskogean, with Creek and Hitchiti, then we are in trouble, for this would imply that the Timucua were primarily in long-term contact not with the coastal Guale but with their Alabama and Koasati neighbors far to the west. This, however, might not be quite as troublesome as it seems on first glance, given the interesting riverine dispersion of the Oconi and Tawasa. These two Timucua groups were distributed along the river systems penetrating later Alabama and Koasati lands, and it is not impossible to envision them as the forefront

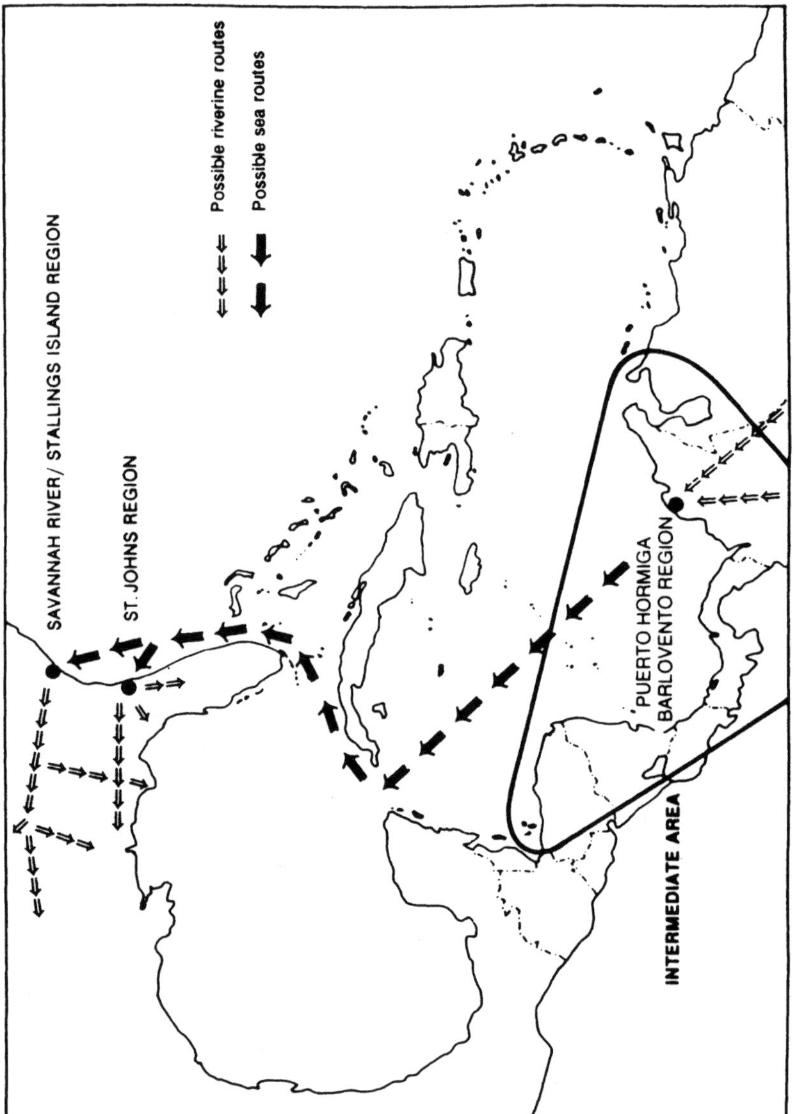

FIG.3
Possible Timucua Trade Routes ca. 1,800 B.C.

of a Timucua trading-wedge into the Southeastern heartland, even though their home-base remained along the Atlantic coast in the Savannah and St. Johns River regions.

Either hypothesis could be tested archaeologically, and the presence of fiber-tempered wares at both the undated Fourche Maline site-complex in eastern Oklahoma (Newkumet 1940) and the Bayou La Batre complex near Mobile Bay (Greenwell 1984), dating to around 1,000-500 B.C., may be an indication that the second hypothesis above is correct. Fiber-tempered wares at both complexes are remarkably similar to Floridian Orange wares, so similar that direct migrations of Orange ware makers have been suggested for the Fourche Maline area (Ford 1969:176).

It may, in fact, be the case that both explanations have some truth to them. The earliest fiber-tempered-ware-bearing sites in the Savannah River region may have been central dispersion points from which riverine trading expeditions put out. Presumably the major item of outgoing trade was pottery, though in return for what we are not sure. The exchange may have involved salt — Timucua *api*, a borrowing from Alabama, Koasati or Choctaw */hapi/* — the Creek */okcán-wa/*, Hitchiti */okcahn-i/*, while cognate with each other, are not cognate with the more westerly stem (Haas 1941:47). Salt is abundant in the central Mississippi Valley and was a major Southeastern trading commodity from very early times on through the Mississippian, both for comestible purposes and as a valuable additive in the manufacture of ceramic wares (Stimmel, Heimann, and Hancock 1982:227). A closer examination of the artifactual inventories of all fiber-tempered sites is certainly called for, particularly in the Savannah and Tennessee River regions.

The present interpretation of Timucua language data, correlated with archaeological information, tends to support a Chibchan-related ultime origin for the language and people somewhere in the Vaupés-Caquetá region of Colombia. The people seem to have been traders, perhaps the famous *mindala*, and to have participated in the trade-network between the northwestern Amazonian jungles and the northwestern

Caribbean coast of Colombia. Eventually they seem to have become one of the prime movers, if not the prime mover, of trans-oceanic trade between that coast and the Southeastern United States. They seem to have established major trading stations on the Savannah and St. Johns Rivers and to have continued to build a Southeastern trading-network along the same lines as in northwestern South America, oriented along major river systems of the region. There is no indication that they migrated to North America in great numbers nor that they came as warlike conquerors. Rather, the archaeological evidence suggests that they came as small, intermittent trading parties, at first perhaps by accident, brought to land by the Gulf Stream and its proximity to the coast of Florida and southern Georgia. They seem to have established themselves in small riverine communities, beginning with settlements on the Savannah and St. Johns Rivers and spreading on inland along the courses of these rivers and their tributaries.

The main outgoing trading commodity seems to have been pottery, to judge from the Fourche Maline evidence, perhaps in return for salt and other items. Such a network must have survived for a considerable period of time — at least until the advent of horticulture as the major form of livelihood and the creation of a more settled way of life. It may, in fact, have been this set of changes which turned the Timucua, still in possession of their South American language and many of their native culture traits, into the Timucua known to the Europeans of the 16th century. By that time they had been a creolized, Muskogeanized, if you will, people with most of the expected attributes of 16th century native Southeastern culture. The data are there — they need only the spade of the competent archaeologist and an expertise in the techniques of modern laboratory and comparative analysis to further test the present hypothesis. Perhaps the Timucua will yet acquire the flesh and blood they have lacked for the past two centuries, since the move of the last few survivors to the Cuban pueblo of San Agustín Nueva — *Ceibamocha*, 'The Speaking Place Under the Ceiba Tree'.

2 A TIMUCUA GRAMMAR

2 A TIMUCUA GRAMMAR

ORTHOGRAPHY & PHONOLOGY

Pareja designed an orthography for use in writing Timucua which was based largely on 17th-century Spanish spelling conventions (*cf.* Spaulding 1948). His keen insight lets us know what some of the salient phonological differences between Spanish and Timucua were, and he overtly describes allophonic detail carefully along with a presentation of minimal-pairs which makes parts of his grammar surprisingly modern (Adam and Vinson 1886:2-3, 26-27). Because of Pareja's attention to phonological detail it is relatively easy to reconstruct the segmental phonemes of Timucua, insofar as this can ever be done with extinct language materials (*cf.* Broadbent 1957). He used this orthography uniformly in all his published works, and Fr. Movilla followed suit. To judge from the orthography of the two surviving Timucua letters it is this set of orthographic conventions which was taught by the Franciscans, who were charged with the education of the native Floridians. We have, in fact, one contemporary attestation (1616) that 'with ease — using Pareja's books — many Indians have learned to read in less than six months and write letters to one another in their own language' (Oré 1616 [1936:103]).

The equations between orthographic symbol and reconstituted phoneme are given in Table 1 in the USER'S GUIDE (pp. xxiv-xxv). All Timucua forms in this volume are, as pointed out in that section, cited in canonical spelling rather than in a phonemic orthography, inasmuch as the canonical spelling is generally identical with Pareja's orthography and is essentially a 1:1 fit with the reconstituted phonemic spelling.

VOWELS

This reconstituted phonemicization agrees essentially with my earlier version (Granberry 1956) except that the three-vowel system reconstructed at that time is clearly incorrect. Pareja provides definite evidence for a five-vowel system with contrast between all members (Adam and Vinson 1886:26-27). Patterns of vowel harmony, discussed later, indicate that */i/* was a high front unrounded vowel, */u/* a high back rounded vowel, */a/* a low central unrounded vowel, */e/* a mid to low front unrounded vowel [*ε*] to [*æ*], and */o/* a lower-mid to low back rounded vowel [*o*] to [*ω*]. Post-junctural, form-initial vowels seem frequently, but optionally, to have been pre-aspirated, as in *aca~haca* 'wind', *aya~haya* 'mountain', *iba~hiba* 'rain'.

There is neither mention nor indication of vowel length. A few forms, such as *tooma* 'all, complete, total', *peemo* 'thrown down', show vocalic doubling orthographically, occurring in all instances of the forms. The phenomenon is rare, however, and it is difficult to imagine that as astute a linguistic observer as Pareja would have missed such a point as vowel length.

Similarly vowel clusters are essentially non-existent, occurring only in the lexical juxtaposition of a morpheme-final vowel with a morpheme-initial vowel under normal transition (see the discussion of transitions in the section JUNCTURE AND TRANSITION later in this chapter), as in *nibiroisticolebonama* 'we are evil men', in which the constituent base morphemes of the compound stem *biroistico* are *biro* 'man' and *istico* 'evil', or *chihubasoteo* 'you love someone', in which the constituent bound-form suffix morphemes are *-te* 'durative' and *-o* 'punctual-intensive'. There is no indication that either the rare <V_1V_1> of *tooma* and *peemo* or <V_1V_2> clusters represent */VbV/* — that is, possibly [*VwV*] or */VyV/*. It should particularly be noted that such <V_1V_2> clusters occur *only* under normal transition, never with an intervening /+/, which is zeroed by the phenomenon called *assimilation* (see the PHONOLOGICAL PROCESSES section of this chapter). In the few instances of <V_1V_2> clusters in morpheme-internal environments, such as *-tiacu* 'proximate time', *aimanta* 'deceased person', *aqio* 'already', it is impossible to make a definitive statement other than to say that /*VbV*/ and /*VyV*/ occur frequently enough as <*VbV*> and <*VyV*> orthographically to render the /*VbV*/, /*VyV*/ interpretation of <V_1V_2> rather unlikely — for example, *aya* 'mountain', *hiyo* 'suffer', *eye* 'path', *colahayo* 'admiration', *huya* 'pulverize', *ebo* 'child', *hiba* 'rain', *cobe* 'successor', *cubita* 'hunger'.

CONSONANTS

The phonetic-phonemic identification of most of the orthographic consonants is relatively straightforward. The only problem is the phonetic definition of the phonemes /*f*/ and /*b*/. The variations in orthographic representation of /*f*/ and /*b*/ suggest that phonetic realization yielded sounds either not present in 17th-century Spanish or not regularly represented by a single or consistent spelling in the Spanish orthography of the times. The <*h*> variation of /*f*/ implies to me the possibility that /*f*/ was, as in the speech of all but the youngest speakers of the Muskogean languages today, a bilabial voiceless spirant [*φ*]. Similarly the <*b*>, <*bu*>, <*gu*>, <*hu*> orthographic variants of /*b*/ imply a voiced bilabial spirant [*β*] rather than voiced stop [*b*], for that variation of spelling was also the norm in 16th and early 17th-century Spanish for the phoneme /*b*/, realized as [*β*] in environments other than post-junctural or post-nasal (Entwistle 1942:185, 260). Additionally the fact that /*f*/ and /*b*/, normally distinct and clearly in contrast — <*bara*> 'filth', <*fara*> 'dislike' — are occasionally interchangeable, as in *iribitela~irifitela* 'it flies', would seem to reinforce the spirant interpretation of /*f*/ and /*b*/.

Geoffrey Kimball (1988:399) has suggested that Timucua /*b*/ was [*b*] on the basis of the Apalachee toponym *Ibitachuko*, which, as he rightly points out, incorporates the Apalachee word

/čoko/ 'dwelling' (Kimball 1988:391) and the Timucua form *ibita* 'it is a river' (*ibi* 'water, river' + *-ta* 'durative time'). The fact that Apalachee, which had a */w/* phoneme, did not borrow the form as */iwitačoko/* indicates to him that the <*b*> symbol as used in both languages represented phonetic [*b*], the normal Muskogean realization of */b/*. While he is certainly correct in pointing out that I erred in initially identifying Timucua <*b*> and its variants as [*w*] (Granberry 1956:104), there is evidence in addition to Spanish orthography which would as definitely suggest that Timucua */b/* was not [*b*]. This comes from the Tawasa vocabulary gathered in 1707 by Lt. Col. John Walker of King & Queen County, Virginia. Walker was an English speaker (Swanton 1929), and he uniformly uses orthographic <*u*> or <*w*> in every Timucua word which occurs with an orthographic <*b*> or one of its variants in Pareja and Movilla. Specifically *soba* 'meat' is rendered as *soúa*, *biro* 'man' is as *Wiedōō*, and *ibi* 'water, river' is as *Wiĕott* (*-t* being the Muskogean 'nominative' or 'subject' suffix). In the same manner the word 'hand', *hue* in the Mocama dialect, is given as *foóley* in Lamhatty's Tawasa, *-ley* being the 'proximate time' suffix *-la~-le* in Timucua (*cf.* pp. 10-11 in Chapter 1). This last word also seems to imply */h/-/f/* variation, be it phonemic or morphophonemic, leading again toward the assumption of a probable [*φ*] value for */f/*. All the evidence, that is, points toward both */b/* and */f/* as bilabial spirants.

STRESS AND PITCH

While suprasegmental phonemes are difficult to suggest from strictly orthographic data, Pareja's descriptive statements enable recovery of a surprising amount of information. Unfortunately nothing can be said about pitch. Stress, however, is easier to document. Pareja specifically states that words of one, two, or three syllables take primary stress (I am using the notation [´]) on the first syllable (Adam and Vinson 1886:5-6). In words of more than three syllables every other syllable after the first bears a secondary stress (I use the notation [ˆ]), though we have no precise idea what that means other than that [ˆ] is of lesser degree than [´] and greater degree than tertiary stress (for which I use the notation [`]). Enclitics, which are well-defined by Pareja, usually drew primary stress (Adam and Vinson 1886:6). Examples of these phenomena are: *yobo* [*yóbò*] 'stone', *nipita* [*nípìtà*] 'mouth', *atimucu* [*átìmûkù*] 'frost', *holatamaqui* [*hôlàtâmàk^{w}í*] 'and the chief'. The total predictability implies, of course, that stress was non-phonemic.

JUNCTURE AND TRANSITION

Transition phenomena and juncture, while not overtly defined as such, are partly recoverable from Pareja's data. It is fairly clear that there were three phonetic transitions involving junctures which may have been similar to the /+/, /|/, and /#/ of other languages. Something like the plus-juncture of other languages, distinct from a presumably longer 'pause' with unknown associated pitch contours, symbolized here as /|/, seems signalled by the rule of vowel alternation called *regressive assimilation*, discussed in the next section of this chapter. This rule does not occur under normal transition in the ordinary flow of vocalization from one phone to another, but only across morpheme boundaries, reducing the non-normal transition to normal transition, as in *tera* + *acola* 'very good' > *teracola*, *coloma* + *uqua* 'not here' > *colomaqua*, reducing what would normally be taken as a sequence of two mono-morphemic lexemes to a single bi-morphemic lexeme.

One is tempted to state simply that the final vowel of one word merges with the initial vowel of the next in favor of the first vowel, except that this does not always happen, as in *istico* + *acola* 'very bad', which never becomes *isticocola* (Adam and Vinson 1886:6-7). Neither does this phenomenon occur internally within morphemes, as in *tooma* 'all, complete, total,' *chie* 'cause', *ofue* 'besides', which never occur as **toma*, **chi*, or **ofu*. That is, some kind of 'pause' longer than normal transition between phones when morpheme-internal separates *tera* and *acola*, and this 'pause' is not the same as that separating *istico* and *acola*. Lastly, it is assumed from Pareja's use of punctuation that utterance-final transition phenomena differ from utterance-internal transitions. Thus a /#/ juncture is defined, presumably as in most languages of longer duration than normal transition, /+/, or /|/. Associated pitch contours are totally unknown for all transitions. Normal transition, in summary, seems orthographically signalled by the lack of printed space between symbols, /+/ transition by the presence of orthographic space, /|/ very frequently, but not always, by the use of orthographic <,>, and /#/ by the use of terminal punctuation marks <.> and <?>.

PHONOLOGICAL PROCESSES

There are two phonological processes in Timucua: *automatic alteration* and *reduplication*. There are in turn two categories of alteration: *assimilation* and *substitution*. Both involve vowels only; there are no instances of automatic consonant alteration. Such vocalic alterations may be characterized as either *regressive* or *non-regressive*, with the former predominating. In regressive alterations it is the nature of the first vowel of the second of two contiguous morphemes which causes a vocalic change in the last vowel of the first morpheme of the pair (numerous examples are provided below). In *regressive assimilation* the changes are conditioned solely by phonological factors. In *regressive substitution*, on the other hand, it is not only the phonological nature of the participating vowels which is important, but also the semological/semantic function of the specific morphemes involved. In *non-regressive alterations*, all substitutions, the conditioning factors are also both phonological and semological/semantic.

ASSIMILATION

All assimilations are regressive. They take place only across morpheme boundaries and then only when the two morphemes are separated by /+/. They occur when the initial morpheme in a pair ends in a vowel and the second morpheme begins in a vowel — /*-V+V-*/. In all such instances the post-junctural initial vowel of the second morpheme is assimilated to the pre-junctural final vowel of the first morpheme. The /+/ juncture is lost in the assimilation. There are two patterns: /-V_1+V_1-/ > /-V_1-/ and /-V_1+V_2-/ > /-V_1-/, as in *tera* 'good' + *acola* 'very' > *teracola* 'very good', *coloma* 'here' + *uqua* 'not' > *colomaqua* 'not here'. As noted above, this alteration does not take place under normal transition or /|/. Instances of /-*VCV* & *VCV*-/ morphemes coming together under normal transition in compound-stem structures, without assimilation regardless of the nature of the two adjacent vowels, are relatively infrequent, but they do occur, as in the example *nibiroisticolebonama* 'we are evil men' cited earlier.

REGRESSIVE SUBSTITUTION

Regressive substitution also occurs solely across morpheme boundaries, but the morphemes are joined by normal transition, never /+/. Unlike regressive assimilation, which may involve any of the five phonemic vowels, regressive substitution involves only first-morpheme low vowels /*e*/, /*a*/, and /*o*/. Also unlike regressive assimilation, substitution occurs whether or not consonants intervene between the two vowels. The second morpheme in all attested examples of substitution, in fact, always has the shape *CV*.

There are three types of regular regressive substitution. In TYPES 1 and 2 the conditioning is such that if the last vowel of the first morpheme is a low vowel it will always alter before the vowel of the second morpheme if that vowel is also a low vowel (see Table 15), the alteration pattern being a raising of the last vowel of the first morpheme (all TYPE 2 forms and most TYPE 1 forms) or a backing of the last vowel of the first morpheme (some TYPE 1 forms). The first morpheme of a TYPE 1 pair is a polysyllabic base of a small, finite set of terms, many, as Pareja indicates, terms of '*parentesco*' (kin-terms), all of which end in -*CV* or -*VV*: *ibine* 'water', *aqe* 'air', *ite* 'father', *isa* 'mother', *qie* 'son' (Adam and Vinson: 1886:24). The second morpheme is a possessive pronominal suffix. It should be reiterated, as pointed out on p. 26, that a pattern paralleling TYPE 1 regressive substitution also occurs in Proto-Maipuran Arawak (Payne 1990:81).

The first morpheme of a TYPE 2 pair is a possessive pronominal suffix, any other low-vowel-containing suffix serving as the second morpheme. While there is the theoretical potential for nine low vowel combinations in TYPE 1 and 2 environments, only five actually occur: */e/-/e/*, */e/-/a/*, */a/-/e/*, */a/-/a/*, and */a/-/o/*. Other combinations are ruled out by the phonological nature of the bases belonging to TYPE 1 and of the possessive pronominal suffixes, none of which end in */o/*.

In TYPE 3 two suffixes, one or both of which must be verbal, come together. While the final vowel of the first morpheme is always a low vowel, the vowel of the second morpheme may be either a high or low vowel, and the alterations do not conform to the TYPE 1-2 pattern, but differ from one morpheme-pair to another (see TYPE 3, Table 15). TYPE 1 is extremely restricted and rare; TYPES 2 and 3 are of very high frequency.

TABLE 15

REGRESSIVE SUBSTITUTIONS

Type/Environment		**Substitution**
1A	Morph 1 = Kin-term; 2 = Poss. pron. suffix	*e-e > a-e*
1B	SAME	*e-a > i-a*
1C	SAME	*a-a > o-a*
2A	Morph 1 = Poss. pron. suffix; 2 = Any suffix	*a-a > i-a*
2B	SAME	*a-o > i-o*
2C	SAME	*a-e > i-e*
3A	*-ma*^{2} + *-la*	*-mo + -la*
3B	*-ma*^{3} + *-bi, -qe, -na*^{3}	*-mo + -bi, -qe, -na*
3C	*-na*^{2} + *-chu*	*-n + -chu*
3D	*-na*^{3} + *-ma*^{4}	*-ni + -ma*
3E	*-no*^{1} + *-chu*	*-n + chu*
3F	*-no*^{2} + *-chu*	*-n + chu*

3G	*-no*^{1} + *-no*^{2}, *-bo*	*-ni* + *-no*, *-bo*
3H	*-si*^{1} + *-la*	*-se* + *-la*
3I	*-so* + *-te~-ta*	*-s* + *-te~-ta*
3J	*-so* + *-la*, *-chu*	*-sa* + *-la*, *-chu*
3K	*-so* + *-ma*^{2}	*-se* + *ma*
3L	*-so* + *-bo*	*-si* + *-bo*
3M	*-bo* + *-chu*, *-ma*^{4}	*-ba* + *-chu*, *-ma*

Examples of regressive substitution types and sub-types are:

TYPE 1 (Base + Possessive Pronoun Suffix):

A. *e-e* > *a-e*:

ite 'father' + *-ye* 'your' > *itaye* 'your father'
qie 'son' + *-ye* 'your' > *qiaye* 'your son'

B. *e-a* > *i-a*:

ite 'father' + *-na* 'my' > *itina* 'my father'
(It should be noted that *qie* 'son' does not conform to TYPE 1B, which would dictate that, for example, 'my son' should become *qiina*. This does not happen; it remains *qiena*, possibly because the /*-ii-*/ combination does not occur in any other attested morpheme or lexeme in the language.)

C. *a-a* > *o-a*:

isa 'mother' + *-na* 'my' > *isona* 'my mother'

TYPE 2 (Possessive Pronominal Suffix + Other Suffix):

A. *a-a* > *i-a*:

ite 'father' + *-ma*^{1} 'his' + *-ma*^{2} 'the' > *itimima* 'his father'

B. *a-o* > *i-o*:

paha 'house' + *-ma*^{1} 'his' + *-no*^{2} 'it is' > *pahamino* 'it is his house'

C. *a-e* > *i-e*:

ite 'father' + *-ma*^{1} 'his' + *-le* 'it is' > *itimile* 'it is his father'

TYPE 3 (Suffix 1 + Suffix 2 — one is always a verbal suffix):

A. *-ma*^{2} 'the' + *-la* 'proximate time' > *-mo* + *-la*:

ibine 'water' + *-ma*^{2} + *-la* > *ibinemola* 'it is the water'

B. *-ma*^{3} '3 pl. subject' + *-bi* 'bounded action', *-qe* 'optative', *-na*^{3} 'habitual action' > *-mo* + *-bi*, *-ke*, *-na*:

i. *ini-* 'be' + *-ma*^{3} + *-bi* + *-la* 'proximate time' > *inimobila* 'they are just now'

ii. *pue* 'go' + *-no*^{1} 'action designator' + *-ma*^{3} '3 pl. subject' + *qe* > *puenomoqe* 'they may go'

iii. *ini-* 'be' + *-ma*^{3} + *-na*^{3} + *-no*^{2} 'proximate time' > *inimonano* 'they usually are'

C. *-na*^{2} 'durative'+ *-chu* 'perfective' > *-n* + *-chu*:

ni- 'lst person' + *ini-* > *-ni-* > *-n-* 'be' + *-ta* 'durative' + *-na*^{2} + *-chu* + *-no*^{2} > *-nu* 'proximate time' > *nintanchunu* 'I have been'

D. *-na*^{3} 'habitual action' + *-ma*^{4} 'proximate time' > *-ni* + *-ma*:

'1st person' + *huba* 'love' + *-so* 'transitive-causative' + *-bo* '1, 2 pl. subject' + *-ta* 'durative' + *-na*^{3} + *-ma*^{4} > *nihubasobotanima* 'we always love (someone)'

E. *-no*^{1} 'action designator' *-chu* 'perfective' > *-n* + *-chu*:

huba 'love' + *-so* 'transitive-causative' + *-no*^{1} + *-chu* + *-no*^{2} > *-nu* 'proximate time' > *hubasonchunu* 'I have loved (someone)'

F. *-no*^{2} 'proximate time' + *-cu* 'subjunctive' > *-n* + *-cu*:

huba 'love' + *-so* 'transitive-causative' + *-ta* 'durative' + *-no*^{2} + *-cu* > *hubasotancu* 'if I love (someone)'

G. *-no*^{1} 'action designator' + *-no*^{2} 'proximate time', *-bo* '1, 2 pl. subject' > *-ni* + *-no*, *-bo*:

i. *ni-* '1st person' + *heba* 'speak' + *-no*^{1} + *-no*^{2} > *nihebanino* 'I am speaking (just now)'

ii. *ni-* '1st person' + *huba* 'love' + *-so* 'transitive-causative' + *-si*^{1} 'reflexive' + *-no*^{1} + *-bo* + *-te* 'durative' + *-la* 'proximate time' > *nihubasosinibotela* 'we love each other'

H. *-si*^{1} 'reflexive' + *-la* 'proximate time > *-se* + *-la*:

chulufi 'bird' and *ni-* '1st person' + *nihi* 'die' + *-si*^{1} + *-la* > *chulufi ninihisela* 'the bird died on me'

I. *-so* 'transitive-causative' + *-te~-ta* 'durative' > *-s* + *-te~-ta*:

ho^{1}*-* '1st person' + *chi-* '2d person' + *mani* 'love greatly' + *-so* + *-ta* + *-la* 'proximate time' > *hochimanistala* 'I love you a lot'

J. *-so* 'transitive-causative' + *-la* 'proximate time', *-chu* 'perfective', *-sa* + *-la*, *-chu*:
   i. *nioco* 'run' + *-so* + *-la* > *niocosala* 'be making something or someone run'
   ii. *huba* 'love' + *-so* + *chu-* + *-la* 'proximate time' > *hubasachula* 'he has loved (someone)'

K. *-so* 'transitive-causative' + *-ma*[2] 'the' > *-se* + *-ma*:
   heba 'speak' + *so* + *-ma*[2] > *hebasema* 'the speaker'

L. *-so* 'transitive-causative' + -bo '1, 2 pl. subject' > *-si* + *-bo*:
   ho[1]*-* '1st person' + *chi-* '2d person' + *mani* 'love greatly' + *-so* + *-bo* + *-ta* 'durative' + *-la* 'proximate time' > *hochimanisibotala* 'we love you very much'

M. *-bo* '1, 2 pl. subject' + *-chu* 'perfective', *-ma*[4] 'proximate time' > *-ba* + *-chu*, *-ma*:
   i. *ni-* '1st person' + *ini-* > *-ni-* 'be' + *-bo* + *-chu* > *ninibachu* 'we have been'
   ii. *ni-* '1st person' + *he-* 'pronoun designator' + *-ca* 'plural' + *-le* 'proximate time' + *-bo* + *-ma*[4] > *nihecalebama* 'it is we'

IRREGULAR REGRESSIVE SUBSTITUTION PATTERNS

There are three additional, aberrant patterns of regressive substitution. Two extremely frequent substitutions, TYPES 4A and 4B, are unusual in that they do not involve low vowels:

4A *ini-* 'be' + *-te~-ta* 'durative' > *in-* + *-te~-ta* as in *intele* 'he is' (*-le* 'proximate time')

4B *ini-* 'be' + *-le~-la* 'proximate time', *-chu* 'perfective' > *ine-* + *-le~-la*, *-chu*, as in *ninela* 'I am' and *ninechunu* 'I have been' (*ni-* '1st person' + *ini-* > *ine-* + *-chu* + *-no*[2] > *-nu* 'proximate time')

TYPE 5, which occurs so sporadically that it may simply represent a typographical misprint in the texts, is unusual in that it does not take place under normal transition, a requirement for all other types of regressive substitution. It occurs only if the form in question is immediately followed by /+/, /|/, or /#/. In this environment *-so* 'transitive-causative' > *-sa*, as in *huquisa* 'cause to rain' (Pareja 1613:150 [misprinted in Gatschet 1878:500 as *uquisa*]).

NON-REGRESSIVE SUBSTITUTION

Non-regressive substitutions, shown in Table 16, though few in number, occur with extreme frequency. TYPES 6 and 7 involve phonological changes in specific semological environments. In TYPE 6 it is the phonological nature of the last vowel of the first morpheme in a morpheme-pair which determines an alteration in the first vowel of the second morpheme. The morpheme-pair consists of verb base plus suffix or of two verbal suffixes. All that can be indicated for TYPE 7 is that verb bases coming after a noun and ending in back vowels /*o*/ and /*u*/ front those vowels to /*a*/ and /*e*/ respectively to identify the resulting phrase semologically as an *agentive noun*. The conditioning factor(s) for TYPE 8, which involves a small set of verbal and nominal suffixes, are at present impossible to define with any degree of certainty. Pareja tells us that the the combination of verbal suffixes *-ta* 'durative' + *-la* 'proximate time' (TYPES 8A, 8B) was the expected combination for first person subject in verbs, while variants *-te* plus either *-le* or *-la*, particularly in the combination *-tele*, were usual for indicating second and third person subjects (Adam and Vinson 1886:14). An examination of the texts verifies this statement, but there are enough exceptions to make it clear that a fuller explanation is needed. Both syntactic and stylistic — that is, semological and semantic — criteria are clearly at work. In TYPE 8C *-bo* is by far the most frequent variant; it occurs as *-ba* after the first and second person plural independent pronouns, as in *hecaba* 'we' (*he-* 'pronoun' *-ca* 'plural' + *-ba* '1, 2 plural subject pronoun'). In TYPE 8D *-ye* is preferred in most constructions. Again further scrutiny of the textual attestations is needed.

TABLE 16

NON-REGRESSIVE SUBSTITUTIONS

Type/Environment		Substitution
6A	Verb base in *-u* + *-no*[1]	*-u* + *-nu*
	Verbal suffix in *-u* + *-no*[2]	*-u* + *-nu*
	Verb base in *-u* + *-so*	*-u* + *-su*
6B	*-ma*[1] + *-te~-ta*	*-ma* + *-ti*
7A	Verb base in *-o* > Agentive noun	*-o* > *-a*
7B	Verb base in *-u* > Agentive noun	*-u* > *-e*
8A	? (*-la* with 1st person)	*-le~-la*
8B	? (*-ta* with 1st person)	*-te~-ta*
8C	?	*-bo~-ba*
8D	?	*-ye~-ya*

Examples of non-regressive substitution types are:

TYPE 6 (Verb Base or Verbal Suffix + Verbal Suffix):

A. Verb base in *-u* or verbal suffix in *-u* + *-no*[1] 'action designator', *-no*[2] 'proximate time', *-so* 'transitive-causative' > verb base or verbal suffix *-u* + *-nu*, *-su*:

i. *ucu* 'drink' + *-no*[1] > *ucunu* 'to drink'

ii. *huba* 'love' + *-so* 'transitive-causative' + *chu-* 'perfective' + *-no*[2] > *hubasochunu* 'I have loved (someone)'

iii. *ucu* 'drink' + *-so* > *ucusu* 'drink something'

B. *-ma*[1] 'his' + *-te~ta* 'durative' > *-ma* + *-ti*:

ite 'father' + *-ma*[1] + *-te* + *-la* 'proximate time' > *itimitila* 'it is his father'

TYPE 7 (Verb Base > Agentive Noun):

A. Noun + verb base in *-o*> Noun + verb base in *-a*:

aye 'wood' + *areco* 'make' > *aye areca* 'carpenter'

B. Noun + verb base in *-u* > Noun + verb base in *-e*:

ano 'man' + *paru* 'sew' > *ano pare* 'tailor'

TYPE 8 (Stylistic Verbal Suffix Variation):

A. *-le~-la* 'proximate time':

i. *nahiabo* 'know' + *-ta* 'durative' + *-la* = *nahiabotala* 'I know'

ii. *nahiabo* 'know' + *-te* 'durative' + *-le* = *nahiabotele* 'he knows'

B. *-te~-ta* 'durative' — see examples above in 8A

C. *-bo~-ba* 'subject pronoun 1, 2 plural':

i. *chi-* '2d person' + *ini* 'fall' + *-bo* + *-te* 'durative' + *-la* 'proximate time' = *chinibotela* 'you are all falling'

ii. *he-* 'pronoun' + *-ca* 'plural' + *-ba* = *hecaba* 'we'

D. *-ye~-ya* '2d person':

i. *paha* 'house' + *-ye* = *pahaye* 'your house'

ii. *isa* 'mother' + *-ya* = *isaya* 'your mother'

REDUPLICATION

Reduplication, always of the entire morpheme or lexeme, is frequently used to indicate intensity of action or to place emphasis on the reduplicated form, as in *noronoromota* 'do it with great devotion' (*noro* 'devotion' + *mo* 'do' + *-ta* 'durative'), *nihubasobilebile* 'I had loved (someone) very much' (*ni-* '1st person' + *huba* 'love' + *-so* 'transitive-causative' + *-bi* 'bounded action' + *-le* 'proximate time').

MORPHEMIC CLASSES

The term *morpheme* is used here to mean a recurring, separable, irreducible language form-unit. Such morphological units may be represented by any variety of segmental and/or supra-segmental phonological structures. In Timucua, where stress is non-phonemic, our sure data on transitions sketchy, and our knowledge of pitch non-existent, we are constrained to definition of segmental morphemes alone.

'Meaning' and usage are not used in the definition of morphemes in the present analysis. On other levels of analysis we may and must, however, define the semantic reference inherent in specific morphemes (their 'meaning') and the associated semological reference inherent in the positional 'slots' in which they occur (their grammatical function).

BASES

Some morphemes may be said to have both semantic and semological reference — *eba* 'left-hand' (particle), *biro* 'male' (noun) — while others, such as *-cu* 'subjunctive', have only semological reference. Those with both semantic and semological reference are here called *bases* (*eba* and *biro* above), those with only semological reference *non-bases* (*-cu* above).

Morphemes may also be characterized in terms of their occurrence. Those which may occur by themselves as lexemes ('words') are here referred to as *free forms.* Those which always occur bound to other forms are called *bound forms.* Bases which are also free-forms are called *free bases* (*eba* or *biro*), those which are bound-forms are called *bound bases.* There are only four bound bases in Timucua: *ini-* 'be', *he-* 'can, be able', *-ni-* 'I', and *-chi-* 'you'. All other bases are free bases.

AFFIXATION

The traditional term *affix* is used for bound, non-base morphemes, of which Timucua has three positional types — *prefixes*, *suffixes*, and *enclitics.*

Free bases in Timucua are not specific parts of speech in and of themselves nor are they semologically selective with regard to part of speech formation. A free base may be designated as *noun*, *verb*, *pronoun*, or *particle* by the presence of various kinds of affixes in the total lexeme. Such affixes are accordingly referred to as *designative affixes* and the resultant parts of speech *morphemic parts of speech* (parts of speech by form). Parts of speech may also be designated by the syntactic usage of the lexeme. The tactical 'slot', that is, in which a form occurs 'contains' the semological function of a specific part of speech. Such parts of speech are therefore called *syntactic parts of speech* (parts of speech by position).

The concept of *transformation* from one part of speech to another applies in Timucua only if a free base which has already been designated a particular morphemic part of speech is altered by the addition of another part of speech-forming affix or by a change in syntactic usage, signaled positionally (see the SYNTAX section later in this chapter). Affixes which specifically transform one part of speech into another are called *derivational affixes*. No derivational affix in Timucua ever functions as a designative affix, and no designative affix ever occurs as a derivational affix — the categories are mutually exclusive. Affixes which alter part of speech usage without transforming the lexeme into another part of speech — singular noun > plural noun, for example — are here called *inflectional affixes*. All affixes are listed in Table 17.

PREFIXES

Timucua makes use of only five prefixes: *ni-* and *ho^1-* '1st person', *chi-* '2nd person' — both Inflectional Prefixes with verbs; *na-* 'instrumental noun', used to derive nouns from other forms, usually verbs, as in *nareconoma* 'the instrument by which something is done' from *na-* + *areco* > *reco* (by regressive assimilation) + *-no^1* 'action designator' + *-ma^2* 'the'; and *ho^2-* 'pronoun', a designative prefix occurring only with the bound-bases *-ni-* 'I' and *-chi-* 'you' to form morphemic pronouns *honihe* 'I' and *hochie* 'you'.

SUFFIXES

Timucua is essentially a suffixing language, making wide and varied use of that mechanism for designative, derivational, and inflectional purposes. There are three noun-designating suffixes — *-tooma* 'all', *-ma^2* 'the', and *-re* 'noun combining-form'. Morpheme *tooma* 'all, total, complete' also occurs as a free base. Morpheme *-re* occurs only in combination with immediately preceding *-ca* 'plural', which is itself used with particles as well as nouns and is, therefore, an inflectional rather than designative

TABLE 17

AFFIXES

Type	Prefix	Suffix	Enclitic	Function*	
VERBAL	*ni-~ho*^{1}			1st person	(If)
	chi-			2d person	(If)
		-bo		1st, 2d plural subject	(Ds)
		-ma^{3}		3d plural subject	(Ds)
		-no^{1}		Action Designator	(Ds)
		-so		Transitive-Causative	(Dr)
		-te~-ta		Durative Action	(If)
		-be		Durative Action	(If)
		-na^{2}		Durative Action	(If)
		-bi		Bounded Action	(If)
		-si^{2}		Potential Action	(If)
		-chu		Perfective Action	(If)
		-co^{1}		Conditional Action	(If)
		-na^{3}		Habitual/Iterative	(If)
		-o		Punctual-Intensive	(If)
		-le~-la		Proximate Time	(If)
		-no^{2}		Proximate Time	(If)
		-ma^{4}		Proximate Time	(If)
		-tiacu		Proximate Time	(If)
		-qua		Distant Time	(If)
		-qe		Optative Action	(If)
		-cu		Subjuntive Action	(If)
		-che		Imperative Action	(If)
NOMINAL	*na-*			Instrumental	(Dr)
		-tooma		'all'	(Ds)
		-re		Noun	(Ds)
		-ma^{2}		'the'	(Ds)
		-siba		Quantitative/ Frequentative	(Dr)
		-na^{1}		1st pers. possessive	(If)
		-ya~-ye		2d pers. possessive	(If)
		-ma^{1}		Possessive	(If)
PRONOM-	*ho*^{2}			Pronoun	(Ds)
INAL		*-(h)e*		Pronoun	(Ds)
NON-		*-ca*		Plural	(If)
SPECIFIC		*-si*^{1}		Reflexive	(If)
			-co^{2}	Noun	(Dr)
			-co^{3}	Interrogative	(If)

-có(co)	Copula/Augment.	(If)
-cho	Interrogative	(If)
-lechu	Vocative	(If)
-qua	Copula/Intensive	(If)
-qui	Copula/Intensive	(If)
-qi	Intensive/Pointer	(If)
-te	Copula/Augmentative/ Intensive	(If)
-leqe	Copula/Augmentative/ Intensive	(If)
-ti	Negative	(If)

*(Ds = Designative, Dr = Derivational, If = Inflectional)

suffix. The morpheme *-re* is noun-designating. In this capacity, which some of my colleagues in Muskogean studies view with incredulity, it plays exactly the same function the */-rV/* morpheme does in the Arawakan languages (Matteson 1972:164, Payne 1990:81) — serving simply to indicate that the total lexical form is nominal in form and usage, without any further nuance of 'meaning'. Its semological freight, so tenuous of description to those not familiar with languages using this device, fits exactly into the category which Charles Hockett (Hockett 1947 [1957:236]) referred to as the *Empty Morph* — English */-it-/* of 'divinity', for example, which has the sole semological function of 'connection'. While English */-it/*, however, is a derivational morpheme, Timucua *-re* is designative. The morpheme *-siba* 'quantitative/frequentative', is noun-deriving, as in *hebasiba* 'talkative'. There are three noun-inflecting suffixes — *-na¹* 'lst person possessive', *-ye~-ya* '2nd person possessive', and *-ma¹* 'possessive' (most frequently, but not exclusively, indicating 3rd person).

There is a single pronoun-designating suffix, *-(h)e*, which, like *-re*, has no other nuances of semological message other than to designate a specific morphemic part of speech. This suffix occurs in *ho-ni-he* 'I' and *ho-chi-e* 'you'.

The majority of Timucua suffixes are verbal in nature. Three are designative — *-bo* 'subject 1, 2 plural', *-ma³* 'subject 3 plural', and *-no¹* 'action designator'. One, *-so* 'transitive-causative', is verb-deriving, and the remainder are inflectional.

There are, finally, two inflectional suffixes which are non-specific with regard to part of speech: *-ca* 'plural' and *-si*[1] 'reflexive', as in *ni-ca* 'we', *paha-ca-re* 'houses', *heta-la-ni-ca* 'we are eating', *paha-ma-si* 'his own house', *ni-huba-so-si-bo-te-la* 'we love each other'.

ENCLITICS

Like suffixes, enclitics are widely used in Timucua. They may be added, under normal transition, to any morpheme or lexeme. They need not be form-final, though this is usually the case. They differ from suffixes, as in many languages, in that they do not fill a rigidly defined tactical slot. In Timucua enclitics usually bear primary stress, indicated in Pareja's orthography by an acute accent over the final vowel of the enclitic, as in *holatamaquí* 'and the chief'. In many instances, however, such an orthographic convention is not used, and it is therefore impossible to say with certainty whether or not enclitics were always the bearers of primary stress.

MORPHOTACTICS

Morphemic parts of speech are discussed in detail in this section, while syntactic parts of speech — parts of speech 'by usage' — are considered in the section of this chapter on syntax.

Bases and affixes combine to form *pronouns*, *nouns*, *verbs*, and *particles*. Each of these may have various additional semological functions on the syntactic level. When morphemes come together to form lexemes as morphemic parts of speech, they are regularly joined by normal phonological transition. This is indicated in Pareja's orthography by the lack of spacing between the constituent morphemes of a lexical item. It seems to be the case that /+/, /|/, and /#/ are used only to separate lexemes, though some lexemes may themselves join with others under normal transition to form various kinds of compound structures (described below as *compound words* and *phrase-*

words). Most of the tactical rules for joining morphemes into larger lexical structures have been discussed earlier in the section on phonological processes.

Morphemic pronouns are those lexemes which have as their final morphemic element the suffix *-(h)e*, as in *ho-ni-he* 'I'. Only *honihe* 'I' and *hochie* 'you' fulfill this requirement. Other independent lexemes used syntactically as pronouns are either morphemic particles or morphemically nominal structures.

Morphemic nouns are those lexemes which may take as their final morphemic element, with or without inflectional suffixes, the designative suffix *-tooma* 'all', as in *paha-tooma* 'houses, all the houses', or those lexemes which have *-re* 'Noun' as one suffix component, not necessarily the final one, as is *paha-ca-re* 'houses', *paha-ca-re-ma* 'the houses'.

Morphemic verbs are those lexemes which may have as one morphemic component either *-bo* 'subject 1, 2 plural' or *-ma*[3] 'subject 3 plural', with or without inflectional suffixes, as in *ini-bo-te-la* 'we are', *huba-sa-ma-chu-nu* 'they loved someone'.

Morphemic particles are those lexemes which normally occur without affixes but which may occur with lexeme-final *-ca* 'plural', as in *beta* 'for', *qua* 'in', *oqe* 'this, that', *he-ca* 'we'.

Lexical free forms (lexemes) contain a *stem* of one of three kinds: a *simple stem*, a *compound stem*, or an *expanded stem*. A simple stem consists of a single free base, as in *yobo* 'stone', *huba* 'love', *tera* 'good'. A compound stem consists of two or more free bases joined under normal transition, as in *nia-paha* 'woman's house', *yaru-ha* 'give in the future'. Expanded stems consist of a simple or compound stem plus derivational affixes, as in *heba-no* 'to speak, speaking' (an expanded simple stem), *heba-tera-siba* 'one who habitually says good things' (an expanded compound stem).

Any stem type may participate in the formation of specific morphemic parts of speech through the addition of affixes, as in *yaha-ma* 'the one' (a simple stem + designative suffix), *nia-paha-tooma-ma* 'all the woman's houses' (an expanded compound stem + designative suffixes).

Simple stems alone as lexical free forms are here called

true words; compound stem free forms are called *compound words*; and expanded stem free forms of either variety (expanded simple stems or expanded compound stems) are called *expanded words*. A fourth lexical free form category will be referred to as the *phrase-word*. Such structures consist of one of the other word types embedded in a new matrix of inflectional endings to form a new lexical form, as in *heba-tera-siba-ma-la* 'it is the person who brings good tidings' (the nominal form *hebaterasibama* 'the one who brings good tidings' verbalized with the inflectional suffix *-la*> 'proximate time'), or *nĭ-biro-istico-ma-le-bo-na-ma* 'we are the evil men' (the nominal compound stem *biro-istico-ma* 'the evil men' is verbalized with a series of inflectional affixes). Such phrase-words are extremely common in Timucua, and the embedding technique, which needs much closer study than it has been given here, is a major method of word formation in the language. What must in English constitute an entire, sometimes lengthy, sentence will frequently occur in Timucua as a single phrase-word.

PRONOUNS

INDEPENDENT PRONOUNS

Only the first and second person singular independent pronouns in Timucua are morphemic pronouns. Other independent pronominals are represented by morphemic particles or nouns (see Table 18).

There are no gender distinctions in pronouns or particles and nouns used as syntactic pronominals. Neither is grammatical case distinguished by form. *Oqe*, for example, may be translated as 'he, him, to him, she, her, to her, it, to it' etc., while *hochie* may be translated as 'you (subj.), you (obj.), to you' etc., as the context demands. Accompanying verbal structures will normally make the usage clear without the explicit use of the independent pronouns, as in *hubasontala* 'I love (someone)', in which *-ta-la*> specifically indicates a first person subject, or *honihe chihubasontele* 'you love me', in which the *-te-le* combination indicates a non-first person subject, demanding that *chi-* be interpreted as verbal subject in the second person and *honihe* as verbal object 'me'.

TABLE 18

INDEPENDENT PRONOUNS

Per./#	Pronoun	Particle	Noun
1st Sg.	*honihe*		
2d Sg.	*hochie*		
2d Sg.		*oqe~∅*	
1st Pl.		*heca~niheca*	
2d Pl.		*yaqe~yeqe~chica*	
3d Pl.			*oqecare*

PRONOMINAL PREFIXES

In the majority of cases verbal subjects are indicated solely by the use of verbal prefixes (see Table 19). The first person prefixes, however, are often not used, the *-te~-ta* and *-le~-la* variation in the 'durative' and 'proximate time' suffixes serving the same purpose — *-ta* and *-la* regularly signaling first person when the verbal prefixes are not used. When the prefixes are used either allomorph of the 'durative' and 'proximate' may be used, as in *hubasontala* vs. *nihubasontela*, *hohubasontala*, *hohubasontela* all meaning 'I love (someone)'. When first person prefixes are used, *ni-* and *ho*[1]*-* occur with approximately equal frequency in contexts which seem stylistically the same. The nuances distinguishing *ni-* from *ho*[1]*-*, if there were any, have so far been impossible to reconstruct.

Verbal pronoun prefixes may be used to indicate either verb subject or verb object, as in the case with the independent pronouns. If both subject and object are indicated by prefix, the object prefix is always in second place, as in *ho-chi-mani-s-ta-la* 'I love you very much'.

TABLE 19

VERB PRONOMINAL PREFIXES

Person	**Singular**	**Plural**
1st	*ni-~ho*^{1}*-*	*ni-~ho*^{1}*- . . . -bo*
2d	*chi-*	*chi- . . . -bo*
3d	*Ø-*	*Ø- . . . -ma*^{3}

POSSESSIVE PRONOUN PREFIXES

Possessive pronouns with nominal structures are expressed with nominal inflectional suffixes (see Table 20). In the third person singular the *-ma*^{1} occurs with much greater frequency than does *-Ø*. The *-ma*^{1} morpheme, however, is not limited to use with the third person. It signals simply 'possessive', regardless of person, as in *paha-mi-ma* 'his house' (*-ma* > *-mi* before the definite article *-ma*^{2}) but *heca paha-mi-ma* 'our house' (specified by the form *he-ca* '1st Plural'). If an independent pronoun, or possessor other than third person is expressed, *-ma*^{1} is taken to mean 'his, her, its'. In most instances *-ma*^{1} is immediately followed, as in the above examples, by *-ma*^{2} 'the'.

TABLE 20

NOUN POSSESSIVE PRONOMINAL SUFFIXES

Person	**Singular**	**Plural**
1st	*-na*^{1}	*-nica*
2d	*-ye~-ya*	*-yaca~-yaqe~-chica*
3d	*-Ø~-ma*^{1}	*-Ø*

In the plural possession is rarely indicated by the possessive suffixes. Instead verbal expressions, given in Table 21, are used. Such forms may be translated literally as 'it is *x*'s *y*', as in *heca paha-mi-le* 'our house', *paha-mi-le yaca* or *paha-mi-le-no yaca* 'your (pl.) house', *paha-mi-ti-le* 'their house', in which 'proximate time' and 'durative' suffixes verbalize the total structure. The third plural is frequently re-nominalized by the addition of *-ma²* 'the', as in *paha-mi-ti-le-ma* 'their house' (='the it-is-their-house').

TABLE 21

NOUN PLURAL POSSESSIVE VERBAL EXPRESSIONS

Person	Form
1st	*heca* + BASE + *-ma¹* > *-mi* + *-le* 'proximate' = 'our'
2d	BASE + *-ma¹* > *-mi* + *-le* + *-no²* 'proximate' + *-yaca* = 'your'
3d	BASE + *-ma¹* > *-mi* + *-ta* > *-ti* 'durative' + *-le* = 'their'

NOUNS

MORPHEMIC NOUN MATRIX

In contrast to the rather complex usage of pronominal structures, nominal forms are simple and straightforward. The noun matrix contains nine slots. Their content may be defined as follows:

SLOT 1	— Base
SLOT 2	— Possessive Pronoun
SLOT 3	— Pronoun Plural
SLOT 4A	— Base plural
SLOT 4B	— Combining Form
SLOT 5	— 'The'
SLOT 6	— Particles
SLOT 7	— Enclitics
SLOT 8	— Reflexive

Of these nine morphotactic slots only Slot 1 (the base itself, not indicated in the table) and 4A (base plural) must be filled to define a lexeme as a noun. Some slots, such as the base slot, may contain more than one morpheme as a compound stem.

TABLE 22

MORPHEMIC NOUN MATRIX

2	**3**	**4A**	**4B**	**5**	**6**	**7**	**8**
1: *-na*[1]	1/2: *-ca*	*-ca* ~	*-re*	*-ma*[2]	*-beta*	*-có(co)*	*-si*[1]
2: *-ye~-ya*	3: *-Ø*	*-tooma*			*-qua*	*-lechu*	
3: *-Ø~-ma*[1]		*-puqua*			etc.	etc.	
		-ara					
		-amiro					
		-inemi					
		-inibiti					
		-achico					
		-amiroqua					

NOUN PLURALIZATION

SLOTS 2 and 3 have been discussed in the previous section on pronouns. SLOT 4 most frequently contains the plural morpheme *-ca* and *-re* 'noun,' (*-ca* never occurs alone with nouns). There are, however, also nine pluralizing particles, always joined to the base under normal transition, which may be used instead of the combination *-care*. Most are used to indicate a *collectivity* rather than simple plurality, and all occur most frequently with non-human animate entities. The most diagnostic of the nine forms is *-tooma* 'all, complete, total', and it is so often used that, though essentially a free base, as in *tooma-ma* 'the end', it may be considered a noun-designating suffix.

POST-POSITIONS

SLOT 5 has been described by example previously. SLOT 6 contains particles which serve the function of post-positional case-indicators. As Pareja points out, 'properly speaking there are no cases, nor are nouns declined, nor do they have more than a single termination' (Adam and Vinson 1886:14). He goes on to indicate that the use of post-positional particles, in normal transition to judge from his orthography, serves the same function that case endings do in Latin and related European languages.

SLOT 7 may be filled by any of the enclitics listed earlier (see Table 17).

REFLEXIVE *-si*[1]

In final position, in SLOT 8, is suffix *-si*[1] 'reflexive', which in nominal structures serves essentially the same function as a genitive, as in *paha-ma-si* 'the house of *x*' ('*x*' referring back to some mentioned owner or other noun, as in *diosi pahamasi* 'the house of God' or *oqe pahamasi* 'his house/the house of him'). While *-si*[1] is always lexeme-final in the morphemic noun, it does not function like an enclitic. It never bears primary stress, as most enclitics do, and it is rigidly limited to occurrence in slot 8. The term 'reflexive' is used to describe this morpheme on the basis of its overall function in the language — it occurs widely with verbs as well (see the next section of this chapter), and in every instance calls attention 'back' to the subject at hand, be it a noun or a verb. Its usage is vaguely reminiscent of the Greek Middle Voice, but it has no real counterpart in any Indo-European language nor in the other native languages of the American Southeast.

As indicated earlier, slot 1 may contain a simple stem true word, a compound word, an expanded word or the oft-occurring phrase-word, as in *paha-mi-ma* 'his house' (true word), *nia-paha-ca-re-ma* 'the woman's houses' (compound word), *na-reco-no-ma* 'instrument for performing a task' (expanded word), *nahiabo-ha-be-ma* 'the one who will know' (phrase-word).

MORPHEMIC VERBS

As indicated earlier, base morphemes in Timucua are rarely selective with regard to part of speech formation. Most may be used indifferently as noun, verb, or particle. The majority may occur with the verb-designating suffixes *-bo* and *-ma*^{3} indicating plurality of 1st/2nd and 3rd person verbal subjects respectively.

MORPHEMIC VERB MATRIX

Table 23 shows the tactical slots in the morphemic verb matrix. It is rare that all thirteen are filled in a given lexical form, but verbs containing eight or nine morphemes are quite frequent as are verbal structures in which SLOT 3, the base, is filled with a complex phrase-word. The nuances of verbal meaning possible in Timucua are many, subtle from our point of view, and quite unlike those of either European languages or of any other native language of the Southeastern United States. It is impossible to talk of tenses in the time-oriented matrix of Indo-European or the better-known languages of North America such as Uto-Aztecan. Time is distinctly *not* of the essence in Timucua, and 'tense' as a concept simply does not exist. Timucua is considerably more interested in defining action in terms of concepts vaguely akin to what we know as *aspect* in, for example, the Slavic languages. Even here, however, this Indo-European label covers a multitude of verbal attributes which are carefully segmented from one another semologically and morphemically in Timucua. Examples of the various kinds of possible constructions are given as they are described below. As pointed out in the *Preface*, considerable work remains to be done before a technically elegant classification of Timucua verbal structures can be finalized. The present incomplete statements are, however, accurate.

Morphemic verbs in Timucua are marked for one of four possible *MODES*: *indicative*, *optative*, *subjunctive*, or *imperative*. Within each mode further semological categories are distinguished. These are herein referred to as: *TRANSITIVITY*, *REFLEXIVE*, *ACTION*, *ASPECT*, *STATUS*, *EMPHASIS*, and *LOCUS*. Some of these semological distinctions have counterparts in more familiar languages, but others, such as *locus* and the *bounded time aspect*, do not. Even familiar verbal concepts are used and arranged in rather unique ways in Timucua.

In some instances a morphemic verb may be immediately preceded by an independent pronoun, as a separate lexeme, either as subject or object. The distinction between subject and object, discussed subsequently in this section, is made clear by the constituent parts of the morphemic verb itself.

VERB SUBJECT

SLOT 1 in the morphemic verb matrix is filled by a pronominal prefix indicating person but not number of the verb subject. The 1st person form variants occur with approximately equal frequency, as in *hontala* 'I am', *chihubasotele* 'you love (someone)', *nihubasola* 'I love (someone)'.

SLOT 13 contains optionally and rarely used subject pronouns. They are identical in form with the nominal possessive pronouns and are found only in questions. They normally take the place of subject pronoun prefixes and subject pronoun plural suffixes, but, very infrequently, SLOTS 1, 7, and 13 are all filled.

VERB OBJECT

SLOT 2, the verb object, may contain the same pronominal prefixes that occur in SLOT 1. This segment of the matrix is rarely filled. Pronominal objects are more usually indicated by the presence of an independent pronoun before the verb and the presence of the *-so* 'transitive-causative' morpheme in the verb. Examples are: *hochihubasotala* (*ho-chi-huba-so-ta-la*) 'I love you', *nihubasotele* (*ni-huba-so-te-le*) 'he loves me' (in which *-tele* indicates a non-1st person subject), *oqe hubasotala* (*oqe huba-so-ta-la*) 'I love him' (in which *-tala* indicates a 1st person subject).

VERB BASE

SLOT 3 contains one or more bases as a simple stem, compound stem, or expanded stem of either variety. Examples have been given earlier. The use of phrase-words in this position,

TABLE 23
MORPHEMIC VERB MATRIX

1	2	3	4	5	6	7	8	9	10	11	12	13
SUBJECT PRONOUN	OBJECT PRONOUN	BASE	TRANSI-TIVITY	RE-FLEXIVE	ACTION DESIGNAT.	SUBJECT PRO. PLURAL	ASPECT	STATUS	EMPHASIS	LOCUS	MODE	SUBJECT PRONOUNS
1: *ho*^{1}-	1: *ho*^{1}-		*-so*	*-si*^{1}	*-no*^{1}	1/2: *-bo*	Durative Action	Perfect. Action	Habitual/ Iterative	Proximate Time	Indicat.	1Sg.: *-na*
~ *ni-*	~ *ni-*					(Slot 13 forms may occur here)	1. *-te* ~ *-ta*	*-chu*	*-na*^{3}	1. *-le* ~ *-la*	∅	2Sg.: *-ye*
2: *chi-*	2: *chi-*						2. *-be*			2. *-no*^{2}		3Sg.: ∅ 1Pl.: *-nica*
							3. *-na*^{2}			3. *-ma*^{4}		2Pl.: *-chica* ~ *-yaqe*
3: ∅	3: ∅					3: *-ma*^{3}				4. *tiacu*		3Pl.: ∅
						(May occur after Slot 8)	Bounded Action	Condit. Action	Punctual Intensive	Distant Time	Optative	(Used primarily in questions)
							-bi	*-co*	*-o*	*-qua*	*-qe*	
							Potent. Action	Non-specific			Subjunct.	
							1. ∅ 2. *-si*^{2}	∅			*-cu*	
											Imperative	
											1. ∅ 2. *-che*	

through the embedding process, is extremely frequent. Examples are given in later in this chapter in the section on verb transformations.

TRANSITIVE-CAUSATIVE

SLOT 4, 'transitive-causative', is limited to the single morpheme *-so*. Pareja gives numerous examples to clarify the usage of this morpheme and explicitly states that 'adding a *so* makes the action transitive with regard to the subject or to another person' (*anidiendoseles a los positiuos vn so hacen transeunte la acçion en si mesmo ó en otra persona*) and that 'It should be noted that verbs which already have SO do not add another in order to become transitive because they already signify that kind of action' (*Item se aduierta que los verbos que de siuo tienen so no admiten otro so para ser transeuntes porque ellos significan la mesma accion*) (Adam and Vinson 1886:104). Examples are: *chi-istitimo-so-ta-la* 'I am hurting you', *nioco-so* 'make him run' (in contrast to *nioco* 'Run!'), *chi-tuqui-so-ta-la* 'I am paining you/causing you pain', *huquisa* (*huqui-so>-sa*) 'make it rain!/cause it to rain!/let it rain!' (in contrast with *huquitele* 'it is raining'), *quo-so* 'to do' (which never occurs simply as *quo* 'do'), *mache tuquisontala* (*mache tuqui-so-no->-n-ta-la)* 'I harm myself' (= 'self I am harming' — semologically reflexive but not reflexive by form). English translation at times requires a 'cause to *x*' phrase to render the meaning of the Timucua adequately; for this reason *-so* has been labelled 'transitive-causative'.

REFLEXIVE

SLOT 5 also contains a single morpheme, *-si*[1], the reflexive suffix. Pareja states that verbs may 'admit a *si*, by which the action is made reciprocal' (*admiten vn si con que se haçe reciproca la accion*) (Adam and Vinson 1886:104), as in *ni-huba-so-si-bo-te-la* 'we love each other', *tuquisosintala* (*tuqui-so-si-no->-n-ta-la*) 'I am harming myself' — like *mache tuquisontala* (*mache tuqui-so-no->-n-ta-la*) = 'Self I am harming', reflexive, but reflexive by form as well as semologically.

When *-si*[1] is used in a traditional reflexive/reciprocal sense it is always preceded by Slot 4 filler, *-so* 'transitive-causative', as in the examples above. Reflexive verbal forms may, however, occur without being morphemically transitive (without *-so*), as in *chara hebuasino* (*chara heba-si-no*) 'to speak by means of a book or document' (*chara* = 'to read'). In such instances *-si*[1] 'reflects' back to the subject, but, from an Indo-European point of view, the usage is instrumental, not reflexive. We have already seen that when *-si*[1] is used with nouns it also 'reflects' back to the subject and has what we would call a genitive function (see the earlier section on nouns in this chapter). The concept as used here, that is, is similar to but not identical with the traditional use of the term 'reflexive' in Indo-European.

ACTION DESIGNATION

SLOT 6 contains the single morpheme *-no*[1], the 'action designator'. While the presence of this morpheme indicates that an action is being described, the lack of *-no*[1] must not be taken to indicate that the form is non-verbal, but, rather, to indicate that the verbal action itself is not emphasized. A structure may, that is, be verbal in function in Timucua without the overt presence of the *-no*[1] morpheme. The typically dualistic Indo-European distinctions of active vs. passive, verbal vs. non-verbal do not apply in Timucua. The closest parallel I can summon up is the */ku-/* morpheme in Swahili, which, like Timucua *-no*[1] when form-final, translates as an infinitive, a present participle, or a noun which ends in *-or/-er*, as in *huba-so-no* 'to love someone/loving/lover' (the latter more usually as *hubasonoma* 'the one who loves'). When followed by other verbal suffixes in the matrix, the morpheme *-no*[1] simply emphasizes the action, as in *oqe chihubuasonotele* (*oqe chi-huba-so-no-te-le*) 'you *love* him' (the action emphasized).

SUBJECT PRONOUN PLURALS

SLOT 7 contains *-bo* 'subject 1/2 plural' or *-ma*[3] 'subject 3 plural'. The absence of a filler in this slot indicates that the verb is singular. Morpheme *-ma*[3] may optionally occur after any Slot 8 filler instead of in Slot 7, particularly in questions or if the Slot 8 filler would otherwise be lexeme-final, as in *hubasotama* 'do they love someone?'

At times the noun-inflectional suffixes *-nica* 'we' and either *-chica* or *-yaqe* 'you (all)' are used in this position, as in *heta-nica-la* 'we are eating', *huba-so-chica-chu-nu* 'you loved someone'.

ASPECTS: DURATIVE, BOUNDED, POTENTIAL

SLOT 8 contains aspect-indicating morphemes of three kinds: *durative action*, *bounded action*, and *potential action.*

The *durative* has parallels in many other languages. It emphasizes lasting action or the ongoingness of the action, without reference to a specific beginning or end. While textual examples indicate that action duration is the major semological function, it is also clear that the durative implies imperfective action — the action is open-ended or unbounded.

There are three durative action morphemes: *-te~-ta*, *-be*, and *-na*[2]. The last two are of infrequent occurrence. The variants of the first morpheme are stylistic variants except that *-ta*, as pointed out earlier, is usual in the first person and obligatory in that person if no pronominal subject prefix occurs in the verb complex. There *seems* to be no semological difference between these three morphemes, though semological verb classes and stylistic variables in Timucua discourse have yet to be explored in detail.

At times the durative nature of a verbal action is emphasized by the use of *-te~-ta* and either of the other durative morphemes together, in that order, in a morphological and semological reduplication paralleling phonological reduplication for emphasis, as in *nintanchunu* (*ni-ini->-ni->-n-ta-na->-n-chu-nu*) 'I *have* been'. Instances of dual duratives are rare, and they always seem to occur in textual passages which might be construed as demanding emphasis on the lasting nature of the action.

The *bounded aspect*, *-bi*, has no parallel in any language of which I am aware. It refers to action as a 'packaged unit', specifically bounded but without finite beginning or end-point — an opposite-image of the durative. The sole emphasis is on the action as encapsulated in a unit of time. There is no reference to 'past', 'present', or 'future' in our sense. The reference is *not* to time; this element, if needed — which it rarely is — is added by the context in which the verb ocurs. The bounded should specifically *not* be equated with perfective action (i.e., over-and-done-with, specifically in the past); there is another morpheme (see the *Status* section below) which covers that kind of action. Examples are: *ho-chi-huba-so-bi-la* 'I am in love with you now (= enamored of you)/I used to love you (= was enamored of you, but am no more)/I have loved you over a definite period of time (= had an affair with you)/I had loved you for a while/I shall be in love with you (= shall have a love-affair with you)', *ninibila* (*ni-ini->-ni-bi-la*) 'I am, right now/I used to be (for a certain time)/I have been (but am no longer)/I had been (but am no longer)/I shall be (for a specific period of time)'.

The *potential aspect* morpheme, *-si*[2], is extremely rare. The auxiliary verb *he-* 'be able (to), can' is usually used in its place. This usage will be discussed in detail later. An example of *-si*[2] is: *ninisela* (*ni-ini->-ni-si->-se-la*) 'I can/could be'.

STATUS: PERFECTIVE, CONDITIONAL

If filled, SLOT 9 will contain either morpheme *-chu* 'perfective' or *-co*[1] 'conditional'. The perfective signals, as in other languages, action over and done with in the past, as in *ninechunu* (*ni-ini->-ni->-ne-chu-nu*) 'I have/had been'. The *conditional* indicates that an action may or might take place given certain circumstances, which may or may not be described in the verbal phrase, as in *huba-so-co* 'he may/might love (someone)'. Frequently, as with the potential, conditional action is indicated by use of the auxiliary verb *he-* 'be able (to), can'.

It is possible that a -Ø morpheme should be set up to mark a *non-specific* or *non-perfective* status, inasmuch as this slot of the matrix rarely makes use of the conditional marker and is essentially concerned with perfective action vs. non-perfective action. It is clear, in any case, that *status* is of a different order than *aspect* since both segments of the matrix are frequently filled in a single verb form, as in *huba-so-te-chu* 'he had loved him for a long time'.

EMPHASIS: HABITUAL/ITERATIVE, PUNCTUAL-INTENSIVE

SLOT 10 has been called *emphasis*. It contains two morphemes: *-na*[3] 'habitual/iterative' and *-o* 'punctual-intensive'. The former is self-explanatory, referring to repeated or usual action, while the latter refers to one-time, punctuated events with an accompanying emphasis on the intensity of the action. Examples are: *huba-so-na-no* 'he is always in love with someone', *chi-huba-so-te-o* 'you are always having love affairs'.

LOCUS: PROXIMATE, DISTANT

SLOT 11 is *vaguely* similar to Indo-European concepts of 'tense' or 'time'. Those terms, however, are not quite appropriate for Timucua, where specific time of action in a past-present-future (or similar) matrix is totally foreign. The difficulty confronting Pareja in the translation of certain Latin and Spanish verb-forms into Timucua and his choice of Timucua forms is very telling in this regard (Adam and Vinson 1886:57-116, esp. 104-116). *Locus* refers, rather, to the distance in time from the speaker that an action takes place.

The *proximate time locus* morphemes indicate that the time of action is temporally near the time of speaking. Near-past, right-now-present, near-future are conflated into a single locus — one can not specify, for example, the near-past or near-future alone without additional lexical explanation. In like manner the *distant time locus* morpheme refers to time distant from the time of speaking, and once again far-past, present-but-not-right-now, and far-future constitute a single 'time' to the speaker. The situation, from textual use, could be charted as in Fig. 4, with 0 representing the speaker and his time of describing the action and the other numbers arbitrary units of time-distance from the time of speaking, only infrequently specified by verbal

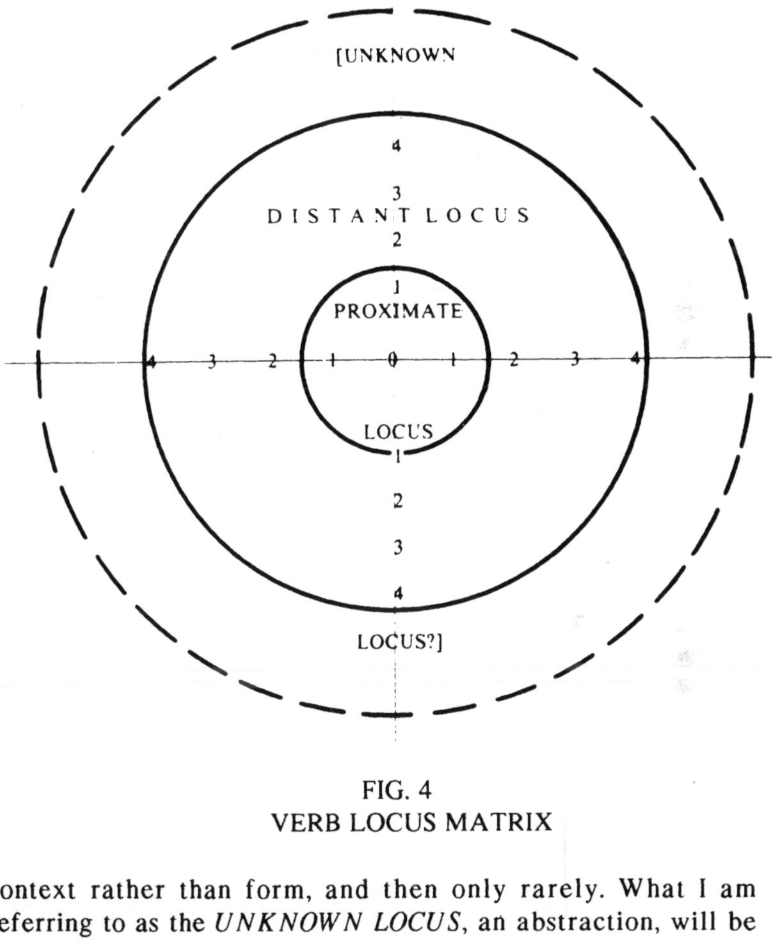

FIG. 4
VERB LOCUS MATRIX

context rather than form, and then only rarely. What I am referring to as the *UNKNOWN LOCUS*, an abstraction, will be discussed later in this chapter under *periphrastic verbs*.

There are four morphemes which are used to indicate proximate time: *-le~-la*, *-no*^{2}, *-ma*^{4}, and *-tiacu*. The latter two occur with extreme rarity, and *-le~-la* is the expected norm. Considerably more work on the contexts of the textual attestations is needed before the usage of these morpheme-variants can be defined. Examples are: *chintele* (*chi-ini->-ni->-n-*

te-le), *chinteno* (*chi-ini->-ni->-n-te-no*), *chintema* (*chi-ini->-ni->-n-te-ma*), *chintetiacu* (*chi-ini->-ni->-n-te-tiacu*) 'you are'. As with the durative, more than one proximate time morpheme may occur in a single morphemic verb. Such usage seems to act as intensifying morphological reduplication, but detailed textual examination is called for to provide an accurate rationale.

MODE: INDICATIVE, OPTATIVE, SUBJUNCTIVE, IMPERATIVE.

SLOT 12 contains four mode moprhemes. The *indicative* is not morphemically marked, and I have postulated a -Ø' morpheme to pattern with the morphemic expression of the other modal affixes. Textual examination corroborates the assumption that a form unmarked as optative, subjunctive, or imperative is always Indicative.

The *optative* expresses, as in other languages, a wish or desire. It is indicated by *-qe*, as in *ini-bi-le-qe* 'if only it might be'. An alternate *periphrastic optative* is discussed later in this section.

The *subjunctive* is also used much as in other languages to express situations contrary to fact or situations with unkown or probable outcomes. The morpheme *-cu* is used, as in *ni-huba-so-bo-bi-le-cu* 'if we had loved (him)'.

The *imperative* is signaled in one of three ways: (1) through use of the verb stem alone; (2) by addition of the morpheme *-che*; or (3) by use of the intensive enclitic morphemes *-qi*, *-qua*, -*có(co)*, *-qui*, as in *hubaso*, *huba-so-che*, *huba-so-qui* 'Love him!' Of these methods by far the most frequent is use of the verb stem alone. A special *periphrastic imperative*, discussed later in this section, is also used.

FINITE VERB FORMS

A morphemic verb with any combination of slots 7-13 filled is a *finite verb*. The most frequent finite verb-forms are discussed below. This list, however, in no way exhausts the possible morphemic combinations inherent in the matrix, but most of the more exotic combinations occurring as text-book examples in Pareja's grammar (Pareja 1614; Adam and Vinson 1886) simply do not occur in the texts themselves except in contrived biblical translation passages. In the grammar they are used as translations of extremely specific Spanish and/or Latin structures, rare even in those languages.

The *durative proximate* (*-tele*, *-tale*, *-tela*, *-tala*) is the most frequent verb form in the Timucua texts. It is translated according to context, of course, but is usually the equivalent of a present-tense form in European languages, as in *hubasotele* 'he loves someone', *hochimanistala* 'I love you very much'.

The *bounded proximate* (*-bile*, *-bila*) and the *durative distant* (*-tequa*, *-taqua*) frequently occur in passages demanding a 'past time' translation in English, as in *hubasobile* 'he used to love him (not so long ago)', *hubasotequa* 'he was in love with him (a long time ago)'.

The *perfective proximate* (*-chunu*, *-chule*) usually signals 'present-perfect' or 'past-perfect' action, as in *hubasochunu* 'he has loved him'.

Other forms of the finite verb are unexceptional and are formed as described in the preceding paragraphs on the morphemic verb matrix.

NON-FINITE VERB FORMS

Non-finite verbs-forms are those in which only slots 3-6 are filled, as in *huba-so-* 'love' (as a transitive verb-stem), *huba-so-no* 'to love, loving' (transitive), *heba-so-si-no* 'to talk to oneself, talking to oneself' (transitive reflexive). There are also three special, frequently occurring participial-like, non-finite verb-forms:

(1) VERB-STEM + OPTATIVE > '-ed':
huba-soqe 'loved'
(2) BASE + DURATIVE *-ta* > '*x* having been done':
heba-ta 'having been said'
(3) VERB-STEM + OPTATIVE + *-re* > '-ing':
huba-so-qe-re 'loving' (= 'one desiring to love')

Type (3) is morphemically nominal, as indicated by the presence of the noun-designating suffix *-re*, but types (1) and (2) remain verbal by form though usually syntactically nominal.

PERIPHRASTIC VERBS

Periphrastic constructions are used when referring to action of uncertain or unknown outcome. All have potential, conditional, optative, or subjunctive meaning, and all relate to times beyond the normal time-loci defined earlier — essentially to what we would call either 'distant future', 'legendary past' or, better, 'unknown' time. The interesting inference, amply borne out by ethnographic and historical data (Granberry MS*a*), seems to be that to the Timucua the outcome of all action outside the normal time-loci is uncertain. One might add, as a dotted-line, a nebulous circle to the verb-locus chart, as we have done in Fig.4, indicating that this kind of extreme locus-distance was probably in the realm of the 'unreal' or even 'unimaginable' to the Timucua.

THE PERIPHRASTIC FUTURE

Future time is expressed periphrastically through the use of the auxiliary verb *ha-* 'be in the future, be ongoing'. A finite form of this verb is added, under normal transition, to a finite form of the main verb, as in *ninibilehabela* (*ni-ini->-ni-bi-le-ha-be-la*) 'I shall have been' (= 'I completed the action of being' + 'such is the case in the future'), *chihubasolehabela* (*chi-huba-so-le-ha-be-la*) 'you will love him' (= 'you love him' + 'such is the case in the future'). While the auxiliary *ha-* is semologically separate from the main verb with which it occurs, it is almost always written without orthographic space between it and the main verb. There are, however, many instances in the texts in which the *ha-*-form is orthographically a separate lexical entity. The frequency of this treatment vs. the single-lexeme treatment has yet to be calculated, and the inference of the usage difference, if any, is unclear.

THE PERIPHRASTIC POTENTIAL

Potential action is also most frequently expressed periphrastically, through use of the auxiliary verb *he-* 'can, be able (to)'. Finite forms of *he-* are added under normal transition to a finite main-verb form, as in *chihubasolehela* (*chi-huba-so-le-he-la*) 'you can love him' (= 'you love him' + 'it can be so'), *nihubasobotehe* (*ni-huba-so-bo-ta-he*) 'it is possible that we love him/we are able to love him' (= 'we love him' + it is possible'). *He-*-form potentials, like periphrastic futures, have conditional, optative, or subjunctive meaning. The periphrastic potential is used much more frequently than potential aspect marker *-si*[2] (Slot 8), conditional marker *-co*[1] (Slot 9), or optative mode marker *-qe* (Slot 12).

THE PERIPHRASTIC OPTATIVE

In addition to the rare Slot 12 morpheme *-qe* and the periphrastic potential, optative meaning is often expressed by a lexical phrase consisting of the verb *-ini-* 'be' in the optative followed by the verb in question joined under normal transition to *he-* 'be able (to), can' and the nominalizing morpheme *-re* in the form *-ro*, as in *inibileqe chihubasohero* (*ini-bi-le-qe chi-huba-so-he-re > -ro*) 'if only you might love him/ if only you were able to love him' (= 'if it might be' + 'you are able to love' > NOUN 'you who are able to love').

THE PERIPHRASTIC IMPERATIVE.

The imperative is often expressed by the durative, proximate, or imperative of *ha-* 'be in the future, be ongoing' added under normal transition to the main verb (finite or non-finite), as in *hubasolehabe* (*huba-so-le-ha-be*), *hubasolehale* (*huba-so-le-ha-le*), *hubasolehano* (*huba-so-le-ha-no*), *hubasohache* (*huba-so-ha-che*) 'Love him!'

TIMUCUA GRAMMAR

PARTICLES

A small number of free bases occur with either no affixation or, at most, with the non-specific pluralizer *-ca*. These constitute the morphemic class called *particles*. Semologically they function as nominals, adverbials, prepositions, or demonstratives. The most frequent particles are:

achico 'much, many'
amiro 'much, many'
ara 'much, many'
arati 'much, many'
abo 'above'
becha 'tomorrow'
beta 'for, with'
cha 'where'
eane 'slow'
eba 'left-hand'
eqete 'near'
farane 'right-hand'
haba 'near'
heca 'now'
huri 'far away'
inemi 'much, many'
inibiti 'much, many'
ca 'this, here'
qela 'near'
qen 'there (far away)'
qibo 'yesterday'
qua 'in'
quana 'for, with'
michu 'that'
miri 'much, many'
na 'this'
ocho 'behind'
ofue 'on top, later'
oqe 'that'
ona 'there (nearby)'
oyo 'beneath'
patafi 'below'
pu 'no'
puqua 'much, many'
reqe 'each'
tulu 'immediately'
u 'no'
ya 'no'
yalaba 'certainly'
yuba 'behind'

Particles frequently compound with one another and with other bases, and they frequently occur with enclitics. For example:

(1) PARTICLE + PARTICLE:
ocho 'behind' + *beta* 'with' > *ochobeta* 'after'

(2) NOUN + PARTICLE:
mucu 'eye' + *beta* 'with' > *mucubeta* 'in front of'

(3) PARTICLE + ENCLITIC:

amiro 'much, many' + *-qua* 'intensive' >
amiroqua 'very much, very many'

A number of particles take on slightly different semological function when combined with enclitics:

na 'this' + *-qi* 'intensive' > *naqi* 'there'
ona 'there (nearby)' + *-qua* 'intensive' > *onaqua* 'enough, then'

Use of *quana* 'for, with' as the second member of a compound particle, under normal transition, gives the resultant lexeme modifying function of the sort we refer to as adverbial, as in *eane* 'slow' + *quana* 'with' > *eanequana* 'slowly'.

Many particles occur with *-ca* 'plural'. In some cases they are transformed into morphemic nouns by the addition of noun-designating *-re*:

ca 'this' + *-ca* 'plural' > *caca* 'these'
miri 'much, many' + *-ca* 'plural' > *mirica* 'very much, very many'
oqe 'that' + *-ca* 'plural' + *-re* 'noun' > *oqecare* 'those, them'

MORPHEMIC TRANSFORMATIONS

I use the term 'morphemic transformation' to mean the alteration of one morphemic part of speech to another through the use of derivational or designative affixes. Only morphemic verbs and nouns can be derived by transformation. There are no derived morphemic particles or pronouns. There are two types of morphemic noun derivation: VERB > NOUN, and PARTICLE > NOUN, and two types of morphemic verb derivation: NOUN > VERB and PARTICLE > VERB.

VERB > NOUN

These transformations are by far the most frequent. Examples are: *hubasoqere* 'loving' (= 'one desiring to love') and *chihubasohero* 'you who are able to love'. While serving as examples of the VERB > NOUN transformation, these two structures are syntactically re-verbalized, occuring only in syntactically verbal contexts. There are, however, seven other VERB > NOUN transformations which occur in strictly nominal contexts:

(1) BASE + *-no*^{1} > VERB STEM + *-ma*^{2} > NOUN:
heba-no-ma 'word' (*heba* 'speak')

(2) BASE + *-te* > FINITE VERB + *-ma*^{2} > NOUN in '-er' (animate):
heba-tema 'speaker' (= 'one who speaks')

(3) *na-* + [BASE + *-no*^{1}> > VERB STEM] + *-ma*^{2} > NOUN in '-er' (inanimate):
na-heba-no-ma 'speaker' (= 'instrument to produce speech')

(4) VERB BASE + *-siba* > '-ive':
heba-siba 'a talkative person'

(5) VERB BASE + final vowel change + *-ma*^{2} > DEFINITE AGENTIVE NOUN:
areca-ma 'a doer' (*areco* 'make, do' > *areca* 'maker, doer')

(6) VERB + *-co*^{2}> 'noun' > NOUN:
nahiabo-te-co 'he who understands' (*nahiabo* 'understand'), *nihi-no-co* 'death' (= 'to die/dying '). Forms in *-co*^{2}> 'noun' may take normal noun-pluralizing constructions, as in *nahiabo-te-co-ca-re* 'those who understand' (= 'he understands + noun + plural + noun')

(7) VERB + *-ma*^{2} > NOUN:
nahiabo-ha-be-ma 'he who will understand' (= 'understand' + 'it will be in the future' + 'the'), *ocoto-bi-ti-ma* 'the one who didn't hear' (= 'he heard' + 'not' + 'the').

PARTICLE > NOUN

These transformations are less frequent. An example is: *oqe-ca-re* 'those, them'.

NOUN > VERB, PARTICLE > VERB

Verb derivation occurs with considerable frequency. Examples of the two varieties are:

(1) NOUN > VERB:
chi-yaha-ma-la 'you are the one' (= 'you' + [*yaha* 'one' + *-ma*[2] 'the' > NOUN] + 'proximate time')

(2) PARTICLE > VERB:
ca-no-ma-be-la 'these are' (= 'this' [particle] + *-no*[1] 'action designator' + *-ma*[3] 'subject 3rd plural' + *be* 'durative' + *-la* 'proximate time'), *ni-heca-le-ba-ma* 'it is we/we are' (= '1st person' + *heca* 'we' [particle] + 'proximate time' + 'subject 1/2 plural' + *-ma*[4] 'proximate time')

SYNTAX

Syntax in my frame of reference involves more than the simple positional patterns of morphologically-defined lexemes in phrases, clauses, and total sentences. Phonological criteria are of equal importance in syntax as semological signals. Most languages have pre-junctural and/or post-junctural allophones of some segmental phonemes, definable paralinguistic phenomena accompanying phrase-, clause-, and sentence-final structures, and highly regular suprasegmental patterns of pitch, stress, and juncture, referred to as *transitions*, at phrase, clause, and sentence boundaries. I have defined the reconstructable transition patterns of Timucua earlier in this chapter in the section on phonology. Without fuller data on phonological transition — which will never be available — it is of course difficult to provide a thorough statement on Timucua syntax. Given Pareja's use of punctuation in the texts and the tentative correlation of punctuation and transition discussed earlier in this chapter, it is possible to suggest the following phrasal and clausal characteristics.

TIMUCUA GRAMMAR

SYNTACTIC PARTS OF SPEECH

While there are only four parts of speech by form in Timucua — verbs, nouns, pronouns, and particles — six syntactic parts of speech may be defined: *verbs*, *nouns*, *pronouns*, *modifiers*, *demonstratives*, and *conjunctions*. One may not assume that morphemic verbs become syntactic verbs, morphemic nouns syntactic nouns, and so on. Syntactic parts of speech are defined by the phrase, clause, and sentence context of lexemes regardless of their morphemic constituents. Such syntactic transformations will be defined below.

PHRASE STRUCTURE

Phrases and clauses are usually defined as lexemic structures bounded by some kind of transition phenomena. The 'phrase' is usually considered a binary lexemic structure in which one member acts as head-word and the second member fulfills various kinds of syntactic functions. Head-word status in most languages is accorded that phrase member which belongs to the statistically more frequent morphemic part of speech of the two members. In Timucua texts finite morphemic verbs occur with the highest statistical frequency, non-finite verbs are second, inflected nouns are third, uninflected nouns fourth, particles fifth, and pronouns sixth and last. This frequency will be taken as the *rank-order* for defining head-words in Timucua binary phrases. Thus a phrase containing a morphemic verb and a morphemic noun will be considered a VERB PHRASE; one containing a morphemic noun and a morphemic particle will be called a NOUN PHRASE. In phrases containing two equally ranked morphemic parts of speech the first member is dominant, to judge from Pareja's translations.

It is technically possible for thirty-six kinds of binary phrases to occur in Timucua. In fact, however, only fourteen are attested to in the texts. There are no phrases in Timucua which have a morphemic particle or a morphemic pronoun as head-word. All binary phrases are either verbal or nominal. In the following discussion of phrase- and clause-types: v = morphemic verb, V = syntactic verb (f = a finite morphemic or syntactic verb, nf = a non-finite morphemic or syntactic verb), n = morphemic noun, N = syntactic noun (i = an inflected morphemic or syntactic noun, non-inflected forms use only the n or N symbol), p = morphemic particle, pr = morphemic pronoun, Pr = syntactic pronoun, M = syntactic modifier, D = syntactic demonstrative, C = syntactic conjunction, s = clause/sentence subject, c = clause/sentence complement, p = clause/sentence predicate, cm = clause modifier, and a = sentence adjunct.

VERB PHRASE TYPES are:

(1) $[v^{nf} + v^{f}] > [M + V^{f}]$:
iniqe nirabonoleqe 'Being thus may make me happy' (= 'being' + 'I may be happy' [*orabo* 'be happy']

(2) $[n + v^{f}] > [N + V^{f}]$:
ano hebanano 'The man is speaking'

(3) $[p + v^{f}] > [Pr + V^{f}]$:
oqe hubasotele 'He loves someone'

(4) $[pr + v^{f}] > [Pr + V^{f}]$:
honihe hontala 'I am'

(5) $[n + v^{nf}] > [N + V^{nf}]$:
soba mahaquano 'meat-selling' (= 'meat' + 'to sell/selling' [*maha* 'sell'])

(6) $[p + v^{nf}] > [Pr + V^{nf}]$:
oqe uquata 'he, having taken . . .'

(7) $[pr + v^{nf}] > [Pr + V^{nf}]$:
honihe uquata 'I, having taken . . .'

(8) $[v^{f} + v^{nf}] > [V^{f} + M]$:
nirabonoleqe uquata 'having done this, I may be happy' (= 'I may be happy' + 'taken')

(9) $[v^{f} + n^{i}] + [V^{f} + M]$:
ibinemola pahama 'tavern' (= ['water' + 'the' + 'it is'] + 'its house')

(10) $[v^{nf} + v^{nf}] > [V^{nf} + M]$:

iniqe uquata 'having been taken' (= 'being' + 'taken')

NOUN PHRASE TYPES are:

(11) [n + n] > [N + M] :
caya biro 'rooster' (= 'chicken' + 'male')

(12) [n + p] > [N + M] :
hachipile michu> 'that animal' (= 'animal' + 'that')

(13) [n + n^i] > [M + N^i] :
chulufi pahama 'bird-house' (= 'bird' + 'its house')

(14) [p + n] > [D + N] :
caqi diosi 'this god'

The relationship between phrasal members is defined from the point of view of the head-word. Thus in Types 1-7, where the verb head-word is the second member, the relationship between the binary elements is referred to as *pre-verbal*. In Types 8-10, where the verb head-word is the first member, the relationship is, accordingly, *post-verbal*. In Types 13-14, where the noun head-word is the second member, the relationship is called *pre-nominal*, and in Types 11-12, where the noun head-word is the first member, the relationship is called *post-nominal*.

As can be seen from the foregoing examples, in any phrase in which the head-word is the first member (Types 8-12, giving a *post-* relationship to the second member) the second member serves a syntactically modifying function. There is in Timucua no formal or syntactic difference between verbal and nominal modification, so the terms 'adjective' and 'adverb', while perfectly satisfactory semological labels, are syntactically inappropriate. Hence the term *modifier* has been used. In any *post-* relationship phrase in which both members are of equal rank (Types 10 and 11) and the head-word is therefore the first member, the second member also acts as a syntactic modifier.

In phrases in which the head-word is the second member

(Types 1-7 and 13-14, giving a *pre-* relationship to the first member) the first member will become:

In VERB PHRASES —

(1) particle or pronoun > Pronoun
(2) noun = Noun
(3) non-finite verb > Modifier

In NOUN PHRASES —

(4) noun > Modifier
(5) particle > Demonstrative

CLAUSE STRUCTURE

Clause-constituents in Timucua are: *subject*, *complement* (= direct or indirect object), *predicate*, and *clause modifier*. Any of these constituents may be single lexemes or phrases. The normal order of these elements is — *SUBJECT*, *COMPLEMENT*, *PREDICATE*. *Clause modifiers* usually occur before the clause-constituent they modify.

Syntactic noun or pronoun material in pre-verbal position, either in-phrase with the verbal material or separated from it by a larger transition, acts either as subject or complement. The precise nature of such pre-verbal material is determined by the morphemic constituents of the finite verb in a predicative utterance. If two syntactic noun or pronoun structures occur in pre-verbal position, the first is always the subject of the clause, the second the complement. Finite verb phrases serve as clause predicates.

The only phrasal clause modifiers in Timucua are phrases whose head-word is a non-finite verb. This type of phrase occurs with high frequency in Timucua (see verb phrase Types 5-7, 10 above) and is equated by Pareja with the ubiquitous *ablative-absolute* of Classical Latin (Adam and Vinson 1886:91-93). In Timucua clause modifiers largely take the place of the separate subordinate clauses of other languages. They are often connected to the rest of the clause by one of the five linking enclitics — *-có(co)*, *-qua*, *-qui*, *-te*, or *-leqe* — having the function of coordinating conjunctions.

SENTENCE STRUCTURE

Most sentences in Timucua consist of single independent clauses. On occasion, however, modifying subordinate clauses also occur, joined to the main clause solely by /I/ (= <,>) or by a syntactic conjunction such as *heqe* 'when' or *cha* 'where'. Such subordinate clauses are here called *ADJUNCTS.*
Examples of clause and sentence constituents are:

(1) *oqe, iniqe uquata, isinoleqe.*
'He may take the opportunity to say something.'
(= 'He, it having been taken, may speak')
$[p > Pr]_s \; [(v^{nf} + v^{nf}) > (V^{nf} + M)]_{cm} \; [v^f > V^f]_p$

(2) *Minolahana, heqe, Pedro ninatila.*
'I won't see Pedro when he arrives.'
(= 'He arrives' + 'it will be', 'when', 'Pedro I do not see')
$[v^f > V^f]_a \; [p > C] \; [n > N]_c + [v^f > V^f]_p$

Syntax is an analytical area in need of considerable additional work. Further careful examination of all the extant Timucua texts will eventually provide a fuller and likely more accurate picture of Timucua grammar. There is room for the work of numerous researchers over many years to come.

3 TIMUCUA – ENGLISH DICTIONARY

3 TIMUCUA-ENGLISH DICTIONARY

Consult the USER'S GUIDE (pp. xvii-xxviii) for a detailed discussion of the entry of forms. The user should bear in mind the fact that inasmuch as many Timucua bases are non-specific with regard to morphemic part of speech — that is, they are unmarked by form — that designation is often left blank in an entry, specific syntactic part of speech usage being shown with the individual usages under the entry. Syntactic part of speech abbreviations used are: V verb, N noun, P particle, Pr pronoun, and M modifier. Consult the grammar section of this volume for a discussion of part of speech designation and usage. Homophonous forms have been given different entries but have been marked with a superscript number at the end of the form, as in **aimanta**^{1} and **aimanta**^{2}. Type 7 vowel alterations (see p. 75) and selected other vowel changes are given in parentheses immediately after the entry form, as in **aboto** (7A).

A

a [**á**] (*a*) 1. Exclamation of satisfaction, 'ah!' 2. Alas!

ababa (*ababa*) *verb* 1. cross.

abala (*abala*) 1. (V) paddle; 2. (V) exert oneself.

abara [**auara**] (*abara*) 1. (N) clearing, field; 2. (N) crop, harvest. [Warao *aba* 'put', *ari-* 'harvest'].

TIMUCUA DICTIONARY

abi[1] (*abi*) 1. (N) clothing, (V) clothe, dress, put on. [Warao *aba* 'put'].

abi[2] 1. (N) hour, time; 2. (P) at each moment.

abi[3] 1. (P) apart.

abi[4] 1. (V) walk (pl.).

abiti (*abi-ti*) *particle* 1. in an instant, at each instant, at each moment, in a moment, at each step.

abo[1] (*abo*) 1. (P) above, up, upward.

abo[2] (7A) 1. (V) travel, wander, go (to) (pl.), run (pl.), go separately.

abo[3] (7A) 1. (V) emulate.

abolo (7A) (*abolo*) *verb* 1. hallow.

abopahama (*abo-paha-ma*) *noun* 1. corn-crib (*lit.* 'above-house-its').

aboqua (*abo-k^{w}a*) *verb* 1. honor (*lit.* 'above praise').

abota[1] (*abota*) *verb* 1. drag, draw.

abota[2] *verb* 1. throw.

abota[3] *verb* 1. say.

aboto (7A) (*aboto*) 1. (V) beat, strike, whip, (N) flagellation, beating.

aca [**haca**] (*aka*) *noun* 1. wind. [Warao *haka* 'wind'].

acata[1] (*akata*) 1. (N) bed.

acata[2] *particle* 1. beneath.

acatala[1] (*akata-la*) *noun* 1. earth, dirt, under the earth's surface. (*lit.* 'it is beneath').

acatala[2] *noun* 1. fishery, fish-weir.

achico (*ačiko*) *particle* 1. much, many.

achitilo (*ačitilo*) *noun* 1. arms, weapons.

aco (*ako*) *particle* 1. most, many.

acoro (7A) (*akoro*) *verb* 1. raise, elevate.

acu[1] (*aku*) 1. (N) moon, month. [Warao *waniku* 'moon', Chocó -*exo*, Sumu *waiku*, Cacaopera *aiku*,
Lokono -*ači*, Baré *k-i*, Yavitero *k-e*, Yamamadí -*axi*].

acu[2] *particle* 1. all, every, another, and, again, any.

ae [**áe, aé**] (*ae*) *particle* 1. Ah!, Alas!

afabo (*afabo*) *particle* 1. light (= 'not heavy'), lightly; 2. swift, swiftly.

TIMUCUA DICTIONARY

afati (*afati*) 1. (N) relief, (M) relieved.
afeta (*afeta*) *noun* 1. chestnut.
aha (*aha*) *noun* 1. white oak.
aho[1] (7A) (*aho*) *verb* 1. declare, say, tell.
aho[2] (7A) *verb* 1. tempt.
aho[3] (7A) *verb* 1. treat.
aho[4] (7A) *verb* 1. concert.
ahono (*ahono*) *noun* 1. son; 2. son; 3. daughter.
ahu (*ahu*) *noun* 1. acorn.
aimanta[1] (*aimanta*) *noun* 1. deceased person.
aimanta[2] *particle* 1. contrary to.
alabina (*alabina*) *verb* 1. remove.
alata (*alata*) 1. (V) kindle or light a fire.
alifila (*alifila*) *noun* 1. boy.
aliho (7A) (*aliho*) 1. (V) go, walk. [Koasati *čayahli* 'walk'].
alobo (*alobo*) *particle* 1. lazy.
altari (*altari*) *noun* 1. altar. [Spanish *altar*].
ama (*ama*) *noun* 1. *Ego*'s (regardless of sex) father's sister's child, regardless of sex (= 'paternal cousin through father's female siblings').
amala (*amala*) *noun* 1. clothing, rope.
amara (*amara*) *noun* 1. candle, fat, grease [Warao *emoera* 'to be soft'].
amiro (*amiro*) *particle* 1. all; 2. much, many.
amita (*amita*) *noun* 1. *Ego* male's younger siblings, regardless of sex (='younger brother', 'younger sister'); 2. *Ego* female's younger sister; 3. *Ego*'s (regardless of sex) father's brother's child, regardless of sex; 4. *Ego*'s (regardless of sex) mother's sisters if younger than *ego*.
amuna (*amuna*) *noun* 1. cloth, clothing, 'sackcloth'; 2. tailor, seamstress.
anacotima (*anakoti-ma*) *noun* 1. counselor.
anapie (*anapie*) *noun* 1. bark of a tree.
anda *see* **anta**
ane (*ane*) *verb* 1. be able to, can.
aneca (*ane-ka*) 1. (V intrans.) be unable to, cannot; 2. (V trans.) disable, prevent; 3. (N) disability, prevention,

impediment; 4. (M) ineffectual, unable to, powerless (< *ane* + *-ca* 'negative', a relic, non-productive suffix).

angeli (*anheli*) *noun* 1. angel. [Spanish *angel*].

ano (*ano*) *noun* 1. male human being, person, man; 2. relative, *specif*. parents; 3. lord, master; 4. neighbor [General Northern Maipuran *ena* 'man', 'human being'].

ano nasimita (*ano nasimita*) *noun* 1. *Ego*'s (regardless of sex) father or mother-in-law.

anorimati (*ano-re>ri-ma-ti*) *noun* 1. mean, wicked, vile, low (*lit*. 'not human').

anoti (*anti*) *noun* 1. house; 2. part of a house. (Der. *ano*).

anta [**anda**] (*anta,* [*anda*]) *particle* 1. before (in time).

apacha (*apača*) *particle* 1. thing.

apalu (*apalu*) *noun* 1. corral, fence, stockade; 2. fort.

ape[1] (*ape*) 1. (V) help.

ape[2] 1. (V) prevent.

api[1] (*api*) *noun* 1. salt; 2. ashes, dust. [Koasati *hapi* 'salt'].

api[2] *noun* 1. tail. [Tariana, Arekana, Carútana, Baré *-i-p/bi* 'tail'].

apichiara (*apichiara*) *noun* 1. hare, rabbit.

apo (7A) (*apo*) 1. (V) break, rupture.

apohola (*apohola*) *noun* 1. buzzard.

apu (*apu*) *noun* 1. palmetto berry.

aqe (1A, B) [**haqe**] (*ake*) *noun* 1. wind, storm, tornado.

aqio (*akio*) *particle* 1. now, presently, already, soon, immediately.

aqui (*ak*^{w}i) *verb* 1. stumble.

aquita (*ak*^{w}ita) *noun* 1. virgin, maiden; 2. girl, damsel.

ara[1] (*ara*) *particle* 1. much, many. [Twahka (Paya) *-rau* 'much, many'].

ara[2] *noun* 1. bear (animal).

ara[3] *verb* 1. help, intercede, succor; 2. favor, advocate; 3. (N) helper.

arati (*arati*) *particle* 1. much, many.

are (*are*) *verb* 1. not to speak.

areco[1] (*areko*) 1. (V) do, make, create, institute, provide; 2. (V) work, labor; 3. (N) creator; 4. (N) creation; 5. *By* *extension* — a person who does any kind of specific work, such as 'blacksmith', 'carpenter', etc.

areco[2] 1. (V) judge, consider, counsel.

ari (*ari*) *verb* 1. lack, be wanting.

aro (7A) (*aro*) *verb* 1. move, go beyond; 2. augment.

arobota iribi (*aro-bo-ta iribi*) *verb* 1. fly (*lit.* 'they are going above').

aruqui[1] (*arukʷi*) 1. (N) *Ego*'s (regardless of sex) father's sister's child, regardless of sex (= 'paternal cousin through father's sister'); 2. (N) boy; 3. (N) girl; 4. *infrequently* 'child', 'descendant', 'generation'. [Warao *araka* 'younger brother', *arao* 'people'].

aruqui[2] 1. (V) be born (*cf.* **aruqui**[1]).

asa (*asa*) 1. (P) beautiful.

asacamaco (*asakamako*) *noun* 1. owl.

asileco (*asileko*) *noun* 1. withered leaf.

asioqe (*asioke*) *verb* 1. say.

asiquita (*asikʷ*ita) *noun* 1. seed.

asisi (*asisi*) *noun* 1. sod, turf, clod.

asisuqua (*asisukʷa*) *noun* 1. foam, froth.

asu (3) (*asu*) 1. (V) plant.

asurupa (*asurupa*) *noun* 1. excrement, dung, manure; 2. filth, sweepings. [Warao *-so-* 'excrement'].

ata (*ata*) 1. (N) viscosity.

atafi (*atafi*) 1. (M) old, ancient; 2. (M) stale.

ataro[1] (7A) (*ataro*) 1. (V) look.

ataro[2] *particle* 1. close to.

ate[1] (*ate*) 1. (N) servant, slave.

ate[2] 1. (N) damage.

atichicolo (*atičikolo*) *noun* 1. soul, spirit.

atimo[1] (*atimo*) *particle* 1. both; 2. all.

atimo[2] *particle* 1. finished.

atimucu (*atimuku*) *noun* 1. frost, ice; 2. bile, gall.

atiqui (*atikʷ*i) 1. (V/N) sneeze.

atofo (*atofo*) *noun* 1. owl.

atulu (*atulu*) *noun* 1. arrow; 2. ray of light. [Warao *atubu* 'arrow'].

auara *see* **abara**

aya (*aya*) *noun* 1. forest. See also **aye**.

ayahibanoma [**ayahibuanoma**] (*aya-hiba-no-ma*) *noun* 1. excrement (*lit.* 'forest-dweller').

aye[1] (*aye*) *noun* 1. tree; 2. wood, timber; 3. stick, post, pole; 4. box; 5. one who works with wood, a 'carpenter'. [Culino *awa* 'tree', Lokono *ada* 'tree, wood', Hitchitit *ahi* 'tree'].

aye[2] 1. mountain.

B

Many entries normally spelled with initial <*b-*> occasionally occur with initial <*bu-*>, <*gu-*>, or <*hu-*>. The most frequently occurring variants are included in the dictionary, but forms with extremely low frequency may not be.

-ba (8C, 3L) (*-ba*) 1. A variant of '1st or 2d plural verb subject pronoun' (= 'we', 'you all') suffix **-bo** (which see). [Warao *-bu*].

bacara (*bakara*) 1. (V) ripen.

bahuru (7B) (*bahuru*) 1. (V) howl.

bali (*bali*) 1. (N) tongue, mouth; 2. *By extension* (V/N) 'wound', 'hunt', (N) 'hunter' (= 'one who wounds') [Baniva *t-ali* 'mouth', Layaná *ba-halo* 'mouth', Cuna *wa-* 'tongue'].

balu (7B) (*balu*) 1. (V) live; 2. (V) restore, regenerate, resurrect, resuscitate, revive, save; 3. (V/N) cure; 4. *By extension* (V) absolve; 5. (N) life, regeneration, restoration, resuscitation, revival, salvation; 6. (M) well, healthy.

balua (*balua*) 1. (V) pay.

banehe [**guanehe**] (*banehe*) *noun* 1. wolf.

bapi (*bapi*) 1. (N) beauty; 2. (M) beautiful, pretty, fair.

bara[1] (*bara*) 1. (V) finish. [Warao *yi-wara* 'finish'].

bara[2] 1. (N) filth, excrement (perhaps by extension from **bara**[1]).

basala[1] (*basala*) 1. (V) cross, pass through, pass by.

basala[2] 1. (N) a river- or stream-bank.

basala[3] 1. (M) from side to side (perhaps by extension from **basala**[1,2]).
basala[4] 1. (V) part, party.
bayeti (*bayeti*) 1. (V/N) doubt, vacillate/vacillation.
-be (*-be*) 1. Durative aspect indicator with verbs (= progressive tenses).
becha[1] [**huecha, buecha**] (*beča*) 1. (P) tomorrow.
becha[2] 1. (V) perform a ceremony.
behe (*behe*) 1. (V) wait, await, wait for, watch for, expect; 2. (V/N) hope, trust.
bele[1] (*bele*) 1. (V/N) hope.
bela[2] 1. (V) ask, call upon.
-belehanima (*-be-le-ha-ni-ma*) 1. 'will always be' (= 'future durative').
benan (*benan*) *verb* 1. lose (< *benano*).
beni [**beny**] (*beni*) 1. (P) laziness, torpor; 2. (P) slowness, slowly; 3. *By extension* (P) 'rude', 'unclean', 'unwholesome', 'lewd', 'crude', 'mock'. [Warao *abani* 'slow'].
beqe (*beke*) TAWASA DIALECT *see* **heqe** 'now'.
beqelo (7A) (*bekelo*) 1. (V) prepare; 2. (N) preparation.
beqenino (*beke-ni-no*) *noun* 1. pillow.
bequa (*bek*^{w}a) TAWASA DIALECT *see* **ca** 'here'.
bere (*bere*) *particle* 1. quickly.
bereta (*bere-ta*) *noun* 1. haste, speed (< *bere*).
beta (*beta*) *particle* 1. by, for, through, towards; 2. more than [Chacobo *-bïta* 'with'].
bete (*bete*) *particle* 1. while.
-bi (*-bi*) 1. Bounded action indicator (= 'past time').
bi (*bi*) TAWASA DIALECT *see* **ibi** 'water'.
bicota (*bikota*) 1. (P) abundantly, plentifully.
bihi (*bihi*) *noun* 1. bunch of grapes. [Choctaw *bihi* 'mulberry'].
-bila (*-bi-la*) 1. 'was', 'was done' (= 'bounded proximate action').
-bile (*-bi-le*) 1. 'was', 'was done' (= 'bounded proximate action').
-bilehabela (*-bi-le-ha-be-la*) 1. 'shall have' (= 'future bounded durative proximate action').
-bileqe (*-bi-le-qe*) 1. 'if I/you/he/she, etc. were' (= 'bounded proximate optative action').

-bima (*-bi-ma*) 1. 'was', 'was done' (= 'bounded proximate action').

-bino (*-bi-no*) 1. 'was', 'was done' (= 'bounded proximate action').

bio (*bio*) 1. (P) distant, far.

biro [**viro, uiro**] (*biro*) *noun* 1. man, male; 2. humanity; 3. son; 4. lover. [Piapoco *-ali* 'man', Taíno *-eri* 'man', Warao *arao* 'people', Yanomama *waro~waru* 'man'].

bisa (*bisa*) 1. (N) name.

biu (7A) (*biu*) 1. (V) fall.

bizcocho (*biskočo*) *noun* 1. biscuit. [Spanish *bizcocho*].

-bo (8C, 3L) 1. 1st or 2d plural subject pronoun (= 'we', 'you all'). [Warao *-bu*, Chacobo *-bo* 'noun plural'].

boco (7A) (*boko*) 1. (V) be drunk; 2. (N) drunkard.

boho (7A) (*boho*) 1. (V) believe, trust; 2. (N) belief, trust, faith; 3. (M) faithful.

boyo (7A) (*boho*) 1. (V) obey; 2. (N) obedience; 3. *By extension* (V) be grateful.

boyoti (7A) (boyo-ti) 1. (V) disobey; 2. (N) disobedience; 3. *By extension* (V) be ungrateful. (Der. *boyo* + *-ti* 'negative' = 'not grateful, unobedient').

bucha (*buča*) 1. (N) yesterday.

C

The user should bear in mind that lexical forms beginning /*ke-, ki-*/ are spelled in Timucua with orthographic <*qe- qi-*>. Lexical forms beginning in /$k^{w}V$-/, where /*V*/ represents any vowel, are spelled with orthographic <*quV-*>.

-ca (*-ka*) 1. plural indicator with nominal forms and particles.

ca (*ka*) 1. (P) here; 2. (P) this; 3. (P) that. [Chacobo *-ka(ya)* 'here'].

caballo (*kabayo*) *noun* 1. horse. [Spanish *caballo*].

cabichi[1] (*kabiči*) 1. (P) about, around; 2. (P) near.

cabichi[2] 1. (V) keep watch.

TIMUCUA DICTIONARY

caca (*kaka*) *noun* 1. crow.

cache (*kače*) *particle* 1. now, it is time.

cachi (*kači*) 1. (P) bitter.

cachu[1] (7B) (*kaču*) 1. (P) beautiful, pretty, fair; 2. (P) delightful; 3. (N) beauty; 4. *By extension* (N) love; 5. *By extension* (V) infatuated with, in love with; (M) enamored of.

cachu[2] 1. (P) disorderly, lawless (probably by extension from **cachu**[1]).

caco[1] (7A) (*kako*) 1. (V) hang upon; 2. (V) crucify.

caco[2] 1. (V) encounter.

cafa (*kafa*) *noun* 1. port, harbor, place of embarkation; 2. wharf.

cala[1] (*kala*) 1. (V) cut, shave.

cala[2] 1. (V) freeze to death.

cala[3] 1. (N) fruit.

calaba (*kalaba*) 1. (P) bald.

caluba[1] (*kaluba*) 1. (V/N) harm; 2. (V) punish; 3. (N) punishment; 4. (V) offend; 5. (N) offence.

caluba[2] 1. *By extension from* **caluba**[1] 'sin'.

calubo (7A) (*kalubo*) 1. (V) condemn. See also **caluba**.

camapata (*kama-pata* ?) 1. (N) lake, lagoon; 2. *By extension* (V) fish. (Der. *cama* + *pata* 'deep' ?).

cana[1] (*kana*) *verb* 1. have to eat.

cana[2] *verb* 1. be without, not to have.

canasta (*kanasta*) *noun* 1. basket. [Spanish *canasta*].

cane[1] (*kane*) 1. (N) drum.

cane[2] 1. (M) meek, softly.

canima (*kanima*) *verb* 1. restore.

canola (*ka-no-la*) *verb* 1. 'Yes, it is true' (*lit.* 'this it is').

cantela (*ka-no>n-te-la*) *verb* 1. 'Yes, it is true' (*lit.* 'this it is').

caqi (*kaki*) 1. (V) suspect; 2. (N) suspicion; 3. (V) despise; 4. (V) persecute; 5. (N) persecution; 6. *by extension (?)* (V) 'set up'.

caraca (*karaka*) *noun* 1. eel.

caramaba (*karamaba*) *noun* 1. turtle.

-care (*-ka-re*) 1. noun plural (= '-s').

caro (7A) (*karo*) 1. (N) light, brightness; 2. (N) splendor; 3. (V) brighten, light, shine, enlighten, reveal, show; 4. (M) light, bright, clear, resplendent. [Warao *o-kera* 'light'].

caru (*karu*) *noun* 1. twin.

casino (*kasino*) *noun* 1. casina (*Ilex vomitoria*), ritual black drink.

cata (*kata*) 1. (N) servant, vassal; 2. (V) impress into work.

cato[1] (7A) (*kato*) 1. (V) wound with words, slander, insult; 2. (M) angry.

cato[2] 1. (V) multiply.

cay (*kay*) 1. (N) strife, discord.

caya (*kaya*) *noun* 1. chicken, partridge, turkey, hen, rooster. [Alabama *aka·ka* 'chicken'].

cayo[1] (7A) (*kayo*) *verb* 1. love, like, fancy.

cayo[2] 1. (P) frequent.

cha[1] (*ča*) *particle* 1. where; 2. whence; 3. whither.

cha[2] *particle* 1. what?

cha[3] *particle* 1. Ah!; 2. Alas!

chaba (*čaba*) 1. (P) open.

chacaba (*čakaba*) *noun* 1. evil; 2. misfortune; 3. disgrace.

chala[1] (*čala*) 1. (V) deceive; 2. (N) deception.

chala[2] 1. (V) conform, fit in.

chale (*čale*) 1. (V) wash, cleanse; 2. (V) purify; 3. (N) purification; 4. *By extension* (V/N) pardon, (V) absolve, (N) absolution, (M) new.

chaleca (*čale-ka*) *noun* 1. cleaning, cleansing.

chano (7A) (*čano*) *verb* 1. point out; 2. see. (Der. *ča-no* 'Is that so?').

chaqueneti (*ča-k*^{w}*ene-ti*) *particle* 1. ignorant (*lit.* 'that + aforesaid + not').

chaqui (*čak*^{w}*i*) 1. (V/N) belch.

chara[1] (*čara*) 1. (V) paint, inscribe, write; 2. (N) book, letter, message, paper, painting (= anything written or painted); 3. (N) writer, painter, artist, reader, messenger, postman; 4. *By extension* (V) sew; (N) seamstress.

chara[2] 1. (N) laundress.

-che[1] (*-če*) 1. Imperative mode indicator.

-che[2] 1. Interrogative enclitic.

chebe (*čebe*) 1. (V) fail, lose; 2. (N) failure, loss, lack; 3. (N) fault.

chepa (*čepa*) *noun* 1. nest.

cheqeta (*čeketa*) 1. (P) four, fourth.

chequa (*ček^{w}a*) 1. (V) despise; 2. (V) ruin; 3. (N) ruin; 4. (N) misfortune.

chequama (*ček^{w}a-ma*) *particle* 1. mean, low, wicked, vile.

chi- (*či-*) 1. 2d plural verbal subject/object indicator (= 'you', 'thou', 'thee'). [Choctaw *či-* 'thou'].

chia (*čia*) *noun* 1. citizen.

chiama (*cia-ma*) *noun* 1. citizen, resident.

-chica (-či-ka*)* 1. 2nd person plural subject of verbs in questions.

chica (*čika*) *verb* 1. add, mix, mingle; 2. stir.

chichi (*čiči*) 1. (P) diminution.

chico[1] (7A) (*čiko*) 1. (N) friend; 2. (M) friendly.

chico[2] 1. (N) saint; 2. (M) saintly, glorious.

chico[3] 1. (n) grace; 2. (M) graceful, delightful.

chico[4] 1. *By extension from* **chico**[1] (V) grant, pardon.

chicolata (*čikolata*) *noun* 1. dumpling, tamale.

chie[1] (*čie*) 1. (V) do, cause, make, create; 2. (N) creation.

chie[2] 1. (V/N) use; 2. (N) instrument.

chie[3] 1. (V/) sign, seal.

chie[4] 1. (V) hatch.

chie[5] 1. (V) baptize, consecrate; 2. (N) baptism, consecration.

chiho- (*či-ho-*) 1. You (subj.) + me (obj.) of verb.

china (*čina*) TAWASA DIALECT *pronoun* 1. he, she, it [Natchez *ičina* 'he']. See **oqe**.

chini- (*či-ni-*) 1. You (subj.) + me (obj.) of verb.

chini (*čini*) *noun* 1. nose, nostrils.

chio (*čio*) *noun* 1. flower.

chipa (*čipa*) 1. (V/N) wound:

chiqe[1] (*čike*) 1. (P) always.

chiqe[2] 1. (V) conceal, hide.

chiqeta (*čike-ta*) *noun* 1. hidden (things), apart.

chiqi (*čiki*) TAWASA DIALECT *see* **chiri**, **qichi**. Probably a metathesized form of the latter.

chiqi[1] (*čiki*) 1. (V/N) revenge; 2. (V) avenge.

chiqi[2] 1. (V) change; 2. exchange.

chiqi[3] 1. *By extension from* **chiqino**, *which see,* (N) vicar.

chiqino (*čiki-no*) *noun* 1. hat; 2. *By extension* (n) vicar.

chiqua (*čikʷa*) *noun* 1. otter, 'weasel', 'ferret'.

chique (*čikʷe*) *noun* 1. raft.

chiri (*čiri*) *noun* 1. little (one), small (one); 2. youth; 3. child; 4. son; 5. daughter; 6. (M) young.

chitaco (*čitako*) *particle* 1. who?

chito (*čito*) *noun* 1. head; 2. forehead, brow; 3. *By extension* the main height of anything — thus: 'roof', 'noon, midday', etc. [Piapoco, Catapolítani *i-w-ita* 'head'].

-cho (*-čo*) 1. Interrogative post-clitic.

choco (*čoko*) *particle* 1. ignorant.

chocolo (*čokolo*) *noun* 1. breast [Apalachee *čokonska* 'breast', Chamicuro *tu-ulu* 'breast'].

chocori[1] (*čokori*) 1. (N) power, force, strength; 2. (M) strong, powerful, forceful [Culino *kara-* 'strong'].

chocori[2] 1. (N) virtue, *by extension from* **chocori**[1].

chofa (*čofa*) *noun* 1. liver [Carútana *č-u-pana* 'liver'].

choho (7A) (*čoho*) 1. (V) to shell corn.

chola (*čola*) 1. (V) drop.

chonco (*čo-no>n-ko*) 1. (P) what?, who? (*lit.* 'who may it be?').

chota (*čota*) 1. (V) drop.

choya[1] (*čoya*) 1. (V) curse.

choya[2] 1. (M) disturbed.

christiano (*kristiano*) *noun* 1. Christian [Spanish *cristiano*].

-chu (*-ču*) 1. 'have, has, had' (= perfective action).

chu[1] (*ču*) 1. (N) charcoal, carbon.

chu[2] 1. (V) pay.

chua (*čua*) *noun* 1. hole, pit.

chubobo (*čubobo*) *noun* 1. stars [Piapoco, Baniva *-wi-*, Yaruro *-boe* 'stars'].

chuca (*ču-ka*) 1. (P) how much?, how many?; 2. (P) how often? (Der. Interrogative clitic **chu** + **-ca** 'this, that, here').

chucu[1] (*čuku*) 1. (N) black(ness), dark(ness); 2. *By extension* 'dirt', 'earth', or anything dark-colored, such as 'dye' [Chacobo *čïkï* 'black'].

chucu[2] 1. *By extension from* **chucu**[1] (N) gourd, squash, pumpkin, or similar products of the earth.

chula (*čula*) *verb* 1. loosen, weaken; 2. relax.

chulufi (*čulufi*) *noun* 1. bird; 2. *By extension* any variety of specific bird, such as 'partridge', 'chicken', etc. [Timote, Cuica *ču*, Koasati *kulu·si* 'bird']

chumosi (*čumosi*) *particle* 1. like.

-chunu (*-ču-nu*) 1. 'have always done' (= perfective habitual action).

chupi (*čupi*) *particle* 1. 100 or larger multiples of tens, such as '1,000' [Koasati, Hitchiti, Creek *čokpi* '100'].

chuteo (*čuteo*) *noun* 1. anger, vexation; 2. (M) angry; 3. *By extension* (N) trouble.

claro (*klaro*) *noun* 1. light [Spanish *claro*].

-co[1] (*-ko*) 1. Interrogative post-clitic.

-co[2] 1. Generalizing post-clitic — 'the one who . . . '

-co[3] 1. 'may, might' (= conditional action). [Warao *-kore* 'conditional'].

-có(co) (*-kó-ko*) 1. Copular post-clitic; 2. *By extension* an augmentative/intensive post-clitic [Warao *-ka* 'diminutive'].

co (*ko*) *verb* 1. say.

cobaqua (*kobak^{w}a*) 1. (P) loyal; 2. (N) loyalty.

cobe (*kobe*) *noun* 1. successor.

cobo[1] (7A) (*kobo*) 1. (V) delight, cherish, please; 2. (N) delight; 3. *By extension* (V) caress.

cobo[2] 1. (N) servant; 2. (V) sustain; 3. (V) obey.

coboso (7A) (*koboso*) 1. (V) entertain, regale, feast.

coche (*koče*) 1. (P) obscene, unchaste.

cocho (7A) (*kočo*) 1. (V) cut; 2. (N) cutter; 3. (N) instrument for cutting (= 'ax') [Proto-Muskogean **kač-* 'cut'].

coesa[1] (*koesa*) *noun* 1. kind, sort; 2. way.

coesa[2] *noun* 1. great-grandafther.

cola (*kola*) *noun* 1. feather, plumage.

colahayo (*kolahayo*) 1. (N) doubt; 2. (V) be in doubt; 3. (P) if, perhaps; 4. *By extension* what?

colala (kolala) *particle* 1. far, at a distance.

colo (*kolo*) *noun* 1. bow; 2. bowman.

colu (*kolu*) TAWASA DIALECT *see* **colo**.

-conacu (*-ka-na-ku*) 1. 'if I may . . . ' (= conditional habitual subjunctive action).

coni (*koni*) *noun* 1. Term used by *ego* male for the child (of either sex) of a sister (= 'cross-nephew', 'cross-niece'). *Cf.* **ebo.**

cono (*kono*) *particle* 1. if.

-coqua (*-ko-k^{w}a*) 1. 'might have . . . ' (= conditional distant action).

core[1] (*kore*) 1. (N) what is left, what remains at the end; 2. *By extension* (N) dessert.

core[2] 1. (V) consume; 2. every (both probably by extension from **core**[1]).

coreso (*kore-so*) *verb* 1. wash at the end of a meal.

cori (*kori*) *noun* 1. oar, paddle.

coto (7A) (*koto*) 1. (V) confirm.

coyo (7A) (*koyo*) 1. (V) tremble.

crusi (*krusi*) *noun* 1. cross [Spanish *cruz*].

-cu (*-ku*) 1. subjunctive mood indicator [Warao *-ku* 'subjunctive'].

cubita (*kubita*) *noun* 1. hunger; 2. famine.

culafo (7A) (*kulafo*) 1. (V) bathe, wash; 2. (N) lavatory, bath.

cume (*kume*) 1. (N) heart, breast, chest; *By extension* — 2. (N) feeling; 3. (V) feel; 4. (N) mind, thought, memory; 5. (V) think, consider, remember; 6. (N) love, compassion, consideration; 7. (V) love; 8. (M) compassionate, merciful, considerate; 9. (V/N) desire, wish; 10. (V) inspire, devote, revere; 11. (N) inspiration, devotion, reverence; 12. (V) believe; 13. (N) belief, custom; 14. (N) virtue; 15. (M) virtuous; 16. (M) gentle, affable, civil; 17. (V/N) command, instruct; 18. (N) commandment, instruction [Warao *kobe* 'heart', Proto-Pre-Andine Maipuran **tsomi* 'heart, breast'].

cumeni (*kumeni*) *particle* 1. restrained.

cumen (*kumen*) *particle* 1. (V) imitate.

cuna[1] (*kuna*) 1. (N) head; 2. (N) neck, throat; 3. *By extension* (N) voice [Manao *kü-na* 'head'].

cuna[2] 1. (V) covet.

cupa (*kupa*) *noun* 1. bark of a tree.

cuque (*kuk^{w}e*) *verb* 1. cover [Warao *kuku-* 'cover'].

cura (*kura*) 1. (V) covet.

curu (*kuru*) *particle* 1. colored.

cuyu[1] (*kuyu*) 1. (V/N) fish [Achagua *ku-* 'fish'].
cuyu[2] 1. (P) ungrateful.

D

In Timucua the orthographic letter <*d*> is found only in words of Spanish origin and, rarely, after /*n*/ to represent /*t*/, which was realized by the allophone [*d*] in that position alone. In the latter instance, however, orthographic <*t*> was more frequent, as in **anda** (rare) vs. **anta** (usual) 'before'.

diosi (*tiosi ?*) *noun* 1. Christian deity [Spanish *dios*].

discipulo (*tisipulo ?*) *noun* 1. disciple [Spanish *dicípulo*].

E

ea (*ea*) *particle* 1. (M) clear, light (in color); 2. (M) transparent.
eane (*eane*) *particle* 1. (M) slow, slowly, gradual, gradually, little-by-little.
eani (*eani*) *particle* 1. gently, slowly.
eba[1] [**ebua**] (*eba*) 1. (V/N) paddle; 2. (N) oar; 3. (V) row (hard).
eba[2] 1. (V) hit, wound (probably by extension from **eba**[1], since the major weapon used by the Timucua was a paddle-shaped war-club).
eba[3] 1. (N) left hand (probably by extension from **eba**[1], implying the left hand as the major paddle-/weapon-using hand). *Cf.* **fara** 'right hand, misfortune'. In Timucua the 'fortunes' of the hand, so frequent in many languages, seem to have been the opposite of what they were in Indo-European — *e.g.*, Latin *manu dextra* 'right hand, dextrous' vs. *manu sinistra* 'left hand, sinister'. For the Timucua the left hand, **eba**, was the hand of power, the good hand, while the right hand, **fara**, was the hand of misfortune, scandal, and ruin.

TIMUCUA DICTIONARY

eba[4] 1. (V) heal, care for; 2. (V) esteem (perhaps by extension from **eba**[1], implying 'to care for' a paddle-caused wound).

ebacalealeno (*eba-ka-le-ale-no ?*) 1. (N) bury, inter; 2. (N) gravedigger.

ebahio (*eba-hio*) 1. (N) compassion, mercy; 2. (N) piety; 3. (M) compassionate, merciful, pious (*lit.* 'heal with compassion').

ebe[1] (*ebe*) 1. (V) intercede, mediate, assist; 2. (N) mediation, assistance; 3. *By extension* (V) advocate, defend, succor, help; 4. (N) defense, help.

ebe[2] 1. (M) open (probably by extension from **ebe**[1]).

ebele (*ebele*) *particle* 1. entirely; 2. most; 3. very.

etea (*ebe-ta*) 1. (V) catch, grasp, take.

ebo (*ebo*) *noun* 1. Term used by *ego* female for the child (of either sex) of a brother (= 'cross -nephew', 'cross-niece'), or the child of ego's father's brother's son (= 'paternal parallel cousin's child'), or the child of mother's brother (= 'maternal cross-cousin'). *Cf.* **coni**.

eca[1] (*eka*) 1. (P) in, into; 2. (V) enter, come in; 3. *By extension* (V) unite, join [Warao *eku* 'in', Warao *eku* 'enter, come in'].

eca[2] 1. (P) equal [Warao *mon-uka* 'equal'].

eca[3] 1. (V) teach, instruct.

eca[4] 1. (N) field.

ecataqere (*ekatakere*) *verb* 1. carry; 2. *By extension* (V) throw (into).

echa[1] (*eča*) 1. (V) come in, go in(to), enter, put into; 2. *By extension* (V) set (sun) (probably related to **eca**[1]).

echa[2] 1. (V) strangle.

echa[3] 1. (M) crazed, possessed.

echaca (*ečaka*) *noun* 1. grass; 2. straw.

echeca (*ečeka*) 1. (V) skate.

ecoya (*ekoya*) 1. (P) in advance (of), before (in time); 2. *By extension* (N) elder, elder brother; 3. *By extension* (V) govern, (N) governor.

ecoyo (*ekoyo*) *particle* 1. before (in space), forward. *Cf.* **ecoya**.

efa (*efa*) *noun* 1. dog [Koasati *ifa* 'dog', Proto-Arawakan **ife-* 'capybara'].

ehe (*ehe*) 1. (N) debt, loan; 2. (V) owe, pay.

ehenta (*ehenta*) 1. (V) ride; 2. (M) mounted on, riding.

ela (*ela*) 1. (N) sun; 2. day; 3. *By extension* (V) show; 4. *By extension* (V) endow [Tariana, Piapoco *-eri* 'moon', Amarizana *eri-* 'fire', Arekena *ale* 'sun', Goajiro *-ali* 'sun', Achagua *eri* 'sun'].

elahiti (*elahiti*) *noun* 1. house.

elatubasa [**elatubuasa**] (*elatubasa*) *noun* 1. snake, serpent, viper.

ele (*ele*) 1. (N) something new, renewal, renovation, regeneration; 2. (V) renew, renovate, regenetrate; 3. (M) new; 4. *By extension* (V) go apart, separate.

eleta (*ele-ta*) 1. (V/M) separate; 2. (V) go apart, walk apart.

elo (7A) (*elo*) 1. (V) sing, whistle; 2. (N) song; 3. (N) singer, choir.

ema (*ema*) *noun* 1. wood; 2. pole, post, stick; 3. *By extension* yard (measure); 4. *By extension* 'one who works with wood', a carpenter.

emi (*emi*) 1. (V/N) hunt.

emo (*emo*) *particle* 1. before (in space), in front of; 2. to, towards; 3. against; 4. *By extension* concerning; 5. *By extension* principally, particularly.

ene (*ene*) 1. (V) see, look; 2. (N) sight, vision; 3. (V) appear; 4. (N) appearance; 5. (V) show, demonstrate, consult; 6. (N) demonstration; consultation; 7. (M) visible; 8. (M) transparent [Machiguenga *nea* 'see, look'].

enemi (*ene-mi ?*) 1. (M) downcast, sad; 2. (N) grief, sadness; 3. *By extension* persecution.

epa (*epa*) 1. (V) help, liberate, save; 2. (N) savior.

epalu (*epalu*) *noun* 1. ring, finger-ring. (*cf.* **apalu** 'enclosure, fort, palisade).

epe (*epe*) 1. (V) guard, watch (over).

epesoha (*epesoha*) 1. (V) spill, leak; 2. *By extension* (V) abandon oneself to pleasure (= 'to spill over').

epo (*epo*) *noun* 1. frost.

eqe[1] (*eke*) 1. (P) so, thus.

eqe[2] 1. (N) force; 2. *By extension* (N) diligence.

eqeta (*eke-ta*) *noun* 1. strength; 2. (M) strong; 3. industry; 4. (M) industrious (Der. *eke* + *-ta*).

eqete[1] (*ekete*) 1. (P) close, close by, near.

eqete[2] 1. (V) play.
equela (*ek^{w}ela*) *noun* 1. day (Der. *ek^w- ?* + *ela* 'sun').
equentequa (*ek^{w}entek^{w}a*) *particle* 1. abominable.
equete (*ek^{w}ete*) 1. (V) dally.
ero (*ero*) *noun* 1. year; 2. season.
esa (*esa*) *noun* 1. shellfish.
esobo (7A) (*esobo*) 1. (V) sustain.
eta (*eta*) 1. (N) womb; 2. *By extension* (N) waist; 3. *By extension* (N) confinement; 4. *By extension* (N) reborn; 5. *By extension* (M) pregnant; 6. *By extension* (M) related by birth.
ete (*ete*) 1. (V) stand, rise; 2. (V) raise, erect; 3. *By extension* (V) fall; 4. *By extension* (V) adore, worship.
eyamoheco (*eyamo-he-ko*) *particle* 1. be so.
eye (*eye*) *noun* 1. path, road, trail, street.
eyo (*eyo*) *particle* 1. other, another; 2. another place, another part.

F

fa[1] (*fa*) 1. (V) go; 2. *By extension* (N) 'one who goes habitually', a highwayman; 3. *By extension* (V) to frequent; 4. *By extension* (V) to be wont to.
fa[2] 1. (V) throw, eject.
fali (*fali*) 1. (N) window; 2. (M) open.
fano (*fa-no*) 1. 'it is so'.
fara[1] (*fara*) 1. (V) dislike, despise; 2. *By extension* (V) ruin; 3. *By extension* (M) weak; 4. *By extension* (N) scandal, misfortune.
fara[2] 1. *By extension* from **fara**[1] (N) right hand. *Cf.* **eba** 'left hand, the healer, the powerful'. In Timucua the 'fortunes' of the hand, so frequent in many languages, seem to have been the opposite of what they were in Indo-European — *e.g.*, Latin *manu dextra* 'right hand, dextrous' vs. *manu sinistra* 'left hand, sinister'. For the Timucua the left hand, **eba,** was the hand of power, the good hand, while the right hand, **fara,**

was the hand of misfortune, scandal, and ruin.

fara[3] 1. (V) return, restore (an extension from **fara**[1]?).

faramiti (*fara-mi-ti*) 1. (P) powerless, overcome; 2. (P) low, mean, wretched, vile (Der. *fara* + *mi* 'move' + *-ti* 'negative' ?).

farane (*fara-ne*) *particle* 1. (on the) right hand.

femiti (*femi-ti* ?) 1. (V) scorn, despise, abhor.

femitima (*femi-ti-ma*) *noun* 1. prostitute (*lit.* 'the despised one').

fere (*fere*) *particle* 1. diligently.

fete (*fete*) 1. (V) beg; 2. (V) borrow, lend. *Cf.* **hete**.

fiche (*fiči*) *particle* 1. late; 2. *By extension* midnight.

flaco (*flako*) 1. (M) wretched, miserable, low [Spanish *flaco*].

fori (*fori*) 1. (P) afternoon; 2. *By extension* (V) turn about.

foriso (*fori-so*) *verb* 1. steer.

foro (7A) (*foro*) 1. (V) cut.

fue (*fue*) TAWASA DIALECT *see* **hue** 'hand'.

G

Phonetic /*g*/ and orthographic form-initial <*g*> occur only rarely in Timucua. In all instances except lexeme-initial <*gu-*> forms with an initial <*g*> are loans from Spanish. The spelling <*gu-*> generally represents <*b-*> (/*b-*/), or, infrequently, <*hu-*> (/*hu-*/), as in **guecha** for **becha** 'tommorow' or **gue** (very rarely) for **hue** 'hand'. All text occurrences of <*gu-*> should first be looked for under **B** in the dictionary; if not found, they will be found under **H**.

gato (*kato ?*) *noun* 1. cat [Spanish *gato*].

gisano (*kisa-no* ?) *noun* 1. cook (Der. *kisa-* + *-no* 'verbalizer') [Spanish *guisar*].

H

Except in the word **hue** 'hand', Timucua lexical forms beginning with <*hue-*> usually represent phonemic /*be-*/ and will be found under **B** in the dictionary — *e.g.* **becha** rather than **huecha** 'tomorrow'.

ha[1] (*ha*) 1. (V) be (in the future); 2. *By extension* (V) have to [Goajiro *-he* 'future', Choctaw *-he* 'future', Warao *ha-* 'have to'].

ha[2] 1. (P) enough.

haba[1] (*haba*) 1. (P) far, far away, away from, apart; 2. (P) separate; 3. (P) outside; 4. (N) absence.

haba[2] 1. (V/N) remedy; 2. (V) purify; 3. (N) chastity [Apalachee *haban sa-či* 'make pure'].

-habe (*-ha-be*) 1. Imperative (= future durative action).

habe (*habe*) *noun* 1. fox [Warao *o-hia* 'fox'].

-habela (*ha-be-la*) 1. 'shall be doing . . . ' (= future durative proximate action).

-habele (*-ha-be-le*) 1. 'shall be doing . . . ' (= future durative proximate action).

habeleta (*ha-be-le-ta*) *particle* 1. for (*lit.* 'it shall be done').

habema [**hauema**] (*ha-be-ma*) *particle* 1. for (*lit.* 'it is done').

habo (7A) (*habo*) 1. (V) embrace; 2. (V) receive; 3. (N) passion.

hacha[1] (*ha-ča*) 1. (P) general interrogative = what, why, how, where, whence, whither.

hacha[2] (*hača*) *particle* 1. something, someone; 2. anything, anyone.

hacha[3] (*hača*) 1. (N) property.

hacha[4] (*hača*) 1. (P) faithful.

hachahiati (*hačahiati*) *particle* 1. agreeable.

-hache (*-ha-če*) 1. Imperative (= future imperative action).

hachi[1] (*hači*) 1. (N) tribute; 2. (N) sacrifice; 3. (N) compensation.

hachi[2] 1. (N) basket.

hachia (*hačia*) *particle* 1. Exclamation of wonder, joy, or satisfaction.

hachibono (*hačibono*) *particle* 1. that; 2. thing.

hachinacachi (*hačinakači*) 1. (V) howl.

hachinara (*hačinara*) 1. (N) extreme feeling: *specif.* suffering, passion, torment, tribulation, torture, punishment.

hachinarami (*hačinara-mi*) *noun* 1. extreme reaction: *specif.* groans.

hachinoroco (*hačinoroko*) *noun* 1. emblem, symbol, sign, ensign, arms.

TIMUCUA DICTIONARY

hachipile (*hači-pile ?*) *noun* 1. animal.

hachitimo (*hači-ti-mo ?*) 1. (N) supernatural.

hacu (*haku*) *particle* 1. though, although, but; 2. and.

halaha (*halaha*) 1. (P) Exclamation of joy.

halaqua (*halakʷa*) *particle* 1. with pleasure, with satisfaction; 2. (N) satisfaction.

-hale (*-ha-le*) 1. Imperative (= future proximate action).

haleqe[1] (*haleke*) *particle* 1. when.

haleqe[2] 1. for.

halifila [**alifila**] (*halifila*) *noun* 1. youth, boy.

halu (*halu*) *noun* 1. saliva, spit.

hami[1] (*hami*) 1. (V) have, own, possess; 2. (N) owner, possessor; 3. *By extension* (N) lord.

hami[2] *particle* 1. that.

-hana (*-ha-na*) 1. 'shall always do . . . ' (= future habitual action).

hana[1] (*ha-na*) *verb* 1. (P) yes (= 'it shall be').

hana[2] (*hana*) *particle* 1. perhaps, if.

-hanano (*-ha-na-no*) 1. 'shall be doing . . . ' (= future durative proximate action).

hani (*hani*) 1. (V) stop, end, cease, abandon, abstain, finish; 2. (V) renounce; 3. (N) end, completion, finish; 4. *By extension* (V) fail, (N) failure; 5. *By extension* (V) deprive, (N) deprivation; 6. *By extension* (V) lose, give up, (N) loss; 7. *By extension* (V) lack, omit, (N) lack, omission; 8. *By extension* (P) without [Warao *ha-* 'stop', Warao *hahinai* 'lose'].

-hanima (*-ha-ni-ma*) 1. 'shall be doing . . .' (= future durative proximate action).

hanima (*hanima*) *particle* 1. although.

-hano (*-ha-no*) 1. Imperative (= future proximate action).

hape (*hape*) 1. (V) present.

hapetaqua (*hape-takʷa*) 1. (P) at present; 2. (P) quickly; 3. (P) suddenly; 4. (P) hastily; 5. (P) diligently; 6. *By extension* (N) archer, bowman (= 'one who does something quickly).

hapo (*hapo*) TAWASA DIALECT *see* **hapu** 'three'.

hapu[1] (*hapu*) 1. (P) three; 2. (P) third [Canamarí *hepü* 'three']

hapu[2] 1. (V) game, gamble; 2. (N) game.

haquentama (*ha-k*^{w}*e-no>n-ta-ma*) *verb* 1. be.

hara (*hara*) 1. (V) despise.

haraca (*hara-ka*) 1. (V) scorn, abhor; 2. (N) prostitute.

hasi (*hasi*) TAWASA DIALECT *see* **ela** 'sun' [Alabama *haši* 'sun'].

hasomi (*hasomi*) *noun* 1. lineage, clan, family; 2. descendant; 3. pedigree.

-hateno (*-ha-te-no*) 1. 'shall be doing . . . ' (= future durative proximate action).

hayaro (7A) (*hayaro*) 1. (V) open.

he[1] (*he*) *verb* 1. eat [Waliperi *he* 'eat', Achagua *-ha* 'eat'].

he[2] *verb* 1. can, be able [Warao *-(bu)hu* 'can, be able'].

he[3] 1. (V) sustain.

heba (*heba*) 1. (V) speak, say, tell, utter; 2. (N) language, word, speech, saying, utterance; 3. (V) sing; 4. (N) song; 5. *By extension* (V) teach, (N) teaching, precept; 6. (V/N) name; 7. *By extension* (N) war council [Warao *ehewere* 'sing'].

hebe (*hebe*) 1. (V) gather.

hebetota (*hebetota*) 1. (V) walk.

heca (*he-ka*) *particle* 1. we, us, our, ours.

heca (*heka*) *particle* 1. now.

heco (*heko*) *particle* 1. if.

-hela (*-he-la*) 1. 'can do . . . ' (= potential proximate action).

hele (*hele*) 1. (N) bald.

helo (*helo*) 1. (N) blind.

hemosi (*hemosi*) *particle* 1. worthy of being.

hepo (7A) (*hepo*) 1. (V/N) rush.

heqe (*heke*) *particle* 1. present time indicating particle = 'now', 'when', 'at times'; 2. *By extension* principally.

here (*here*) 1. (V/N) lust.

hero (*hero*) *particle* 1. Pray God!

hete[1] [**fete**] (*hete*) 1. (V) borrow, lend; 2. (N) loan.

hete[2] 1. (P) quickly, in a hurry.

heya (*heya*) TAWASA DIALECT *see* **hiyaraba** 'lion'.

hi (*hi*) TAWASA DIALECT *see* **hochie** 'you'.

hia (*hia*) 1. (V) know.

hiamiqua[1] (*hiamik*^{w}*a*) 1. (V) cool.

hiamiqua[2] 1. (P) easy.

hiba[1] [**hibua**] (*hiba*) 1. (V) live, dwell; 2. *By extension* (V) remain; 3. *By extension* sit; 4. *By extension* (V) marry.

hiba[2] 1. (V) be wont to (by extension from **hiba**[1]?).

hiba[3] 1. (V/N) rain [Baré *hiya* 'rain', Goajiro *huyá* 'rain', Cuna *iya* 'rain'].

hibatelaqe (*hiba-te-la-ke*) *verb* 1. affirm (*lit.* 'to be saying').

hibe (*hibe*) 1. (N) louse.

hibi (*hibi*) 1. (V) capture; 2. (V) drive away.

hibino (*hibino*) TAWASA DIALECT *see* **hinino** 'tobacco'.

hica (*hika*) *noun* 1. settlement, town, village, city; 2. citizen.

hiereba [**hyereba**] (*hiiereba*) *noun* 1. metal of any kind: *specif.* gold, iron, silver; 2. *By extension* money; 3. *By extension* 'one who works with metals', blacksmith.

hima[1] (*hima*) *noun* 1. health.

hima[2] 1. mercy (perhaps by extension from **hima**[1]).

hime (*hime*) *verb* 1. come.

himi (*hiomi*) 1. (V) cure, heal; 2. (N) cure, health.

hinino (*hinino*) *noun* 1. tobacco [Taíno *hynino* 'tobacco'].

hio[1] (7A) (*hio*) 1. (V) offer; 2. (N) offering; 3. *Perhaps by extension* (N) sacred.

hio[2] 1. (V/N) curse; 2. (V) tempt; 3. (N) temptation [Warao *hio* 'curse'].

hio[3] 1. (N) compassion; 2. (N) piety.

hioco (7A) (*hioko*) *verb* 1. greet, salute.

hiosa (*hiosa*) *noun* 1. The term used by *ego* male for an elder brother or the elder son of father's brother or mother's sister; 2. Term used by children for each other after the death of one parent.

hiqi (*hiki*) 1. (V/N) dream; 2. (V) sleep.

hiqitima (*hikiti-ma*) *noun* 1. acid.

hiqui[1] (*hik*^{w}*i*) 1. (V) end, finish, complete, conclude, terminate; 2. (N) end, finish, completion, conclusion, termination; 3. (M) final, complete(d), finished, concluded.

hiqui[2] 1. (P) afterwards (probably by extension from **hiqui**[1].

hiquo[1] (*hik*^{w}*o*) 1. (N) miracle; 2. (M) miraculous(ly).

hiquo[2] 1. (V) scandalize.

hiri[1] (*hiri*) *noun* 1. diligence; 2. promptness; 3. quickness; 4. (P) diligently; 5. (P) promptly; 6. (P) quickly.

hiri[2] 1. (N) lack.

hite (*hite*) *particle* 1. Hello!

hiti (*hiti*) *noun* 1. demon, evil spirit, devil; 2. hell.

hitiqire (*hiti-ki-re*) *noun* 1. owl (Der. *hiti* + *qi* 'wish' + *-re* 'noun-combining form').

hito (*hito*) *particle* 1. now; 2. Well, then!

hitumo (7A) (*hitumo*) 1. (V) run.

hituqua[1] (*hituk^{w}a*) *verb* 1. esteem.

hituqua[2] *verb* 1. understand.

hiyaraba (*hiyaraba*) *noun* 1. lion, panther, wildcat (*not* 'domestic cat') [Gê Remokamekran *orobo* 'jaguar', Gê Xavante *hu-* 'jaguar'].

hiyo (7SA) (*hiyo*) *verb* 1. suffer.

ho- (*ho-*) 1. 1st person verb subject pronoun (= 'I'); 2. 1st person verb object pronoun (= 'me').

ho[1] (*ho*) *verb* 1. eat [Warao *ho* 'eat', Island Carib *háo* 'eat'].

ho[2] *verb* 1. go.

hoba (*hoba*) 1. (V/N) love; 2. *By extension* (N) charity; 3. (M) devoted; 4. *By extension* (N) heat [Warao *obo* 'love']. *Cf.* **huba**.

hocha (*hoča*) *noun* 1. marsh, swamp, quagmire.

hochi- (*ho-či-*) 1. 'I' (subject) + 'you' (object) of transitive verb.

hochie (*ho-či-e*) *pronoun* 1. you, thou; 2. you (object), thee; 3. your, thy; 4. yours, thine.

hocho (7A) (*hočo*) *verb* 1. drop; 2. fall; 3. lose.

hola (*hola*) *noun* 1. an agricultural crop: *specif.* corn; 2. the first corn; 5. *By extension* (N) farmer.

holata (*holata*) *noun* 1. chief [Apalachee *holahta* 'chief'].

homa[1] (*homa*) 1. (V) finish, complete, end, cease; 2. (N) finish, completion, end, cessation; 3. *By extension* the last.

homa[2] 1. (N/M) infinite (perhaps by extension from **homa**[1]).

homa[3] 1. (M) include.

homa[4] 1. (N) love.

homo (*homo*) *particle* 1. quick(ly).

honihe (*ho-ni-he*) *pronoun* 1. 1st person, regardless of usage — 'I', 'me', 'my', 'mine'. [Warao *ine* 'I'].

hono (7A) (*hono*) 1. (N) hunger; 2. (M) hungry; 3. *By extension* (N) food; 4. *By extension* (V) vomit [Warao *nõhõ* 'hunger'].

honoso (*honoso*) *noun* 1. deer.

honosta (*honosta*) *noun* 1. shellfish [Warao *hunu* 'shrimp'].

hoqe (*hoke*) *particle* 1. That (one); 2. there.

horo[1] (*horo*) *particle* 1. together; 2. joined.

horo[2] 1. without.

hororo (*hororo*) *noun* 1. owl.

hoto[1] (7A) (*hoto*) 1. (V) guard, watch, care for; 2. *By extension* (V) search.

hoto[2] 1. (V) unite; 2. *By extension* (N) spouse; 3. *By extension* (P) together. All **hoto[2]** forms probably by extension from **hoto[1]**.

huba[1] (*huba*) *verb* 1. love [Warao *obo* 'love'].

huba[2] [**uba**] (*uba*) *verb* 1. swim. *Note:* The form without <*h-*> occurs with slightly greater frequency than the form with <*h-*>.

hue [**gue**] (*hue*) *noun* 1. hand; 2. *By extension* fingernail [Non-Maipuran Arawak *we-~wa-* 'hand', Proto-Tucanoan **wã* 'hand', Chocó *hua* 'hand'].

hulubo (*hulubo*) *noun* 1. laborer; 2. farmer.

hupu (*hupu*) *particle* 1. Exclamation of joy.

huque (*hukʷe*) *noun* 1. rain; 2. flood, inundation; 3. storm, hurricane [Proto-Muskogean **umkʷa* 'rain'].

huqui (*hukʷi*) *noun* 1. shoulder.

hura (*hura*) 1. (V) suddenly change position — 'appear', 'disappear'.

huri[1] [**uri**] (*huri*) 1. (V) free, liberate, deliver, save, redeem; 2. (N) freedom, liberation, redemption, deliverance; 3. (N) savior; 4. *By extension* give (in general).

huri[2] 1. (V) deny, refuse; 2. (N) denial, refusal.

huri[3] 1. (P) out, away, outside.

huri[4] 1. (N) forest.

huru[1] (7A) (*huru*) 1. (N) boy; 2. (M) small, little.

huru[2] 1. (V) heal; 2. (V/N) benefit; 3. (N) health.

huri[3] 1. (N) extremity.

huta[1] (*huta*) 1. (V) take, seize; 2. (V) grasp.

huta[2] 1. *By extension from* **huta**[1] (V) unite; 2. *By extension* (V) have intercourse, sleep with, cohabit, lie with; 3. (N) intercourse; 4. *By extension* (V) seduce, (N) seduction; 5. *By extension* (V) commit adultery, (N) adultery; 6. *By extension* (M) lascivious.

huta[3] 1. (V) assist, help.

hutano (*hutano*) *noun* 1. frost.

huya (*huya*) *verb* 1. pulverize, pound up.

I

iba (*iba*) *noun* 1. dew.

ibatele[1] [**iguatele**] (*ibatele*) *verb* 1. watch, wait, await.

ibatele[2] 1. (V) keep.

ibi(ne) (1A, B) (*ibi~ibine*) 1. (N) water; 2. (N) liquid; 3. *By extension* (N) lake, pond, lagoon; 4. *By extension* (N) river, stream, canal, channel; 5. *By extension* (N) ocean, sea; 6. *By extension* (N) rain; 7. *By extension* (N) tear; 8. *By extension* (N) wave; 9. *By extension* (N) dew; 10. *By extension* (N) rainbow; 11. *By extension* (V) wash, bathe; 12. *By extension* (V) drink; 13. *By extension* (V) anoint; 14. *By extension* (V) menstruate; 15. *By extension* (N) sign [Baniva, Yavitero, Maipuré *weni* 'water', Baré *uni* 'water', Yaruro *wi* 'water', Esmeralda *wivi* 'water'].

ibiri (*ibiri*) *noun* 1. regulations.

ibora (*ibora*) 1. (V/N) thunder.

ica [**yca**] (*ika*) 1. (V/N) dispute, quarrel, fight; 2. *By extension* (N) affront; 3. *By extension* (N) anger, (M) angry.

icacheti (*ikačeti*) *verb* 1. frequent.

icatu (7A) (*ikatu*) *verb* 1. break a law.

icha (*iča*) TAWASA DIALECT *see* **echa** 'enter'.

ichaca (*ičaka*) *noun* 1. root.

ichali (*ičali*) *noun* 1. fish-weir.

ichico (7A) (*ičiko*) *verb* 1. bite [Baré *n-ike* 'eat'].

ichicosa (*ičikosa*) 1. (V) cool, refrigerate; 2. (N) cold.

TIMUCUA DICTIONARY

ichiqe[1] (*ičike*) 1. (N) shoe; 2. (N) shoemaker. *Cf.* **ichiqi.**
ichiqe[2] 1. (V) replace; 2. *By extension* (V) imitate.
ichiqeche (*ičike-če*) *noun* 1. boot (*lit.* 'large shoe').
ichiqi[1] (*ičiki*) 1. (N) foot.
ichiqi[2] 1. (V/N) revenge; 2. (V) avenge; 3. (N) vengeance.
ichiqi[3] 1. (V/N) exchange.
ichiqi[4] 1. (N) vicar.
ichira (*ičira*) *noun* 1. winter; 2. wind; 3. *By extension* (N) hell.
ichito (7A) (*ičito*) 1. (V) begin; 2. (N) beginning; 3. *By extension* (N) principle.
icho (7A) (*ičo*) 1. (V) pierce, bore (into), chisel, lay open; 2. (N) worm; 3. (N) disembowelment.
ichu (7A) (*iču*) 1. (V) carry away; 2. (V) throw away, throw down; 3. (V) drive away; 4. (V) discharge; 5. *By extension* (V) sleep with.
ico (*iko*) *particle* 1. all.
icupata (**ikupata**) *verb* 1. gnaw, chew on.
iglesia (*iklesia ?*) *noun* 1. church [Spanish *iglesia* 'church'].
iguatele *see* **ibatele.**
ihiriba (*ihiriba*) 1. (M) long; 2. (M) tall.
ihoco (7A) (*ihoko*) 1. (V) carry; 2. (N) load.
iholo (7A) (*iholo*) 1. (V) uproot, pull up; 2. (V) transplant.
ihoto (7A) (*ihoto*) 1. (V) pierce, bore (into), chisel; 2. (N) auger, drill, chisel.
ilaqe [**ylaqe**] (*ilake*) *noun* 1. night; 2. afternoon [Piro *ilači-nu* 'night', Proto-Muskogean **niNaki* 'night'].
ilifo (7A) (*ilifo*) *verb* 1. kill.
imo (7A) (*imo*) *verb* 1. treat (an illness or wound); 2. heal.
indo *see* **into.**
ine[1] (*ine*) 1. (P) anything; 2. (P) something; 3. (N) thing.
ine[2] 1. (V) do; 2. (V) work; 3. (V) commit.
ine[3] 1. (V/N) damage, harm; 2. *By extension* (V/N) sin.
inemi (*inemi*) *particle* 1. all; 2. much, many.
infierno (*infierno*) *noun* 1. hell [Spanish *infierno* 'hell'].
-ini- (4A, B) (*-ini-*) *verb* 1. be, exist.
ini (*ini*) TAWASA DIALECT [Alabama *nihta* 'day'] *see* **equela** 'day'.
iniba (*iniba*) *noun* 1. state or condition with regard to degree of

goodness — *i.e.*, 'good', 'goodness', 'evil', 'wickedness'.

inibi (*inibi*) 1. (P) great; 2. (P) many, more.

inibiti (*inibiti*) 1. (M) leading, principal; 2. (P) much.

inibo (*inibo*) *particle* 1. commonly.

inihama (*iniha-ma*) *noun* 1. counselor (Der. *iniha* 'counselor' + *-ma* 'the') [Creek *hiniha* 'councilman, counselor'].

iniheti (*iniheti*) 1. (N) sin.

inihi (*inihi*) 1. (N) spouse, consort; 2. *Specif.* husband; 3. *Specif.* wife; 4. (V) marry.

inimi (*inimi*) *particle* 1. lightly.

inino[1] (7A) (*inin-no*) 1. (V) do; 2. (N) deed; 3. (V) commit; 4. (V/N) exercise; 5. (V/N) work. *Cf.* **ino.**

inino[2] 1. (V/N) benefit, merit; 2. (N) virtue. All probably by extension from **inino**[1].

inino[3] 1. (V) sustain; 2. (N) sustenance (probably by extension from **inino**[2]).

iniqe[1] (*inike*) 1. (V) happen, occur; 2. (N) happening, occurrence, occasion.

iniqe[2] 1. (N) motive.

iniqe[3] 1. (P) so.

ino[1] (7A) (*ino*) 1. (V) do; 2. (N) deed.

ino[2] 1. (V) serve; 2. (N) servant; 3. (V/N) work. All probably by extension from **ino**[1].

ino[3] 1. (V) suffer, bear (up with) — probably by extension from **ino**[2].

incochie (*ino-ko-čie*) 1. (V/N) praise, esteem, respect, honor; 2. (V) revere; 3. (N) reverence; 4. (V) venerate; 5. (N) veneration. (Der. *ino* 'do' + *co* 'say' + *chie*[5] 'consecrate').

inoni(ma) (*ino-ni-ma*) 1. (N) instrument (Der. *ino* 'do' + *-ni*[3] 'habitual action' + *-ma* 'the').

inquenenela (*in-kʷene-ne-la*) *verb* 1. 'it is (what is) left', 'there is little' (remaining); 2. (M) little; 3. (V) remain.

intafayela (*in-tafaye-la*) *particle* 1. much (*lit.* 'it is much' ?).

intaribala (*in-tari-ba-la*) *verb* 1. lack (*lit.* 'they are few' ?).

inteca (*in-te-ka*) *particle* 1. if only (*lit.* 'it is that').

inti (*in-ti* ?) *noun* 1. bad (*lit.* 'it is not' ?).

intichiqe (*in-ti-či-ke* ?) *particle* 1. although.

into [**indo**] (*into*) *particle* 1. now then; 2. 'all together'; 3. *By extension* 'Come!', 'Let's go!', 'Let's do this!'.

ipalo (7A) (*ipalo*) 1. (V) snuff up. [Koastai *-ipá* 'eat']. *Cf.* **iparu**.

iparu (7A) (*iparu*) *verb* 1. drink; 2. eat (something which requires chewing); 3. crush, grind, or break (with the teeth) [Warao *hobi* 'eat', Koasati *-ipá* 'eat'].

ipita (*ipita*) 1. (V) take off, undress, shed.

ipo (7A) (*ipo*) *verb* 1. charm, bewitch; 2. *By extension* take medicine; 3. *By extension* blow; 4. *By extension* baptize. *Cf.* **ipopi**.

ipopi (*ipo-pi*) 1. (V/N) smoke; 2. (N) *Specif.* tobacco (*Cf.* also **hinino**).

ipulu (7B) (*ipulu*) *verb* 1. restore.

ipunu (*ipunu*) *noun* 1. spear, lance.

iputu (7B) (*iputu*) 1. (V) conquer; 2. (N) conquest; 3. (N) offensive (on the).

iqe^{1} (*ike*) 1. (N) earth; 2. (N) dirt, mud, clay, soil [Culino *-iki* 'earth', Baniva Piapoco *-ipe* 'earth'].

iqe^{2} 1. *By extension from* **iqe**^{1} wash, bathe; 2. (V) clean, cleanse, purify.

iqi^{1} (*iki*) 1. (V) rise, ascend, go up; 2. (N) ascension.

iqi^{2} 1. (N) hood (probably by extension from **iqi**^{1}).

iqi^{3} 1. (V) revive (probably by extension from **iqi**^{1}).

iqibi (*ikibi*) 1. (V) laugh; 2. (M) disrespectful.

iqilaba (ikilaba) *noun* 1. sickness; 2. (M) sick; 3. *By extension* (N) charity.

iqili (*ikili*) 1. (V) resist.

iqua^{1} (*ik^{w}a*) 1. (V) shout, cry out; 2. (V) proclaim, declare; 3. (N) shout, cry; 4. (N) proclamation, declaration; 5. *Specif.* (N) war-cry.

iqua^{2} 1. *By extension from* **iqua**^{1} (V) order an attack.

ique (*ik^{w}e*) *verb* 1. polish, scour; 2. (V) clear (away).

iquente (*ik^{w}ente*) *verb* 1. imitate.

iqui^{1} (ik^{w}*i*) *verb (transitive)* 1. kill; 2. destroy, crush, extinguish; 3. *By extension* win at a game, defeat; 4. *By extension* hunt [Apalachee *ibi* 'kill', Koasati *i·bi-* , Proto-Muskogean **abi* 'kill'].

iqui[2] *verb (intransitive)* 1. die; 2. *By extension* (N) ancestors, ancient ones (= 'those who have died or been killed'); 3. (M) old, ancient; 4. *By extension* (N/M) past; 5. *By extension* (V) fulfill (life).

iqui[3] 1. *By extension from* **iqui**[2] (N) superstition (= 'belief in the past'); 2. (M) superstitious.

iquile (*ikʷi-le* ?) 1. (V) offend (Der. *iqui* 'destroy' + *-le* 'proximate time' ?).

iquilo (*ikʷilo*) *noun* 1. *Ego* male's wife's sister's husband (= 'brother-in-law').

iquimi (*ikʷmi*) *noun* 1. cause, reason; 2. fault, guilt, sin.

iquimileqe (*ikʷimi-le-ke*) *particle* 1. for (the reason of), because, on account of (Der. *iqui* 'reason' + *-leqe* 'augmentative').

iquine (*ikʷine*) *noun* 1. milk; 2. teat; 3. *By extension* mother.

iquita (*ikʷita*) 1. (V) reach.

iquiti (*ikʷi-ti*) *noun* 1. dishonor; 2. insult; 3. (M) ignominious (Der. *iquo* 'honor' + *-ti* 'not'). *Cf.* **iquo.**

iquito (7A) (*ikʷito*) *verb* 1. ask, inquire; 2. say something good.

iquo[1] (7A) (*ikʷo*) 1. (V/N) honor, esteem, praise, respect; 2. (V) venerate; 3. (N) veneration.

iquo[2] 1. (N) mortal.

iri (*iri*) 1. (N) war, attack; 2. (N) enemy, adversary; 3. *By extension* (N) warrior, war-prince, war-councilor.

iribo[1] (*iribo*) 1. (V) remain, stay; 2. (V) hold; 3. (V) stand (up), rise; 4. (V) fly.

iribo[2] 1. *By extension from* **iribo**[1] (N) midday, noon; 2. *By extension* (N) mother-in-law of a chief.

is (*is*) *verb* 1. want, wish.

isa[1] (1) (*isa*) 1. (N) *Ego* male or female's mother and mother's sisters; 2. *By extension* (N) beauty, (M) beautiful; 3. *By extension* (N) grace, (M) graceful; 4. *By extension* (N) goodness, (M) good; 5. *By extension* (M) neat; 6. *By extension* (M) wholesome [Northern Maipuran *isa* 'good', Koasati *iskí* 'mother'].

isa[2] 1. (V) do; 2. (V) cause; 3. (V) accomplish. All possibly by extension from **isa**[1].

isamola (*isamola*) 1. (V) signify.

isaqi[1] (*isaki*) 1. (V) scatter.

isaqi[2] 1. (V) share.

isaco (7A) (*isa-ko*) 1. (V) please; 2. (N) pleasure; 3. (M) pleasing; 4. (V) rejoice; 5. (N) joy; 6. (V) satisfy; 7. (N) satisfaction; 8. (M) satisfied, content; 9. (N) happy; 10. (M) happy; 11. (V) agree; 12. (N) agreeableness; 13. (M) agreeable; 14. (V) know. All probably by extension from **isa**[1] (Der. *isa* 'good(ness)' + *-co* 'augmentative').

isaco (7A) (*isako*) *verb* 1. move in any direction.

isahio (*isa-hio*) *noun* 1. glory (*lit.* 'sacred goodness'. Der. *isa* 'good(ness)' + *hio*[1] 'sacred').

isamola (*isamola*) *verb* 1. signify, indicate.

isamolacoco (*isamola-koko*) *noun* 1. purpose (Der, *isamola* 'signify' + *-coco* 'augmentative').

isamolo (7A) (*isamolo*) *verb* 1. teach. *Cf.* **isamola** 'signify'.

isapu (7B) (*isapu*) *verb* 1. run; 2. move quickly by any means — *e.g.*, 'row quickly', 'paddle quickly'.

isaqi (*isaki*) 1. (V) spread, distribute.

isi[1] (*isi*) 1. (N) blood [Marawa *isa* 'blood', Catapolítani *iti* 'blood', Proto-Tucanoan **zie* 'blood'].

isi[2] 1. (V/N) name; 2. (N) word; 3. (V) say; 4. (N) saying; 4. (N) speech, declaration; 5. (V) declare, speak, tell; 6. (N) admonition; 7. (V) call; 8. (V) sing; 9. (V) agree, affirm; 10. (V) repeat. All probably by extension from **isi**[1].

isi[3] 1. Probably by extension from **isi**[2] (N) ceremony.

isi[4] 1. (V) crackle.

isimi (*isimi*) *particle* 1. only, sole, alone; 2. self.

isinihimiti (*isini-himi-ti* ?) *particle* 1. miserable; 2. mean, low, vile; 3. ruined (Der. *isini* '??' + *hima* 'health' + *-ti* 'not' ?).

iso[1] (7A) (*iso*) 1. (V) make, do; 2. (V/N) cause, effect; 3. (V) work; 4. (N) deed; 5. (V) work; 6. (N) manner; 7. (N) instrument; 8. (N) treatment; 9. *By extension* (N) process.

iso[2] 1. (V) be able (to).

iso[3] 1. (V) own.

iso[4] 1. (V) sustain.

iso[5] 1. (V) give quickly.

iso[6] 1. (N) virtue.

isotamale (*isotama-le* ?) *verb* 1. eat.

isote (*isote*) *verb* 1. have, possess.

istico (*istiko*) 1. (N/N) bad, evil, sin(ful); 2. (N) offense; 3. *By extension* (N) villain, rogue; 4. *By extension* (N) sadness; 6. *By extension* (M) sad; 7. *In Christian context* = 'pagan'.

isticoco[1] (*isti-koko* ?) 1. (P) much, many.

isticoco[2] 1. (N) grief, pain, suffering, torment (probably by extension from **istico**).

isticoco[3] 1. (N) labor (by extension from **isticoco**[2] ?).

isu (*isu*) *noun* 1. doctor, herbalist, medicine man, sorcerer, wizard; 2. *By extension* (N) herb, medicine; 3. *By extension* (M) possessed (used as 'crazed' in a Christian context).

ita[1] (*ita*) 1. (P) sole, only, limited.

ita[2] 1. (V) stumble.

ita[3] 1. (V) multiply, increase.

ite (1) (*ite*) *noun* 1. *Ego* male or female's father and father's brothers; 2. *By Christian extension* monk, priest [Lokono *itʰi* 'father'].

itinochiqequana (*itinočikekʷana*) *verb* 1. walk.

itora (*itora*) *noun* 1. *Ego* male or female's father's father and mother's father (= 'grandfather') and *ego* male's father-in-law; 2. *By extension* governor; 3. *By extension* (M) noble.

itori (*itori*) *noun* 1. alligator, crocodile; 2. *By extension* (M) fast [Warao [*duru-duru*] 'cayman', Proto-Tucanoan **iSo-ri* 'cayman, crocodile', Proto-Arawakan **(iy)akare* 'cayman, crocodile', Chocó *kore* 'crocodile'].

itufa (*itufa*) 1. (V) conjure; 2. (N) conjurer, wizard, sorcerer. *Cf.* **ituhu**.

ituhu[1] (7B) (*ituhu*) 1. (V) conjure, charm, bewitch; 2. (N) conjurer, sorcerer, wizard, doctor; 3. (N) exorcism; 4. (N) doctrine; 5. (V) invoke.

ituqua (*itukʷa*) *noun* 1. tongue [Sumu, Ulua *tuke* 'tongue', Chibcha *p-kʷa* 'tongue', Brunca *-kʷa* 'tongue', Cuna *-wa* 'tongue', Manare *kʷa* 'tongue'].

iyebana (*ieybana*) TAWASA DIALECT *noun* 1. chair.

iyeno (*iyeno*) *particle* 1. great

iyobo (7A) (*iyobo*) 1. (V) murmur.

iyola (*iyola*) *noun* 1. snake, serpent, viper [Natchez *ula* 'snake'].
iyorona (*iyorona*) *noun* 1. eel.

L

-la (4B) (*-la*) 1. Proximate time indicator with verbs (= 'now', close to the event described, regardless of time).
laca (*laka*) *noun* 1. dark; 2. black; 3. (M) shady [Alabama, Koasati *loča* 'black'].
lacalacama (*laka-laka-ma*) *noun* 1. obscure.
lame (*lame*) 1. (V) mix.
lapa (*lapa*) 1. (N) secret; 2. (M) secretly.
lapu (7B) (*lapu*) *verb* 1. ask, ask for; 2. beg; 3. petition; 4. require (of someone).
-le (4B) (*-le*) 1. Proximate time indicator with verbs (= 'now', close to the event described, regardless of time).
leba (*leba*) *verb* 1. appear.
-lechu (*-lechu*) 1. Vocative post-enclitic.
lehe[1] (*lehe*) *verb* 1. be able to.
lehe[2] 1. be worthy of.
lenaqe (*lenake*) *particle* 1. already; 2. now.
lepeti (*lepeti*) *particle* 1. moderate.
-leqe (*-leke*) 1. and.
leta (*leta*) *particle* 1. certain.
lico (*liko*) 1. (N/M) blue.
licofaye (*likofaye*) *noun* 1. fog, mist, haze.
lucha (*luča*) TAWASA DIALECT *noun* 1. fight [Spanish *lucha(r)* 'fight'] *see* **ica**.

M

-ma[1] (2) (*-ma*) 1. Possessive indicator with nouns (usually = 'his', 'her', 'its', but may be used with any person).

TIMUCUA DICTIONARY

-ma^{2} (5A) (*-ma*) 1. Definite goal-marker with nouns (= 'the') [Warao *-ma* 'goal-marker'].

-ma^{3} (5B) (*-ma*) 1. 3rd plural verb subject (= 'they') [Warao *-ma* 'plural agent'].

-ma^{4} (*-ma*) 1. Proximate time indicator with verbs (= 'now', close to the event described, regardless of time).

ma (*ma*) *verb* 1. call; 2. speak; 3. say; 4. talk; 5. tell; 6. *By extension* command; 7. *By extension* name; 8. *By extension* (N) sentence; 9. *By extension* (V) correct.

maca^{1} (*maka*) 1. (N) laziness; 2. (N) negligence; 3. (M) lazy; 4. (M) negligent; 5. *By extension* weakness, feebleness.

maca^{2} 1. (N) citizen (?).

machaba (*mačaba*) *noun* 1. marsh, swamp.

mache (*mače*) *particle* 1. self (reflexive).

machi^{1} (*mači*) 1. (N) resting place; 2. (V) rest.

machi^{2} 1. (N) depths.

machi^{3} 1. (N) basis.

maha^{1} (*maha*) *particle* 1. alone, only; 2. any; 3. some.

maha^{2} *particle* 1. always.

maha^{3} *particle* 1. in vain.

maha^{4} 1. (N) evil, malice; 2. (N) apprehension; 3. *By extension* (V) offend; 4. *By extension* (V) desecrate.

maha^{5} 1. (V) gain.

maha^{6} 1. (V) raise the eyes.

mahaqua (*mahak*^{w}*a*) 1. (V) exchange (= 'buy', 'sell', 'trade', 'purchase'); 2. (N) shop, store.

malu (7B) (*malu*) *verb* 1. administer.

man^{1} (*man*) 1. (V) think; 2. (N) thought.

man^{2} 1. *By extension from* **man**^{1} (V) behave; 2. (N) behavior.

man^{3} 1. *By extension from* **man**^{1} the resultant of almost any form of thought or behavior — **man**^{3} is defined by its context: *e.g.*, 'want', 'wish', 'suggest', 'swear', 'agree', 'consent', 'forgive', 'repent', 'regret', 'grieve', 'sanctify', *etc.*

manan (*manan*) *verb* 1. be so.

mani^{1} (*mani*) 1. (V) understand (Der. *man* 'think').

mani^{2} 1. *By extension from* **mani**^{1} the resultant of almost any act of understanding — *e.g.*, 'wish', 'desire', 'mediate', 'law', 'play'.

-maqua (*makʷa*) 1. 'in the'.
maquima (*makʷima*) *particle* 1. old, long-established.
maracay[1] **[maracai]** (*marakay*) *particle* 1. single.
maracay[2] 1. (M) garrulous.
mareca (*mareka*) *particle* 1. six; 3. sixth.
mareheba (*mare-heba*) *noun* 1. madman; 2. (M) insane, mad, crazy (Der. *mare* '?' + *heba* 'speak, say').
marema (*marema*) *particle* 1. soon; 2. quickly.
marica (*marika*) TAWASA DIALECT *see* **mareca** 'six'.
maru (7B) (*maru*) *verb* 1. shut.
marua (*marua*) *particle* 1. five; 2. fifth [Chocó *kʷĩ mare* 'four, five'].
mas (*mas*) *verb* 1. say.
masi (*masi*) *particle* 1. in.
mayu[1] (7B) (*mayu*) 1. (V) drink; 2. *By extension* (V) smoke.
mayu[2] 1. (V/M) faint; 2. (M) pale; 3. (M) weak.
mecalala (*mekalala*) *noun* 1. sword-maker.
mela (*mela*) 1. (N) heat, warmth; 2. (M) hot, warm; 3. *By extension* (N) piety, (M) pious; (N) devotion.
mele (*mele*) *verb* 1. censure; 2. (V) blaspheme; 3. (V) desecrate.
meleni (*meleni*) *noun* 1. medicine.
melo (*melo*) 1. (N) mollusk, shellfish; 2. *By extension* (M) bitter.
meloni (*meloni*) *noun* 1. melon [Spanish *melón*].
mera (*mera*) *noun* 1. the social world, the world of man.
mero (7A) (*mero*) 1. (V) weaken; 2. (M) luke-warm.
meta (*meta*) *noun* 1. heat.
metaba (*meta-ba*) 1. (N) heat, warmth; 2. (M) hot, warm (Der. *meta* 'heat' + *-ba* '?').
mete (*mete*) *noun* 1. past.
metele (*metele*) *noun* 1. feather; 2. *By extension* ear of an owl.
meya (*meya*) *verb* 1. fly.
-mi[1] (*-mi*) 1. Possessive indicator with nouns (usually = 'his', 'her', 'its', but may be used with any person). *Cf.* **-ma**[1].
-mi[2] 1. Definite goal-marker with nouns (= 'the'). *Cf.* **-ma**[2].
mi(qe) (*mi-ke*) *verb* 1. move in any direction (= 'come', 'go', 'approach', 'arrive', 'leave', *etc.*) [Atakapa *mo·k-* 'go'].

michu[1] (*miču*) *particle* 1. that (one).

michu[2] 1. what?; 2. which?; 3. who? [Warao *bitu* 'which'].

mili (*mili*) 1. (V) light (= 'make a light shine'); 2. (M) resplendent [Apalachee *miłli*, Koasati *miłł-n* 'clean by scrubbing'].

milisuru (*milisuru*) *noun* 1. eyebrow.

miltiba (*miltiba*) TAWASA DIALECT *noun* 1. night [Alabama *niła* 'night'] *see* **ilaqe** 'night'.

mine (*mine*) *noun* 1. first; 2. great, large; 3. *By extension* (N) lord, sir; 4. *By extension* (N/M) prior, preceding; 5. *By extension* that one.

mirica (*miri-ka*) *particle* 1. all; 2. (N) neighbors.

miso (*miso*) *noun* 1. old man; 2. *By extension* (N) wise man, wizard; 3. *By extension* (N) demon, devil [Warao *misi-* 'demon, devil'].

missa (*misa*) *noun* 1. Christian mass [Spanish *misa* 'mass'].

mistachcaqe (*mistačkake*) *particle* 1. that (one).

-mitila (*-mi-ti-la*) 1. 'their' (Der. *-ma*[3]>*-mi* '3d plural subject' + *-te*>*-ti* 'durative action' + *-la* 'proximate time').

-mitile (*-mi-ti-le*) 1. 'their' (Der. *-ma*[3]>*-mi* '3d plural subject' + *-te*>*-ti* 'durative action' + *-la*>*-le* 'proximate time').

miya (*miya*) *noun* 1. splendor; 2. (M) resplendent.

-mo[1] (*-mo*) 1. Definite goal-marker with nouns (= 'the'). *Cf.* **-ma**[2].

-mo[2] 1. 3rd plural verb subject (= 'they'). *Cf.* **-ma**[3].

mo[1] (*mo*) 1. (V) be able to, can; 2. (V) do.

mo[2] 1. (V) call (to); 2. (V) speak, say; 3. (V) affirm; 4. *By extension* (V) command; 5. *By extension* (V) consent; 6. *By extension* (V/N) name; 7. *By extension* (N) speech, utterance.

moca (*moka*) *noun* 1. sea, ocean.

mochase (*mo-čase* ?) *noun* 1. beginner, learner, novice, apprentice; 2. *By extension* disciple.

moco (7A) (*moko*) *verb* 1. smoke.

mocoro (*mokoro*) *noun* 1. crowd.

mofa (*mofa*) *verb* 1. drown.

moha[1] (*moha*) *verb* 1. be.

moha[2] *verb* 1. can, be able to.

moqeti (*moketi*) 1. (V/N) belch.

mora (*mora*) *particle* 1. Contrastive particle (= 'great', 'very', 'little', 'slight', *etc.*).

mosi (*mosi*) 1. (V) appear.

mucu[1] (7B) (*muku*) 1. (N) eye [Warao *mu* 'eye', Manao *uku-* 'eye', Choctaw *muču-* 'wink'].

mucu[2] 1. *By extension from* **mucu**[1] (N) face.

mucu[3] 1. *By extension from* **mucu**[1] (P) before, in front of.

mucu[4] 1. *By extension from* **mucu**[1] (V) undertstand.

mucu[5] 1. *By extension from* **mucu**[1] (N) tear.

mucu[6] 1. *By extension from* **mucu**[1] (?) (V) be ignorant (of), not to know.

mulu (*mulu*) 1. (N) root; 2. (N) source; 3. (N) principal; 4. (M) principally.

muqua (*muk^{w}a*) 1. (V) dance.

muti (*muti*) *noun* 1. temper.

N

-n (*-n*) 1. Active voice indicator (action designator) with verbs.

-na[1] (2A-C) (*-na*) 1. 1st person possessive pronoun with nouns (= 'my', 'our').

-na[2] (3C) 1. Durative aspect indicator with verbs (= progressive tenses).

-na[3] (3D) 1. Habitual action indicator with verbs (= 'usually') [Chacobo *-na-* 'become'].

na[1]**-** (*na-*) 1. (V) move in any direction (*i.e.*, 'come', 'go' [Warao *nao-* 'come', Cuna *naa-* 'come'].

na[2]**-** 1. Nominalizer with verb stems [Warao *-na* 'nominalizer with verb stems'].

na[1] (*na*) *particle* 1. if.

na[2] *particle* 1. same.

na[3] *particle* 1. this, that.

naba[1] (*naba*) *particle* 1. about, around, near;. 2. inside, within; 3. *By extension* underground.

naba[2] *particle* 1. enough.

naba[3] *particle* 1. away (?).

nabo (7A) (*nabo*) *verb* 1. honor, esteem; 2. revere, venerate; 3. *By extension* praise.

nabucha [**nagucha**] (*na-buča*} 1. (N) day (Der. *na-* '?' + *bucha* 'yesterday').

naca (*naka*) *verb* 1. deliver; 2. *By extension* trust, entrust.

nacacha (*nakača*) 1. (V/N) wound.

nacaqi (*nakaki*) 1. (V) meet, encounter; 2. (N) meeting, encounter.

nachiliqi (*načiliki*) 1. (V) wash; 2. (V) water, irrigate; 3. *By extension* (V) purge.

nachua (*načua*) *noun* 1. nail.

naco (*nako*) 1. (N/M) blind.

nacu (*naku*) *particle* 1. but, however; 2. if.

nacume (*nakume*) *verb* 1. ripen.

nacumo (*nakumo*) 1. (N) mulch.

nacumono (*nakumo-no*) *noun* 1. cover for plants.

nacupa (*nakupa*) 1. (V) enjoy; 2. (V) delight (in); 3. (V) desire; 4. *By extension* (?) (V) last, (M) lasting.

naeyanele [**naeianele**] (*na-eya-ne-le* ?) *particle* 1. just; 2. suitable.

naeye (*naeye*) *verb* 1. mitigate.

naha (*naha*) 1. (V) leave.

nahan (*naha-n*) *verb* 1. be (Der. *naha* 'leave' + *-no* possibly 'action designator' ?).

nahaqui (*nahak^{w}i*) 1. (V/N) sneeze.

nahe[1] (*nahe*) 1. (N) effect.

nahe[2] *particle* 1. near.

nahe[3] 1. (M) resplendent.

nahela (*nahe-la*) *particle* 1. around, about, near (Der. *nahe*[2] 'near' + *-la* 'durative action'; *lit.* 'it is near').

naheleo (*nahe-le-o*) 1. (M) shining, resplendent (Der. *nahe*[3] + *-le* 'durative action' + *-o* 'punctual/intensive'; *lit.* 'it is very resplendent').

nahi[1] (*nahi*) 1. (V) be able to, can.

nahi[2] 1. (V) have, own, possess; 2. (V) hold; 3. *By extension* (V) remain; 4. *By extension* (M) powerful (= 'in possession of').

nahe[3] 1. (V) oblige; 2. (V) forbid.

nahe[4] 1. (V) measure.

nahe[5] *particle* 1. at a distance.

nahiabo (7A) (*nahiabo*) 1. (V) know, understand; 2. (N) knowledge, understanding; 3. *By extension* (V) recognize; 4. *By extension* (V) reveal; 5. *By extension* (V) instruct, show [Warao *nahobo* 'understand, know'].

nahico (7A) (*nahiko*) 1. (V) fail, fall short.

nahio (*nahio*) 1. (N) advantage; 2. (M) useful; 3. *By extension* (V) provide.

naho (7A) (*naho*) 1. (M) complete; 2. (P) ultimately; 3. *By extension* (N) reward.

nahomo (7A) (Inahomo) 1. (P) about to, on the point of, at the hour of; 2. *By extension* (V) come to die.

nahulu (7B) (*nahulu*) 1. (V) adorn oneself.

nalepeti (*nalepeti*) 1. (V) mitigate.

nali(sono) (*nali-sono*) *noun* 1. (N/M) yellow, gold [Alabama, Koasati *la¯na* 'yellow', Creek *lá·ni* 'yellow'].

nalimo (*nalimo*) *noun* 1. heaven.

naliqui (*nalik^{w}i*) *noun* 1. laurel.

namequa (*namek^{w}a*) *particle* 1. particularly.

namere (*namere*) 1. (V) contend.

nameya (*nameya*) 1. (V) faint.

namono (*namono*) *particle* 1. commonly, ordinarily.

namoqua[1] (*namok^{w}a*) 1. (P) worthy of; 2. (N) worth, merit; 3. *By extension* (V/N) favor.

namoqua[2] *particle* 1. apart.

namoro (7A) (*namoro*) 1. (V) obstinate; 2. *By extension* (V) wrangle.

namoyo (7A) (*namoyo*) 1. (V) meet.

nancu (*nanacu*) *particle* 1. because; 2. as follows; 3. *By extension* (N) past.

nanareqe (*nanareke*) 1. (M) variegated.

nanemi (*nanemi*) *particle* 1. always, forever; 2. (M) eternal, eternally, perpetual(ly).

nanibeti (*nanibeti*) 1. (V) stop.

nano (*nano*) 1. (V) be so, be thus, be true.

napirala (*napira-la*) *particle* 1. after, afterwards (Der. *napira* '?' + -*la* 'durative action').

napona (*napona*) *noun* 1. hair; 2. *By extension* scalp [Proto-

Tucanoan **poa* 'hair'].

napoti (*napoti*) 1. (V) rub.

napula (*napula*) *noun* 1. sky; 2. *By extension* storm, tempest.

napura (*napura*) 1. (V) hold in contempt, scorn, despise, abhor.

naqi^{1} (*naki*) 1. (V) laugh.

naqi^{2} 1. (V) embroil.

naqua (*nak^{w}a*) *particle* 1. sufficient.

naquana (*nak^{w}na*) *particle* 1. at once, immediately; 2. without interruption.

naquate (*nak^{w}te*) *particle* 1. angry.

naque (*nak^{w}e*) 1. (V) trust.

naquere (*nak^{w}ere*) 1. (V/N) jest.

naquero (*nak^{w}ero*) 1. (V) imitate.

naquilu^{1} (*nak^{w}ilu*) 1. (V) decorate; 2. *By extension* (V) dye, tint.

naquilu^{2} 1. (N) house-cover (probably by extension from **naquilu**^{1}).

naquo (7A) (*nak^{w}*) 1. (V) trust, esteem.

nararaca (*nararaka*) 1. (M) bitter.

nariba [**naribua, narigua**] (*nariba*) *noun* 1. (N/M) old; 2. old man; 3. (M) ancient; 4. *By extension* (V) venerate. This term is frequently used to designate any male relative on G^{+3} (great-grandfather, *etc.*) or higher. It is a term of extreme respect [Warao *nibora* 'man'].

narutuqua(sota) (*narutuk^{w}a-so-ta*) *verb* 1. throw down, cast out; 2. *By extension* (V) disinherit (Der. *narutuk^{w}a* '?' + *-so* 'transitive/causative' + *-ta* 'durative action').

nasaqi (*nasaki*) 1. (V) participate.

nasi (*nasi*) *noun* 1. Used by both *ego* male and *ego* female to indicate affinal kin, male or female (= 'in-law').

nata (*nata*) 1. (V) be born; 2. *By extension* (V) come (together); 3. *By extension* (V) go (together); 4. *By extension* (V) draw out.

nataite^{1} (*nataite*) 1. (V) arrive.

nataite^{2} 1. (V) succeed in having (probably by extension from **nataite**^{1}).

nataitema^{1} (*nataite-ma*) *noun* 1. fish (cooked); 2. *By extension* (V) have for food (Der. *nataite*^{2} 'suceed in having' + *-ma*^{2} 'the'; *lit.* 'that which one suceeds in having').

nataitema[2] 1. *By extension from* **nataite**[1] 'arrive' (V) come.
nate (*nate*) 1. (V) give oneself up to (something); 2. *By extension* (V) pardon.
natela (*na-te-la*) *particle* 1. also; 2. it is so (Der. *na*[3]- 'that' + *-te* 'durative action' + *-la* 'proximate time'; *lit.* 'that is so').
natori (*natori*) 1. (V) teach.
natoya (*natoya*) 1. (V) burn.
nayame (*nayame*) 1. (V) add.
nayele (*nayele*) 1. (V/N) honor.
nayo (7A) (*nayo*) 1. (N/M) white(ness), silver; 2. *By extension* (N) snow; 3. *By extension* (V/N) bleach; 4. *By extension* (P) in the morning.
nayomoqe (*nayo-mo-ke*) *particle* 1. tomorrow (Der. *nayo* 'white(ness)' + *-ma*[2]>*-mo* 'the' + *-qe* 'optative action'; *lit.* 'the whiteness (= morning) which may come'. The use of the optative for unknown, future time is typical of Timucua — *cf.* GRAMMAR, pp. 96-97, 101 — which considers all events which have not yet occurred only as potentialities, not certainties).
nayuchami (*nayučami*) 1. (M) faithful; 2. (M) fearless.
neba (*neba*) *noun* 1. *Ego* male or female's mother's brother (= maternal uncles).
neca[1] (*neka*) 1. (V/N) sleep; 2. (M) asleep [Proto-Muskogean **nuči-* 'sleep'].
neca[2] 1. (N) the desire to imbibe (perhaps by extension from **neca**[1]).
neche (*neče*) 1. (V/N) fear.
necoa (*nekoa~nekoba* ?) TAWASA DIALECT *noun* 1. potato.
neha (*neha*) *noun* 1. fat, grease; 2. *By extension* gravy [Koasati *niha* 'fat'].
nela (*nela*) *particle* 1. clear(ly), open(ly), public(ly); 2. *By extension* well.
neme[1] (*neme*) *particle* 1. toward.
neme[2] *particle* 1. opposite.
neqero (7A) (*nekero*) 1. (V) kneel [Culino *i-ku-buti* 'knee'].
nequa (*nek^{w}a*) 1. (V) hit.
-ni[1] (*-ni*) 1. 1st person possessive pronoun with nouns (= 'my', 'our'). *Cf* **-na**[1].

-ni[2] 1. Habitual action indicator with verbs (= 'usually'). *Cf.* **-na**[3].

-ni[3] 1. Active voice indicator (action designator) with verbs. *Cf.* **-no**[1].

ni- (*ni-*) 1. 1st person verbal subject (= 'I', 'we'); 2. 1st person verbal object (= 'me', 'us').

nia (*nia*) *noun* 1. female, woman, lady; 2. *By extension* any female relative on one's own generation; 3. *By extension* mistress, concubine [Baré, Tariana, Piapoco, Achagua, Baniva *ina-* 'woman, female'].

nibe (*nibe*) *noun* 1. *Ego* male or female's father's sister (= paternal aunt). *Cf.* **neba** 'mother's brother' (= maternal uncle).

nibi (*nibi*) 1. (N) image, figure; 2. (N) picture, painting, drawing; 3. (N) sign; 4. *By extension* (N) face; 5. (V) draw, paint; 6. (V) signify; 7. (V) represent

nibili (*nibili*) *noun* 1. mouse, rat.

nibira (*nibira*) *noun* 1. *Ego* male or female's paternal and maternal grandmothers and great-grandmothers.

-nica (*-ni-ka*) 1. 1st plural subject with verbs in questions (Der. *-ni-* '1st person' + *-ca* 'plural').

nichi- (*ni-c̊i*) 1. 'I' (subject) + 'you' (object) of verb.

niha (*niha*) *noun* 1. *Ego* male's elder brothers.

-nihero (*-ni-he-re>-ro*) 1. 'if I could' (= potential durative action) (Der. *-ni* '1st person' + *he* 'be able to' + *-re>-ro* 'noun combining-form').

nihi (*nihi*) 1. (N) death; 2. (V) die; 3. (M) dead; 4. *By extension* (V) kill; 5. *By extension* (V) lose in gambling [Warao *na-* 'kill'].

niho [**nijo**] (*niho*) 1. (N) something fire-colored; 2. (N) something burned; 3. *By extension* (N) heat; 4. (M) inflamed; 5. *By extension* (M) gloomy, obscure, murky; 6. *By extension* (M) sad, melancholy.

nihona (*nih-ona* ?) *noun* 1. *Ego* female's elder sisters.

nimi (*nimi*) 1. (V) be delighted, delight oneself with.

nioco (*nioko*) *noun* 1. letter, message; 2. mail, post; 3. messenger.

nipati (nipati) 1. (V) threaten.

nipita (*nipita*) *noun* 1. mouth; 2. tongue [Chocó *itae* 'mouth', Choctaw *itopa* 'mouth'].

niquisa (*nik^{w}isa*) *noun* 1. A female's husband's sisters.

niroco (*niroko*) 1. (M) dead; 2. (M) extinct.

nitimu (*nitimu*) 1. (M) dead; 2. (M) extinct.

niye (*niye*) *noun* 1. herb; 2. medicine.

-no[1] (3E, 3G, 6A) (*-no*) 1. Active voice indicator (action designator) with verbs [Chacobo *-noʔo* 'locative transitive'; Warao *-ne* 'gerundive'].

-no[2] (3F, 6A) 1. Proximate time indicator with verbs (= 'now' close to the event described, regardless of time).

no (*no*) *noun* 1. honor; 2. (M) honored.

nocomi (*nokomi*) *noun* 1. truth; 2. (M) true; 3. (P) truly.

-noma (*-no-ma*) 1. instrument by which an action is performed (Der. *-no*[1] 'action designator' + *-ma*[2] 'the').

noqua (*nokʷa*) *noun* 1. (N/M) powerful.

noro (*noro*) 1. (N) attention, devotion; 2. (M) with attention, with devotion; 3. *By extension* (N/M) great.

noti (*no-ti*) 1. (V) despise, scorn; 2. *By extension* (N) prostitute (Der. *no* 'honor' + *-ti* 'not').

noyuque (*no-yukʷe*) YUFERA DIALECT *see* **yuque**.

-nte (*-n-te*) 1. 'it is' (Der. *ini* 'be' + *-te* 'durative action').

-nu (*-nu*) 1. Active voice indicator (action designator) with verbs. *Cf*. **-no**[1].

nu (*nu*) 1. (V) know someone physically; 2. (V) rape, violate [Baré *nu-* 'know'].

nuba (*nuba*) 1. (P) downcast, face downward; 2. (V) throw down; 3. *By extension* (V) praise, revere, (N) reverence.

nubo (*nubo*) *noun* 1. *Ego* male or female's daughter-in-law.

nula (**nula**) 1. (V) flirt; 2. (V) fool; 3. (V) tickle; 4. *By extension* (V) delight.

nulufo (7A) (*nulufo*) 1. (V) keep watch.

numa (*numa*) *noun* 1. sky, heaven; 2. *By extension* thunderbolt.

nuque (*nukʷe*) 1. (V) carry away, take away; 2. (V) steal; 3. (N) theft; 4. (N) thief; 5. (P) away.

nura (*nura*) 1. (V) lie, prevaricate; 2. (N) lie, prevarication.

nute (*nu-ti>-te*) *verb* 1. not to know, be ignorant of. (Der. *nu* 'know (physically)' + *-ti>-te* 'not').

O

-o (*-o*) 1. Emphatic mood indicator in verbs [Warao *-u* 'intensive'].

o (o) *particle* 1. yes, certainly (TAWASA DIALECT *see* **ho-**).

obacha (*obača*) 1. (V/N) kiss.

obe (*obe*) *noun* 1. dove.

obo (*obo*) *noun* 1. hook; 2. thorn.

oboqi (*oboki*) 1. (V) generate.

oca (*oka*) *particle* 1. this; 2. that [Campa *oka* 'this, that', Alabama *ak-* 'this'].

ocho (*očo*) 1. (P) after, behind, back of; 2. (N) shoulder [Chacobo *-čo* 'behind'].

oco[1] (*oko*) *noun* 1. body; 2. flesh.

oco[2] 1. (N) side.

oco[3] 1. (N) part.

oco[4] 1. (V) run.

oco[5] TAWASA DIALECT 1. (V) drink *see* **uku**.

ocora (*okora*) 1. (P) all; 2. (P) with, together, united; 3. *By extension* (N) assembly, congregation; 4. *By extension* (N) companion.

ocoto (7A) (*okoto*) 1. (V) hear; 2. (V) listen; 3. (V) observe [Warao *noko* 'hear'].

ofue[1] (*ofue*) *particle* 1. above, over, on top (of).

ofue[2] *particle* 1. after, later, afterwards; 2. beyond; 3. besides. All probably by extension from **ofue**[1].

oha (*oha*) 1. (V) give.

ohi (*ohi*) *particle* 1. that

oho (7A) (*oho*) 1. (V) teach; 2. (N) teacher.

ona[1] (*ona*) *particle* 1. enough, sufficient; 2. no more.

ona[2] *particle* 1. this; 2. that; 3. there.

ona[3] *particle* 1. true.

opomo (*opomo*) *noun* 1. rope.

oqe (*oke*) *noun* 1. that; 2. he, she, it; 3. there [Campa *oka* 'this, that', Alabama *ak-* 'this'].

orabo (7A) (*orabo*) *noun* 1. joy, happiness, contentment; 2.

pleasure, satisfaction; 3. (V) enjoy, be happy; 4. (V) please, satisfy; 5. (V) rejoice.

oroba (*oroba*) 1. (V) cast as spell, bewitch, charm; 2. (N) spell, charm.

orobisti (*orobo>orob-isti*) *noun* 1. counsel; 2. (M) cunning, sly; 3. *By extension* (N) rogue. *Cf.* **orobo** (Der. *orobo* 'advise' + *isti(co)* 'bad'; *lit.* 'bad advice' — could the Timucua have been as disenchanted with politicians as we are today!).

orobo[1] (7A) (*orobo*) 1. (V) advise; 2. (N) advice; 3. *By extension* (N) understanding; 4. *By extension* (N) wisdom in the sense of cunningness.

orobo[2] 1. *By extension from* **orobo**[1] (N) doctor; 2. (V) treat with herbs, heal.

orobo[3] 1. *By extension from* **orobo**[1] (N) rogue; 2. (M) roguish.

oroco (*oroko*) *noun* 1. child; 2. (M) little, small. *Cf.* **aruqui**.

oso[1] (7A) (*oso*) 1. (V) hasten, hurry; 2. (V) run; 3. (M) quick(ly).

oso[2] 1. (N) sweetness.

osobota (*oso-bo-ta*) *verb* 1. rush, go quickly; 2. *By extension* (P) much, greatly (Der. *oso*[1] 'hurry' + *-bo* '1st, 2d plural subject' + *-ta* 'durative action'; *lit.* 'they are hurrying').

ostanu (*os-ta-nu*) *particle* 1. quickly (Der. *oso*[1]*>os-* 'hurry' + *-ta* 'durative action' + *-no*[1]*>-nu* 'action designator'; *lit.* 'hurrying').

oto (*oto*) *noun* 1. corner.

otorota (*otorota*) *particle* 1. abundantly, plentifully.

oyo[1] (*oyo*) 1. (P) in, inside, within; 2. (N) interior, inside.

oyo[2] 1. (P) beneath.

oyo[3] 1. (V) run.

oyo[4] 1. (M) obstinate(ly).

P

paca[1] (*paka*) 1. (P) in, inside; 2. *By extension* (N) street.

paca[2] 1. (V) engender.

paca[3] 1. (V) neglect.

TIMUCUA DICTIONARY

pacanihino (*paka-nihi-no*) 1. (M) careless, negligent, thoughtless, heedless (Der. *paca* 'neglect' + *niho>nihi* 'inflamed' + the *-no*[1] 'action designator'; *lit.* 'with extreme neglect').

pacano[1] (*pacano*) 1. (N) single, unmarried; 2. bachelor, spinster.

pacano[2] 1. (M) second; 2. (M) subsequent. Probably by extension from **pacano**[1], given the fact that the married state was considered the normal adult state among the Timucua.

pacha (*pača*) 1. (N/M) ancient, old; 2. (M) very.

pachiqua[1] (*pačik*^{w}*a*) *particle* 1. before (in time).

pachiqua[2] 1. (N) anything.

pacu (7B) (*paku*) *verb* 1. cover; 2. *By extension* (V) double; 3. *By extension* (P) close to.

paha (*paha*) *noun* 1. house, dwelling, habitation [Eastern Maipuran *pa-* 'house', Goajiro *pe-* 'house', Apolista *pi-* 'house', Guahibo *po-* 'house'].

pala (*pala*) 1. (V) break, shatter; 2. (N) defect.

pale[1] (*pale*) 1. (V) consent.

pale[2] 1. (V) rub.

pali[1] (*pali*) 1. (V) cut (open), lay open; 2. (N) knife.

pali[2] 1. (V) think.

paloco (7A) (*paloko*). 1. (V) injure; 2. (V) wound; 3. *By extension* (V) fear.

palu (7B) (*palu*) 1. (V) accomplish.

palucu[1] (7B) (*paluku*) 1. (N) fear, fright, terror.

palucu[2] 1. (V) rest.

pana (*pana*) 1. (V) enjoy, delight; 2. (N) enjoyment, delight.

panta (*pa-n-ta*) *verb* 1. be (Der. *pa-* '?' + *ini* 'be' + *-ta* 'durative action').

paqe[1] (*pake*) 1. (V) forget.

paqe[2] 1. (V) forgive.

paqe[3] 1. (V) satisfy; 2. (N) satisfaction; 3. (M) satisfied.

paqe[4] 1. (V) spy upon.

paqetosa (*paketosa*) 1. (N) poverty; 2. (M) poor.

paqua (*pak*^{w}*a*) 1. (V) touch.

paracusi [**parucusi**] (*parakusi*) *noun* 1. prince, war-prince [Yuchi *pá'län ku-siä*^{n} 'village chief'].

pari (*pari*) *particle* 1. around, round about.

parifo (7A) (*parifo*) 1. (V) fly around, circle about.

paritima (*pari-ti-ma*) *noun* 1. everywhere (Der. *pari* 'around' + -*te*>-*ti* 'durative action' + -*ma*^{2} 'the').

paru (7B) (*paru*) 1. (V) sew; 2. (N) any work involving sewing — *e.g.*, seamstress, tailor, cobbler, shoemaker, *etc.*

parucusi *see* **paracusi.**

pasi (*pasi*) *particle* 1. together.

pata^{1} (*pata*) 1. (P) below; 2. *By extension* (M) deep.

pata^{2} 1. (V) protect; 2. *By extension* (V) conquer.

pata^{3} 1. *By extension from* **pata**^{2} (N) sexual intercourse; 2. (V) cohabit, unite with sexually; 3. *By extension* (N) adultery.

pata^{4} 1. (V) stretch.

pata^{5} 1. (V) blow.

pata^{6} 1. (V) measure.

patafi (*pata-fi*) *particle* 1. below; 2. *By extension* (N) obedience (Der. *pata*^{1} 'below' + -*fi* '?').

pataqui (*patak*^{w}*i*) 1. (N) fatigue, exhaustion; 2. (M) tired, fatigued, exhausted, weary; 3. *By extension* (M) miserable; 4. *By extension* (M) mean, low, vile.

pataro (7A) (*pataro*) 1. (V) surround.

patu (*patu*) 1. (N) cold; 2. (N) frost.

pecherereca (*pečere-re-ka*) *noun* 1. floor (Der. *pečere* '?' + -*re* 'noun combining-form' + -*ca* 'plural').

peemo (*peemo* ?) 1. (M) thrown down.

penani (*pe-nani* ?) *particle* 1. with the hands [General Northern Maipuran -*p*/*bi* 'hand'].

peqe (*peke*) 1. (V) hang up.

peqecheqeta (*peke-čeketa*) *particle* 1. nine; 2. ninth (Der. *peke*- 'hand, 5' + *čeketa* '4'; *lit.* '5 + 4') [Shipibo-Conibo *piči-ka* '5', Cavineña *piši-ka* '5', Reyesano *piši-ka* '5', Cuna *pakka*- '5', Quechua *pička* '5'].

pequa (*pek*^{w}*a*) *noun* 1. skin; 2. *By extension* leather.

pequata (*pek*^{w}*ata*) *noun* 1. servant; 3. vassal.

pera(mo) (7A) (*pera-mo*) 1. (V) contend, fight; 2. (V) wrangle, quarrel; 3. *By extension* (V) persist.

perefo[1] (7A) (*perefo*) 1. (V) clear.

perefo[2] 1. (V) negate. Perhaps by extension from **perero**[1].

pesa[1] (*pesa*) 1. (N) blade, knife.

pesa[2] 1. (V) pollute.

pesanoma (*pesa-no-ma*) 1. (N) weight, measure; 2. (V) weigh, measure [Spanish *peso* 'weight, measure'].

pesola (*pesola*) *noun* 1. adz; 2. hoe, spade, shovel.

pesolo (*pesolo*) *noun* 1. bread.

pia[1] (*pia*) 1. (V) carry away.

pia[2] 1. *By extension from* **pea**[1] (V) finish, complete; 2. (V) consume; 3. *By extension* (V) defecate.

picha (*piča*) 1. (V) accomplish; 2. (V) complete; 3. *By extension* comply with.

pichi (*piči*) 1. (V/N) remedy; 2. (V) accomplish; 3. (V/N) benefit.

picho (*pičo*) *noun* 1. knife.

picu (*piku*) *noun* TAWASA DIALECT 1. arrow [Spanish *pico* 'sharp pointed object'] *see* **atulu** 'arrow'.

pilani (*pilani*) *particle* 1. in the morning; 2. (N) morning; 3. at dusk, in the evening; 4. *By extension* tomorrow. NOTE: The semantic spread of this form seems to imply that **pilani** referred to any time of day during which the sun was not at its height or to a time in the future, which, by Timucua definition of time, fell in the *unknown time locus*, undefinable until it actually occurred — *cf.* GRAMMAR, pp. 96-98.

pile[1] (*pile*) 1. (N) hut, cabin, shed; 2. *By extension* field.

pile[2] 1. (V) tie.

pileno (*pileno*) *noun* 1. dumpling, tamale.

pilenoma (*pileno-ma*) *noun* 1. lungs. Probably by extension from **pileno**.

pili (*pili*) *verb* 1. drag.

piliqua (*pilik^{w}a*) *noun* 1. Term used by a parent for his or her children after the death of the parent's spouse; 2. *By extension* orphan.

pilu (*pilu*) 1. (V) turn, overturn, upset; 2. (V) return; 3. *By extension* (V) vomit.

piqi (*piki*) *verb* 1. envy; 2. begrudge.

piqicha (*piki-ča*) *particle* 1. seven; 2. seventh (Der. *piki-* '5' + *(yu)cha* '2'; *lit.* '5 + 2') [Shipibo-Conibo *piči-ka* '5', Cavineña *piši-ka* '5', Reyesano *piši-ka* '5', Cuna *pakka-* '5', Quechua *pička* '5'].

pi(qi)ch(e)cuta (*piki-č(e)kuta*) TAWASA DIALECT *particle* 1. nine. *See* **peqecheqeta**.

piqinaho (*piki-naho*) *particle* 1. eight; 2. eighth (Der. *piki-* '5' + *naho* '3' ?; *lit.* '5 + 3') [Shipibo-Conibo *piči-ka* '5', Cavineña *piši-ka* '5', Reyesano *piši-ka* '5', Cuna *pakka-* '5', Quechua *pič-ka* '5'].

piqui (*pik^w*) 1. (V) hide, conceal; 2. *By extension* (V/N) escape.

pira[1] (*pira*) 1. (N/M) red; 2. *By extension* (?) (N) infidel [Paumarí *puru* 'black'].

pira[2] 1. (V) add; 2. (V) continue, go beyond; 3. (M) continually; 4. (M) more; 5. (M) last; 6. *By extension* (N) past.

piri[1] (*piri*) *noun* 1. scowl, grimace.

piri[2] 1. (M) small, little, lesser; 2. *By extension* (M) low.

piso (*piso*) TAWASA DIALECT *noun* 1. bread. *See* **pesolo.**

pisoco (*pisoco*) *noun* 1. arms, weapons.

pita (*pita*) *verb* 1. finish, complete; 2. (P) enough.

pite (*pite*) *verb* 1. hide.

plato (*plato*) *noun* 1. dish, plate [Spanish *plato* 'dish, plate'].

po (*po*) *particle* 1. that sort of thing, such-and-such a thing.

pocha (*poča*) 1. (V) grow, produce; 2. (N) produce; 3. *By extension* a growing ditch.

pole (*pole*) *noun* 1. herb (a particular variety, but the species is unknown).

polo (7A) (*polo*) 1. (V) weave; 2. (N) weaving-stick.

polon (*polon*) 1. (N) anger; 2. (N) disgust; 3. *By extension* (V) humble oneself.

po(na) (*pona*) *verb* 1. arrive, come; 2. bring.

poranacu (*poranaku*) *noun* 1. homosexual; 2. *By extension* sodomite.

poy (*poy*) *noun* 1. *Ego* female's brothers and sons of father's brothers (= paternal cross-cousins), regardless of age.

pu (*pu*) *particle* 1. no.

puchi (*puči*) *noun* 1. hair of the head
puchu (*puču*) *particle* 1. empty, vacant.
pue(n) (*puen*) *verb* 1. go [Proto-Muskogean **(x^{w}u/hu)pun-* 'go'].
pufi (*pufi*) *noun* 1. fox (male only).
pulu (7B) (*pulu*) 1. (N) adz; 2. (N) hoe, spade, shovel; 3. (V) dig, hollow out.
punu (7B) (*punu*) *verb* 1. add; 2. mix.
-puqua (*-pu-k^{w}a*) *particle* 1. much, many (Der. *-bo>-pu* ? 'plural' + *-k^{w}a* 'intensive').
purgatorio (*purkatorio* ?) *noun* 1. purgatory, hell [Spanish *purgatorio* 'purgatory, hell'].
puru (7B) (*puru*) *verb* 1. flee; 2. shake out; 3. *By extension* shell corn.
putisi (*puti-si* ?) *verb* 1. fight with, war with (Der. *putu>puti* 'war' + *-si*[1] 'reflexive'). *See* **putu**.
putu (7A) (*putu*) *verb* 1. war, fight against; 2. *By extension* hate, dislike, abhor; 3. *By extension* flee.
puya (*puya*) *noun* 1. vegetables; 2. *Specif.* greens.
puye (*puye*) *noun* 1. fish-trap, fish-basket.

Q

qa (*ka*) *particle* 1. Exclamation of fear.
-qe[1] (*-ke*) 1. optative mode indicator with verbs (= 'may', 'might') [Chacobo *-ki* 'conditional', Warao *-ko* 'optative'].
-qe[2] 1. Variant of intensive/pointer post-clitic **-qi** (which see).
qé (*ke*) *particle* 1. Exclamation of terror.
qe[1] (*ke*) *particle* 1. that; 2. what; 3. there; 4. where.
qe[2] 1. (V) attack; 2. (V/N) hunt; 3. (V) hurt; 4. (V) bruise; 5. *By extension* (V) seek, look for; 6. *By extension* (N) sport, game.
qeba (*keba*) 1. (V) arrange.
qeba(ni) (*keba-ni*) *verb* 1. prepare; 2. provide; 3. dispose (of).
qeche (*keče*) 1. (V) scale a fish.
qechela (*kečela*) *noun* 1. skin; 2. bark of a tree [Proto-Tucanoan

kasero~katsero 'skin, bark'].

qela[1] *(kela) particle* 1. about, near.

qela[2] 1. (N) relationship, lineage. *Cf.* **qele** 'line'.

qele[1] *(kele) particle* 1. in the same manner.

qele[2] 1. (V) pass through or by; 2. (N) line (= 'what passes through'); 3. *By extension* (N) mark, sign; 4. *By extension* (V) wound (with an arrow).

qen *(ken) particle* 1. over there (far away).

qena (kena) *particle* 1. self.

qenele *(kenele) particle* 1. later, subsequently.

qepe *(kepe) noun* 1. claws; 2. fingernails; 3. *By extension* (M) scabby; 4. *By extension* (M) whitish; 5. *By extension* (M) clean.

qere[1] *(kere) particle* 1. after; 2. immediately (= following).

qere[2] *particle* 1. when; 2. while.

qere[3] *particle* 1. thus, so.

qere[4] 1. (V) drag, draw; 2. (V) *By extension* (V) scrape; 3. *By extension* (V) erase.

qere[5] 1. (V) speak, tell; 2. *By extension* (V) belch (out).

qereba *(kereba) noun* 1. pearl.

qete *(kete) particle* 1. now.

-qi *(-ki)* 1. intensive/pointer post-clitic (= 'that').

qi *(ki) verb* 1. wish, desire, want.

qibe[1] *(kibe) particle* 1. especially.

qibe[2] 1. (N) start, beginning, first, initial; 2. *By extension* (M) principal.

qibo *(jibo) particle* 1. yesterday.

qichi *(kiči) noun* 1. little ones, small ones, innocents.

qie (1A, B) *(kie) noun* 1. *Ego* male's children of either sex, the children of either sex of his brothers, the children of his father's brothers' sons, and the children of his mother's brothers' (= 'child', 'nephew/niece' through males, paternal male cross-cousins' children, and cousins through the male line on the mother's side); 2. *Often specif.* the male children of the above (= 'son').

qilabo *(kilabo) noun* 1. pity, compassion; 2. mercy; 3. *By extension* contrition, piety; 4. *By extension* grief; 5. *By* *extension* sickness.

qili (*kili*) 1. (V/N) fight, combat; 2. (V) quarrel, be angry; 3. (N) quarrel; 4. (M) angry.

qiruma (*kiruma*) *noun* 1. wager.

qisa (*kisa*) *noun* 1. earth, dirt, ground; 2. dust.

qiso (*kiso*) *noun* 1. *Ego* male or female's grandchildren and the children of father's sister (= paternal cross-cousins).

qiti (*kiti*) 1. (V) move quickly, perform quickly; 2. (N) promptness, quickness, diligence; 3. (M) diligently, quickly, promptly.

qitu (7B) (*kitu*) *verb* 1. anoint.

-qua[1] (*-k^{w}a*) 1. distant time indicator with verbs.

-qua[2] 1. copular/intensive post-clitic (= '<u>and</u>').

qua[1] (*k^{w}a*) *particle* 1. similar to; 2. equal (to or with); 3. thus, so.

qua[2] 1. (V) glorify, exalt; 2. (V) sanctify; 3. (V/N) honor; 4. (V) venerate; 5. (N) veneration; 6. (N) glorification.

quachi (*k^{w}ači*) 1. (V) give; 2. *By extension* (V) teach, instruct; 3. *By extension* (N) teacher, instructor.

quale[1] (*k^{w}ale*) *particle* 1. with.

quale[2] *particle* 1. enough; 2. *By extension* an exclamation of wonder; 3. *By extension* (N) admiration.

quana[1] (*k^{w}ana*) *particle* 1. like; 2. together, with.

.quana[2] *particle* 1. for.

quana[3] *particle* 1. self.

quanimaca (*k^{w}animaka*) 1. (M) sad, downcast.

qunata (*k^{w}anta*) *particle* 1. same.

quanu[1] (*k^{w}anu*) 1. (V) dress; 2. (V) adorn oneself in any manner — *specif.* paint the face, arrange the hair.

quanu[2] 1. (V) praise; 2. (V) respect.

quara (*k^{w}ara*) *noun* 1. slivers, splinters.

quehasi (*k^{w}ehasi*) *particle* 1. thus, so.

quela[1] (*k^{w}ela*) 1. (V) fish, catch fish.

quela[2] 1. (V)burn; 2. (V) melt.

quela[3] 1. (V)withdraw; 2. *By extension* (V) wither.

quelo (*k^{w}elo*) *noun* 1. rabbit.

quene[1] (*k^{w}ene*) *particle* 1. because, so, thus, truly in that way; 2. then; 3. *By extension* aforesaid.

quene[2] *particle* 1. like, similar (to).
quene[3] *particle* 1. which, whatever, who.
quenele (k^{w}*enele*) *particle* 1. after, afterwards.
queta[1] (k^{w}*eta*) 1. (N/M) plane, flat.
queta[2] 1. (V) wash a wound.
-qui (-k^{w}*i*) 1. copular/intensive post-clitic (= 'and').
quilo (k^{w}*ilo*) *noun* 1. *Ego* male or female's great-grandparents and great-grandchildren; 2. an adopted kinsman (= godmother, godfather, *etc.*).
quimo (ik^{w}*imo*) *particle* 1. so, as, like, in that way, in that manner.
quimosi (k^{w}*imosi*) *particle* 1. between; 2. to(wards).
quiri (k^{w}*iri*) *verb* 1. curse; 2. *By extension* cause disgrace.
quisoti (k^{w}*soti*) *noun* 1. *Ego* male or female's father's sister's child.
quiti (k^{w}*iti*) 1. (V) fry; 2. *Specif.* (V) make soup; 3. *Specif.* (V) cook fritters; 4. *Specif.* (V) shake while cooking; 5. *By extension* (N) spoon, spatula for stirring.
quitulu (k^{w}*itulu*) *verb* 1. accompany.
quo (k^{w}*o*) 1. (V) admire, respect, esteem; 2. (V/N) honor, praise; 3. *By extension* (V) venerate; 4. (N) admiration, respect, esteem; 5. *By extension* (N) veneration; 6. *By extension* (V) satisfy, (N) satisfaction; 7. *By extension* (M) noble; 8. *By extension* chaste.
quoso[1] (k^{w}*oso*) *verb* 1. do; 2. use; 3. (N) usage.
quoso[2] *verb* 1. praise, honor; 2. *By extension* thank, be grateful.
quoto (k^{w}oto) *noun* 1. load.

R

-re (*-re*) 1. noun combining-form (usually = 'plural', but frequently occurs when any noun base is combined with any other type of base and/or affix).
reqe (*reke*) *particle* 1. each, every; 2. everywhere; 3. whatever.
rey (*rey*) *noun* 1. king [Spanish *rey* 'king'].

ruqui (*rukʷi*) TAWASA DIALECT *noun* 1. child *see* **aruqui**.

S

-s (*-s*) 1. transitive/causative verb indicator *see* **-so**.
-sa (*-sa*) 1. transitive/causative verb indicator *see* **-so**.
sa (*sa*) 1. (M) attractive, pretty, handsome; 2. (M) gracious; 3. (M) agreeable; 4. (M) salutary.
sacasisota[1] (*sakasi-so-ta*) *particle* 1. apart (Der. *sacasi* '?' + *-so* 'transitive/causative' + *-ta* 'durative action'; *lit*. 'cause to *x*').
sacasisota[2] *verb* 1. come apart; 2. walk apart; 3. fall apart. All by extension from **sacasisota**[1].
saliqi (*saliki*) *noun* 1. beans.
samo (7A) (*samo*) 1. (V) wash, bathe.
sandia (*santia* ?) *noun* 1. watermelon [Spanish *sandía* 'watermelon'].
santo (*santo*) *noun* 1. saint [Spanish *santo* 'saint'].
sapato (*sapato*) *noun* 1. shoe [Spanish *zapato* 'shoe'].
sara (*sara*) 1. (V) judge; 2. (N) judgement; 3. (V) criticize.
sare (*sare*) *noun* 1. quarrel (probably by extension from **sara**).
sario (*sario*) 1. (N) condition.
saro(ma) (*saro-ma*) noun 1. jug, jar (Der. *saro* 'jug, jar' + *-ma*[2] 'the') [Spanish *jarro* 'jug, jar'].
-se[1] (*-se*) 1. reflexive goal-marker with nouns, verbs, and particles *see* **-si**[1].
-se[2] 1. transitive/causative verb indicator *see* **-so**.
sea (*sea*) *noun* 1. eel.
seca (*seka*) TAWASA DIALECT *noun* 1. leg.
secucheno (*seku-čeno*) TAWASA DIALECT *noun* 1. stocking.
seqe (*seke*) 1. (V/N) saw; 2. *By extension* (N) mountains.
-si[1] (3H) (*si*) 1. reflexive goal-marker with nouns, verbs, and particles [Warao *-si* 'goal-marker'].
-si[2] 1. potential action indicator with verbs (= 'perhaps', 'if').
-si[3] 1. transitive/causative verb indicator *see* **-so**.

si (*si*) *particle* 1. same.

siapu (*siapu*) *noun* 1. palmetto berry.

-siba (*-siba*) 1. qunatitative/frequentative action indicator, deriving nouns from verbs (= '-ative', as in 'talkative').

sibato (*sibato*) *noun* 1. prune.

sicali (*sikali*) *noun* 1. oyster.

sicuri (*sikuri*) *noun* 1. crane; 2. goose.

sile (*sile*) *noun* 1. perspiration, sweat.

sili (*sili*) *noun* 1. brains; 2. senses; 3. *By extension* forehead; 4. *By extension* tomato.

silibacara (*sili-bakara*) *noun* 1. scorpion (Der. *sili* 'brains' + *bacara* 'ripened'; *lit.*, 'ripened brains' — perhaps a reference either to the physical or mental state induced by a severe scorpion bite).

sipaca (*sipaka*) *noun* 1. coward; 2. (M) cowardly; 3. *By extension* (M) miserable, mean, vile, low; 4. *By extension* (M) weak, tired, sick.

siqi (*siki*) 1. (V) create; 2. (N) creator; 3. (V trans.) give birth; 4. (V intrans.) be born; 4. *By extension* (N) child (of either sex).

siricale (*sirikale*) *noun* 1. candlewood; 2. torch.

siso (7A) (*si-so*) *verb* 1. (V/N) dispute, quarrel, fight; 2. (M) angry; 3. *By extension* (V) say (in anger).

-so (6A, 3H, 3I, 3J, 3K) (*-so*) 1. transitive/causative verb indicator [Chacobo *-šo* 'transitive']. *Cf.* **so**.

so (*so*) *verb* 1. cause.

soba (*soba*) *noun* 1. flesh; 2. meat; 3. food [Warao *toma* 'meat'].

soldado (*soltato* ?) *noun* 1. soldier [Spanish *soldado* 'soldier'].

soqua (*sok^{w}a*) TAWASA DIALECT *particle* 1. how many? *see* **chuca**.

sono (*sono*) *noun* 1. agent.

soti (*soti*) *particle* 1. carefully, diligently; 2. promptly, quickly; 3. *By extension* vehemently; 4. *By extension* proudly.

-su (*-su*) 1. transitive/causative verb indicator *see* **-so**.

sula (sula) *noun* 1. drum.

sulu (*sulu*) *noun* 1. sin.

suluquita (*suluk^{w}ita*) *noun* 1. ant.

suluquita pahama (*sulukwita paha-ma*) *noun* 1. ant-hill.
suquo (7A) (*sukʷo*) *verb* 1. bathe.

T

-ta (6B, 8B) (*-ta*) 1. durative aspect indicator with verbs (= progressive tenses) [Warao *-ta* 'momentaneous occurrence'].
tabi[1] (*tabi*) 1. (V) eat with; 2. *By extension* (N) condiment.
tabi[2] 1. (V) take with.
taca[1] (*taka*) 1. (N) fire; 2. (V/N) light; 3. (V) burn; 4. *By extension* (N) candle; 5. *By extension* (N) charcoal [Warao [*dokia*] 'flame', Pre-Andine Maipuran *titi* 'fire', Pre-Andine Maipuran *tak-* 'sun', General Eastern Maipuran *tike* 'fire', Alabama, Koasati *tikba* 'fire', Creek *tó·tka* 'fire'].
taca[2] 1. *By extension from* **taca**[1] (N) offering; 2. *By extension* (N) reverence.
tacato (*taka-to*) *noun* 1. offering, sacrifice (Der. *taca* 'fire' + *ta*>-*to* (?) 'durative action'; *lit.* 'something which is burnt').
tacu[1] (*taku*) *particle* 1. comparative particle (= 'also').
tacu[2] *particle* 1. although, if.
tacuba (*takuba*) 1. (V) judge; 2. (M) just.
tafarela (*tafarela*) 1. (V) arrive.
tafi (*tafi*) *noun* 1. Term used by *ego* male to refer to the wives of his brothers; 2. Term used by *ego* female to refer to her husband's brother.
taima (*taima*) 1. (V) fail; 2. (V) lack; 3. *By extension* (V) vanish.
-tala (*-ta-la*) 1. durative (*-ta*) proximate (*-la*) action suffix combination with verbs.
talaca (*talaka*) 1. (V) learn; 2. (N) catechism.
talama (*talama*) 1. (V) despise; 2. *By extension* (N) prostitute.
tamalo (7A) (*tamalo*) 1. (V) ask; 2. (V) pray, supplicate, call upon, beg.

tani[1] (*tani*) 1. (V) die.

tani[2] 1. (V) know. Perhaps by extension from **tani**[1].

tapa (*tapa*) 1. (M) cowardly; 2. (M) mean, low; 3. *By extension* (M) thin, lean; 4. *By extension* (M) flat.

tapita (*tapita*) 1. (V) descend (into).

tapo (*tapo*) 1. (N) protestation.

tapola (*tapola*) *noun* 1. maize, corn [Terena *so-poro* 'maize', Guaná *tso-poro* 'maize', Chocó *pe* 'maize', Chibcha *aba* 'maize', Manare *epa* 'maize'].

taqe (*take*) 1. (V) contradict; 2. *By extension* (V) impress.

taqua (*takʷa*) 1. (V) pertain to, concern.

tara (*tara*) 1. (V) embrace.

tari[1] (*tari*) 1. (V) sustain; 2. (N) strength; 3. (N) force; 4. (M) strong, firm; 5. *By extension* (N) patience, (M) patient [Warao *taera* 'strong'].

tari[2] 1. (V/N) work, labor; 2. (N) worker, laborer. All by extension from **tari**[1].

tarua (*tarua*) 1. (V) appear.

tasi (*tasi*) *see* **tafi**.

tasoro (7A) (*tasoro*) 1. (V) pass through or by; 2. *By extension* (V) wound.

tato (7A) (*tato*) 1. (V) draw out.

-te[1] (6B, 8B) (*-te*) 1. durative action indicator with verbs (= progressive tenses) *see also* **-ta** [Warao *-ta* 'occurrence-momentaneous'].

-te[2] 1. copuilar/augmentative/intensive post-clitic (= 'and').

-tela (*-te-la*) 1. durative (*-te*) proximate (*-la*) action indicator with verbs.

tele (*te-le*) 1. durative (*-te*) proximate (*-le*) action indicator with verbs.

-tema (*-te-ma*) 1. 'the one who' (Der. *-te* 'durative action' + *ma*[2] 'the').

-teno (*-te-no*) 1. durative (*-te*) proximate (*-no*) action indicator with verbs.

-tequa (*te-kʷa*) 1. durative (*-te*) distant (*-qua*) action indicator with verbs.

tera (*tera*) 1. (N) good(ness), virtue; 2. (M) good, better, best, well; 3. (M) attractive (= 'pretty', 'handsome').

teyalo (7A) (*teyalo*) 1. (V) melt.

-ti (*-ti*) 1. negative post-clitic (= 'no', 'not') [Campa *-te* 'not', Alabama, Koasati *-ti* 'not'].

-tiacu (*-tiaku*) 1. proximate time indicator with verbs (= 'now', close to the event described, regardless of time).

tico (*tiko*) *noun* 1 canoe; 2. boat, ship.

tilipachua (*tilipa-čua*) *noun* 1. window (Der. *tilipa* '?' + *chua* 'hole, opening').

tilo (*tilo*) *noun* 1. feather.

tilono (*tilono*) *noun* 1. pond.

timoso (7A) (*timo-so*) *verb* 1. loosen.

timu (7B) (*timu*) 1. (V) extinguish.

tinibo (*tinibo*) *noun* 1. woodpecker.

tipari (*tipari*) 1. (V) embrace.

tipopili (*tipo-pili*) 1. (V) roll about, turn about, turn over; 2. (V) writhe; 3. (V) move about (Der. *tipo* '?' + *pili* 'drag').

tiqi (*tiki*) 1. (N) ear; 2. (V) hear; 3. *By extension* border [Manao *teki* 'ear', Lokono *-dike* 'ear'].

tiquemota (*tik^{w}emo-ta*) 1. (N/M) stumbling.

tiqui (*tik^{w}i*) *noun* 1. resin, rosin, pitch, tar.

tiquire (*tik^{w}ire*) *noun* 1. fragments.

to (*to*) *particle* 1. in, into; 2. (V) put, place.

tobo (7A) (*tobo*) 1. (V) swear.

toca (*toka*) *particle* 1. more; 2. other.

tocala (*toka-la*) 1. comparative particle (= 'more', 'most').

toco (7A) (*toko*) 1. (V) to move away from a place (= 'go out', 'come out', 'withdraw', 'proceed', 'walk out', 'pour out'); 2. *By extension* (V) desire.

tofa (*tofa*) *noun* 1. wound.

tola[1] (*tola*) *particle* 1. up, in the air; 2. *By extension* (N) paddle, oar.

tola[2] 1. (N) laurel.

tolo (7A) (*tolo*) 1. (V) open; 2. (N) opening; 3. *By extension* (V) open the mouth, say.

tolobo (7A) (*tolobo*) 1. (V) declare, show; 2. (V) publish; 3. *By* *extension* (V) explain. *Cf.* **tolo.**

tomo (7A) (*tomo*) *particle* 1. immediately, directly; 2. *By extension* (V) guide.

tomoti (*tomoti*) *particle* 1. right (*vs.* 'wrong'); 2. straight.

-tooma (*-tooma*) 1. plural indicator with nouns [Warao *-tuma* 'noun plural']. *Cf.* **tooma.**

tooma (*tooma*) *particle* 1. all, every; 2. *By extension* (N) the last, end.

tori (*tori*) 1. (V) burn.

toro (*toro*) *particle* 1. without; 2. nothing; 3. 'Is there not?'

torobo (*torobo*) *noun* 1. frost, ice.

tuba (*tuba*) 1. (V) fail, fall short, not to arrive or reach; 2. (V) lack.

tucu (*tuku*) *noun* 1. live-oak; 2. *By extension* acorn.

tufa (*tufa*) 1. (V/N) spit.

tulu (*tulu*) *particle* 1. immediately, right away.

tuluqua[1] (*tulukʷa*) *particle* 1. closely; 2. repeatedly; 3. continually.

tuluqua[2] 1. (V) condense; 2. (M) diminshed in size.

tuma (*tuma*) *particle* 1. ten; 2. tenth. *Cf.* **tooma.**

tupi (*tupi*) *particle* 1. separate.

tuqua (*tukʷa*) 1. (V) bury; 2. (N) grave, tomb, sepulcher.

tuqui[1] (*tukʷi*) 1. (V) arise; 2. (V/N) return; 3. (V) restore, resurrect; 4. (N) restoration, resurrection; 5. *By extension* (M) united; 6. *By extension* (P) together.

tuqui[2] 1. *By extension from* **tuqui**[1] (V) grieve.

tuqui[3] 1. (V) touch.

tuquita[1] (*tukʷita*) 1. (V) torment, afflict.

tuquita[2] 1. (N) crowd.

tutca (*tutka*) TAWASA DIALECT *noun* 1. fire [Creek *tóˑtka* 'fire'] *see* **taca.**

tutu (*tutu*) 1. (V) provoke, incite; 2. (V) tempt; 3. (N) temptation.

TIMUCUA DICTIONARY

U

Text occurrences of words beginning in <*u*>+ vowel represent /*b*/ + vowel and are consequently given under **B** in the dictionary.

u (*u*) *particle* 1. no, not.

uba [**huba**] (*uba*) 1. (V) swim; 2. (V) *By extension* (V) catch [Alabama, Koasati *opahk-* 'swim'].

ube[1] [**ubue, vbue**] (*ube*) 1. (V) weep; 2. (N) grief.

ube[2] *particle* 1. on account of.

ube[3] *particle* 1. toward; 2. there.

ubeta [**ufueta**] (*ubeta*) *noun* 1. prostitute.

ubu (*ubu*) *noun* 1. widow, widower.

uchu (*uču*) *noun* 1. whale.

ucu[1] (7B) (*uku*) 1. (V/N) drink; 2. *By extension* (N) cup [Proto-Tucanoan **ũkũ* 'drink', Pre-Andine Maipuran *-ika* 'eat'].

ucu[2] 1. (V/N) cover

ucuchua (*uku-čua*) *noun* 1. door, gate (Der. *uku*[2] 'cover' + *chua* 'hole, opening') [Alabama, Koasati *okhiča* 'door'].

ucutu[1] (*ukutu*) 1. (V/N) need; 2. (N) necessities.

ucutu[2] 1. (N) end.

ufube (*ufube*) *noun* 1. grief. *Cf.* **ube**.

uhubi (*uhubi*) *noun* 1. grief; 2. *By extension* pain; 3. *By extension* sickness. *Cf.* **ube**, **ufube**.

ulechi (*uleči*) 1. (V) humiliate; 2. (N) humility.

ule (*ule*) *noun* 1. Term used by *ego* female only for her own children and the children of her sister.

uli (*uli*) *noun* 1. pot, pottery; 2. *By extension* drum [Spanish *olla* 'pot'].

ulubatari (*ulubatari*) *noun* 1. worker, laborer, workman.

una[1] (*una*) *particle* 1. if; 2. since.

una[2] 1. (N) body.

upa (*upa*) 1. (V) decay, rot; 2. (N) stench; 3. (V/N) stink.

upaha (*upaha*) 1. (V) taste, savor.

uqua[1] (*ukʷa*) *particle* 1. besides, in addition to.

uqua[2] 1. (V) undertake; 2. *By extension* (V) teach; 3. *By* *extension* (V) learn; 4. *By extension* (N) pupil, disciple.

uqua[3] 1. (V) obey.

uqua[4] 1. (N) forenoon, morning.

uqua[5] (*u-k^{w}a*) *particle* 1. not (Der. *u* 'not' + *-qua* 'copular, intensive'; *lit.* 'and not') {Proto-Muskogean **ik- . . . -a* 'not'].

uquale[1] (*uk^{w}ale*) *particle* 1. along with, side by side, by the side of, together (with), with, close to, close by; 2. *By extension* (V) bring, carry.

uquale[2] 1. (V) steal.

uque (*uk^{w}e*) *noun* 1. oil, grease; 2. *By extension* snare, trap.

ura (*ura*) *noun* 1. sport.

uri (*uri*) 1. (V) sweep.

uru (7B) (*uru*) 1. (V) accompany; 2. (V) come next, come afterward; 3. (P) accompanying, in the company of, together, with.

urunu (*urunu*) *particle* 1. same.

utasi(nino) (*utasi-nino*) 1. (V/N) attack, assault [Warao *ataihase* 'attack'].

utata (*utata*) *particle* 1. apart.

uti (*uti*) *noun* 1. earth; 2. land; 3. country; 4. world [Warao *-hota* 'high land, mountain', Baré *-ati* 'earth'].

utimala (*uti-ma-la*) *noun* 1. snake (Der. *uti* 'earth' + *-ma*[2] 'the' + *-la* 'proximate time'; *lit.* 'it is (of the) earth').

utina (*uti-na*) *noun* 1. region, province; 2. *By extension* (V) command; 3. *By extension* (N) power, (M) powerful (Der. *uti* 'land' + *-na* 'my').

utiti (*utiti*) *noun* 1. reverence.

V

All words beginning in <*v*> + vowel represent /*b*/ + vowel and are entered under **B** in the dictionary. The sole exception, always occurring with form-initial <*v*->, is given below.

vichubi (*bičubi*) 1. (V) break.

Y

-ya (8D) (*-ya*) 1. 2nd person possessive pronoun with nouns (= 'your', 'thy') [Warao *hia-* 'your', 'thy'].

ya[1] (*ya*) *particle* 1. no, not.

ya[2] 1. (N) satisfaction.

yaba (*yaba*) 1. (N/V) charm, spell; 2. (N/V) curse; 3. (V) threaten; 4. *By extension* (N) omen; 5. *By extension* (N) wizard, witch.

yabi[1] (*yabi*) *noun* 1. bone; 2. *By extension* (?) fishhook [Warao *yaba-* 'to fish'; Baré *-abi* 'bone', Piapoco *api* 'bone', Achagua *-ahe* 'bone'].

yabo (*yabo*) *noun* 1. majesty; 2. (M) majestic.

yaca (*yaka*) 1. (M) ignorant.

yacfa (*yakfa*) TAWASA DIALECT *particle* 1. one; 2. first. *Cf.* **yaucfa**. *Also see* **yaha**.

yacha (*yača*) *noun* 1. Term used by *ego* male for his sisters' children and the children of his mother's sisters (= 'niece', 'nephew', female maternal cross-cousins).

yache[1] (*yače*) *noun* 1. elderly person; 2. *specif.* old man, old woman; 3. *Specif.* great-grandmother; 4. (M) old.

yache[2] *noun* 1. corn-crib.

yachi (*yači*) *noun* 1. Term used by *ego* female for her elder sister.

yafaraba (*yafaraba*) *noun* 1. iron.

yaha (*yaha*) *particle* 1. one; 2. first; 3. (M) once; 4. (M) single, sole; 5. (M) limited; 6. (N) first-born.

yahati (yahati) *noun* 1. hunter.

yahi (*yahi*) *noun* 1. ax.

yala[1] (*yala*) 1. (N) feelings.

yaha[2] 1. (N) sorcery.

yala[3] 1. (M) clear; 2. (M) transparent, diaphonous.

yalaba (*yalaba*) *particle* 1. certainly.

yalabaquana (*yalabak*^{w}*ana*) *particle* 1. openly.

yale[1] (*yale*) 1. (V) watch, observe; 2. (V) guard; 3. (N) guardian; 4. (V) keep.

yale[2] 1. (V) bury.

yale[3] 1. (V) load; 2. *By extension* (V) embark.

yalu (*yalu*) *noun* 1. marsh, swamp.

yame[1] (*yame*) *noun* 1. Term used by *ego* male for his brothers' wives.

yame[2] 1. (V) add, count; 2. *By extension* (V/N) increase; 3. *By extension* (N) abundance.

yamu (7B) (*yamu*) 1. (V) weigh; 2. *By extension specif.* (M) heavy.

yanachu (*yanaču*) *particle* 1. and (contrastive), but, or.

yano (7A) (*yano*) *particle* 1. yes; 2. (V) affirm.

yanulema (*yan-ule-ma*) *noun* 1. Term used by *ego* female for a sister as the mother of a child (?).

yapi (*yapi*) *noun* 1. palm, palmetto.

-yaqe (*-yaqe*) 1. 2nd person plural subject with verbs in questions.

yaqequa (*yakek*^{w}*a*) *particle* 1. same; 2. one's own.

yaraha (*yaraha*) *noun* 1. panther, lion, wildcat [Gê Xavante *hu~ru* 'jaguar'].

yari (*yari*) 1. (V) march in line, move in a procession; 2. *By extension* (V) move quickly; 3. *By extension* (M) quickly.

yaru[1] (7B) (*yaru*) 1. (V) give (of one's own free will).

yau[2] 1. (V) tremble.

yata (*yata*) 1. (V) feel; 2. (M) felt.

yatacunachicosanco (*yatakunačiko-sa-n-ko*) *verb* 1. do (Der. ?).

yate[1] (*yate*) 1. (V) give; 2. *By extension* (V) administer.

yate[2] 1. (V) can, be able to.

yate[3] 1. (V) find.

yate[4] 1. (N/M) bad.

yati (*ya-ti*) *noun* 1. evil, bad; 2. *By extension* sin; 3. *By extension* (M) worthless; 4. *By extension* (V) offend (Der. *ya*[1] 'no, not' or *ya*[2] 'satisfaction' + *-ti* 'not'; *lit.* 'not' or 'no satisfaction').

yaucfa (*yaukfa*) TAWASA DIALECT *particle* 1. one; 2. first.

Cf. **yaha**. *See also* **yacfa**.

yayi[1] (*yayi*) 1. (N) strength, power; 2. *By extension* (N) power; 3. *By extension* (N) force; 4. *By extension* (M) important; 5. *By extension* (P) more, much; 6. *By extension* (N) virtue; 7. *By extension* (M) strong, powerful, forceful.

yayi[2] 1. (N) witness.

-ye (8D) (*-ye*) 1. 2nd person possessive pronoun with nouns (= 'your', 'thy').

yechi (*yeči*) 1. (V) ask; 2. (V/N) question.

yeho (7A) (*yeho*) 1. (V) rot.

yelo (*yelo*) *noun* 1. frost [Spanish *hielo* 'frost, ice'].

yemo (*yemo*) *particle* 1. aforesaid.

yereba (*yereba*) *noun* 1. weight. *Cf.* **hiereba** 'metal'.

yinti inino (*yi-n-ti ini-no*) *verb* 1. (V/N) sin. (Der, *ya²>y* 'satisfaction' + *ini>n* 'be' + *-ti* 'not' & *ini* 'be' + *-no* 'action designator'; *lit.* 'to be in an unsatisfactory situation').

yo[1] (*yo*) *particle* 1. that; 2. 'the one'; 3. *By extension* (?) part.

yo[2] *particle* 1. both.

yo[3] *particle* 1. 'the other place'.

yobo (*yobo*) *noun* 1. stone, rock [Achaguda, Goajiro, Piapoco *i-ba* 'stone, rock', Baré *-i-ba* 'stone, rock', Manao *i-pa* 'stone, rock'].

yoco (7A) (*yoko*) 1. (V) terrify; 2. (N) terror; 3. *By extension* (V/N) blame.

yoho[1] (*yoho*) 1. (V) run.

yoho[2] 1. (V) succor.

yolo (7A) (*yolo*) 1. (V) become.

yoloqua (*yolo-k^{w}a*) *verb* 1. grow old (Der. *yolo* 'become' + *qua* 'distant time indicator').

yoloquala (*yolo-k^{w}a-la*) *verb* 1. (M) old, aged (Der. *yoloqua* 'grow old' + *-la* 'proximate time').

yo manta (*yo manta*) *particle* 1. exclamation of fear or terror.

yoroba (*yoroba*) *noun* 1. snake, serpent, viper [Lokono *óri* 'snake', Warao *ni-hara-baka* 'cayman'].

yoso (*yoso*) 1. (M) lukewarm.

yualu (7B) (*yualu*) 1. (V) save, liberate, free.

yuba[1] [**yuba**] (*yuba*) *particle* 1. above; 2. *By extension* (V) go beyond.

yuba[2] *particle* 1. behind, back (of); 2. *By extension* (N) sodomy.

yuba[3] *particle* 1. more than.

yube (*yube*) 1. (N) wound.

yucha (*yuča*) *particle* 1. two; 2. second.

yuchi[1] (*yuči*) 1. (V/N) insult, affront; 2. *By extension* (V) cry out; 3. *By extension* (V) confess.

yuchi[2] 1. (M) ashamed. Probably by extension from **yuchi**[1].

yuchino (*yučino*) *noun* 1. male genitalia.

yucsa (*yuksa*) TAWASA DIALECT *particle* 1. two; 2. second *see* **yucha**.

yucuta (*yukuta*) *noun* 1. wild berry.

yunco (*yunko*) *noun* 1. frost.

yuparala (*yupara-la*) *verb* 1. have wrinkles; 2. (M) wrinkled.

yuqua (*yuk*^{w}*a*) *noun* 1. past.

yuque[1] (*yuk*^{w}*e*) 1. (N) port, harbor, place of embarkation; 2. *By extension* (N) wharf; 3. *By extension* (V) arrive by sea.

yuque[4] 1. (N) the last.

yurico (7A) (*yuriko*) 1. (V) be angry; 2. (V) offend; 3. (N) anger, vexation; 4. (M) angry [Warao *oriki* 'anger'].

yururuca (*yururuka*) *noun* 1. (N/M) sweet.

yutusu (*yutusu*) 1. (V) stir a fire; 2. *By extension* (V) incite, inflame.

4 ENGLISH – TIMUCUA INDEX

4 ENGLISH-TIMUCUA INDEX

This section should be used solely as an index to the English meanings of Timucua forms. It is not intended as a dictionary in any sense, but simply as a guide to refer the interested reader to a fuller treatment of each form in the dictionary itself.

A

abandon Hani.
abandon oneself to pleasure Epesoha.
abhor Napura, putu, femiti, haraca.
able, to be Ane, hela, lehe, mo, yate, iso, nahi, he-.
abominable Equentequa.
about Cabichi, naba, nahela, qela.
about to Nahomo.
above Abo, yuba, ofue.
absence Hela.
absolution Chale.
absolve Chale, balu.
abstain Hani.
abundance Yame.
abundantly Bicota, otorota.
accompany Uru, quitulu.
accomplish Palu, isa, picha, pichi.
accuse Man.

ENGLISH-TIMUCUA INDEX

acid	Hiqitima.
acorn	Tucu, aha.
add	Chica, yame, punu, pira, nayame.
administer	Yate, malu.
admiration	Quo, colahayo, quale.
admonish	Isi.
adore	Ete.
adorn oneself	Quanu, nahulu.
adultery	Huta, pata.
advance, in	Ecoya.
advantage	Nahio.
adversary	Iri.
advice	Orobo.
advocate	Ebe, ara.
adze	Pesola, pulu.
affable	Cume.
affection	Niho.
affirm	Mo, isi, yano, hibatelaqeno.
afflict	Tuquita.
afflicted	Hachinara.
affront	Ica, yuchi.
aforesaid	Quene, yemo.
after	Qere, ocho, ofue.
after, to be	Napirala.
afternoon	Fori, ilaqi.
afterwards	Ofue, hiqui, quenele.
again	Acu.
against	Emo.
age, to	Yoloquala.
agent	Sono.
agree	Isi, man.
agreeable	Man, sa, isaco, hachihiati.
ah!	A, aé, áe, cha.
alas!	see **ah!**
alive	Balu.
all	Tooma, achico, acu, amiro, atimo, ico, inemi, mirica, ocora.

ENGLISH-TIMUCUA INDEX

alligator	Itori.
all together	Into.
alone	Yaha, isimi, maha.
along with	Uquale.
already	Lenaqe, aqio.
also	Tacu, natela.
altar	Altari.
although	Hanima, hacu, intichiqe, tacu.
always	Maha, chiqe, nanemi.
ancestors	Iqui.
ancient	Atafi, pacha, nariba, iqui.
and	Acu, hacu, leqe, qe, qui, te, yanacu.
anew	Ele.
angel	Angelil.
anger	Polon, chuteo, yurico.
angry	Cato, chuteo, yurico, ica, siso, qili, naquate.
animal	Hachipile.
anoint	Qitu, ibi.
another	Acu, eyo.
ant	Suluquita.
anthill	Suluquita pahama.
any	Acu, maha, mo.
anyone	Hacha.
anything	Hacha, ine, pachiqua.
apart	Abi, haba, chiqeta, namoqua, sacasisota, utata.
appear	Mosi, ene, hura, tarua, leba.
apprehension	Maha.
apprentice	Mochase.
approach	Mi.
arise	Tuqui.
arms	Pisoco, achitilo, hachinoroco.
around	Naba, pari.
arrange	Qebe.
arrange the hair	Quanu.
arrive	Mi, pona, tafarela, nataite.

ENGLISH-TIMUCUA INDEX

arrive by sea	Yuque.
arrive, not to	Tuba.
arrow	Atulu.
as	Quimo.
as follows	Quene, nanacu.
ascend	Iqi.
ashamed	Yuchi.
ashes	Api.
ask	Bele, iquito, lapu, tamalo, yechi.
ask for	Lapu.
asleep	Neca.
assault	Utasinino.
assembly	Ocora.
assist	Ebe, huta.
associated	Ocora.
at once	Naquana.
attack	Iri, utasinino, qe.
attack, order an	Iqua.
attain	Mi.
attention	Cume, noro.
attention, with	Noro, melaba.
augur	Ihoto.
augment	Aro.
aunt	Isa, neba, nibe.
avenge	Chiqi, ichiqi.
await	Behe, ibatele.
away	Huri, naba, nuque.
away from	Haba.
ax	Cocho, yahi.

B

bachelor	Pacano.
back	Yuba.
back of	Yuba, ocho.

ENGLISH-TIMUCUA INDEX

bad	Istico, inti, yate, yati.
bad things	Hachinarami.
bald	Calaba, hele.
bank	Basala.
baptism	Chie, ipo.
bark (tree)	Anapie, cupa.
basis	Machi.
basket	Hachi, canasta.
bathe	Ibi, iqe, culafo, samo, suquo.
be	Ano, ea, bahesi, haquentama, ine, fa, le, lenima, leta, nahan, nahela, nahi, hatela, -no, cantela, panta, toto, hana, quanta, mo, moha, monima.
be so	Eyamoheco, fano, quene.
be that	Isote.
be, wont to	Hiba.
beans	Saliqi.
bear (animal)	Ara.
bear	Ino, uqua.
beat	Aboto.
beautiful	Isa, asa, bapi, cachu.
beauty	Isa.
because	Nanacu, quene.
become	Yolo.
bed	Acata.
before	Anta, mucu, pachique.
before (position)	Ecoyo, emo, mucu.
beg	Fete, tamalo, lapu.
beget	Siqi.
begin	Ichito.
beginning	Ichito, qibe.
begrudge	Piqi.
behave	Man.
behind	Ocho, yuba.
belch	Chaqui, moqeti, qere.
belief	Boho.
believe	Boho, cume.

ENGLISH-TIMUCUA INDEX

below	Pata.
beneath	Acata.
benefit	Inino, pichi, huru.
berry (palmetto)	Apu.
besides	Ofue, uqua.
best	Tera.
better	Tera.
between	Quimosi.
bewitch	Ipo, oroba, ituhu.
beyond	Ofue.
beyond, to go	Aro, pira, yuba.
bile	Atimucu.
billiards (?)	Torobo.
bird	Chulufi.
biscuit	Bizcocho.
bite	Ichico.
bitter	Melo, hiqiti, cachi, nararaca.
black	Chucu, laca.
blackness	Chucu.
black drink	Casino.
blacksmith	Areca, hiereba.
blade	Pesa.
blame	Yoco.
blaspheme	Mele.
bleach	Nayo.
bleat	Heba.
blind	Helo, naco.
blood	Isi.
blow, to	Ipo, pata.
blue	Lico.
boat	Tico.
body	Oco, una.
bolster	Beqenino.
bone	Yabi.
book	Chara.
boot	Ichiqeche.
border	Tiqi.

bore	Icho, ihoto.
born	Nata, ule, aruqui.
borrow	Fete, hete.
both	Atimo, yo, quene.
bow (for arrows)	Colo.
bowman	Hapetaque, colo.
box	Aye.
boy	Aruqui, alifila, chiri, huru, biro, pequata.
brains	Sili.
bread	Pesolo.
break	Iparu, pala, bichubi.
break a law	Icatu.
breast	Cume, chocolo.
brief	Talaca.
brightness	Caro.
bring	Pona, uquale.
broken	Yame.
brother	Amita, niho, piliqua, yacha, yachi, yuba.
brother (elder)	Ecoya, hiosa, miso, niha.
brother-in-law	Tafi, tasi, yame, iquilo.
brow	Chito.
bruise	Qe.
bunch of grapes	Bihi.
burn	Taca, natoya, quela, tori.
burned	Niho.
bury	Ebacalealeno, tuque, yale.
but	Hacu, nacu, yanacu.
butcher shop	Soba, mahaqua.
buy	Mahaqua.
buzzard	Apohola.
by	Beta.

ENGLISH-TIMUCUA INDEX

C

cabin	Pile.
call	Heba, ma, mo, isi.
call upon	Bele, tamalo.
can (be able to)	Ane, hela, moha, he-.
canal	Ibi.
candle	Amara, taca.
candlewood	Siricale.
cannot	Aneca.
canoe	Tico.
capture	Hibi.
carbon	Chu, taca.
care for	Hoto.
carefully	Soti.
careless	Pacanihino.
caress	Cobo.
carpenter	Areca, aye, ema.
carry	Uquale, ecataqere, ihoco.
carry away	Ichu, nuque, pia.
casina	Casino.
cast out	Narutuqua.
cat	Gato
catch	Ebeta, uba.
catch fish	Quela.
catechism	Talaca.
cause	Iquimi, chie, isa, iso, mo, so.
cease	Hani, homa.
censure	Mele.
ceremony	Isi.
certain	Leta, mani, quene.
certainly	O.
change	Chiqi.
channel	Ibi.
charcoal	Chu, taca.
charity	Hoba, iqilaba, melaba.

ENGLISH-TIMUCUA INDEX

charm	Yaba, ipo, ituhu.
chaste	Quo.
chastity	Haba.
cherish	Cobo, homa.
chestnut	Afeta.
chicken	Caya.
chief	Holata, parucusi.
child	Aruqui, qie, ahono, aiman(ta), ebo, piliqua, siqi, oroco, ule.
childless (?)	Ule.
chisel	Icho, ihoto.
choir	Elo.
choke	Ipo.
Christian	Christiano.
church	Iglesia, diosi pahama.
circle about	Parifo.
citizen	Hica, chia, maca.
city	hica.
civility	Cume, chale.
clan	Hasomi.
clarity	Caro.
claws	Qepe.
clay	Iqe.
clean	Qepe, chale, iqe.
cleansing	Chaleca.
clear	Ique, caro, ea, perefo.
clear of	Yala.
clearing	Abara.
clearly	Nela.
clearness	Caro.
clod	Asisi.
close to	Ataro, pacu, eqete.
close by	Eqete, uquale.
closely	Tuluqua.
cloth	Amuna.
clothe	Abi.
clothing	Abi, amuna, amala.

coal	Chale.
coal fire	Taca.
cobbler	Paru.
cohabit	Huta, pata.
cold	Patu, ichicosa.
colored	Curu.
combat	Qili.
Come!	Into.
come	Hime, isaco, mi, nataitema, pona.
come afterwards	Uru.
come in	Eca, echa.
come next	Uru.
come out	Toco.
come to die	Nahomo.
come together	Nata.
command	Ma, mo, utina.
commandment	Man, cube, heba.
commit	Ine, inino.
commonly	Inibo, namono.
companion	Ocora.
compassion	Cume, melaba, hio, qilabo.
compassionate	Cume, ebahio.
compensation	Hachi.
complaint	Hachinara.
complete	Hani, homa, naho, picha, pita.
comply with	Iqui, picha.
compound	Iso.
conceal	Piqui, chiqe.
concern	Taqua.
concerning	Emo.
concert	Aho.
conclude	Hiqui.
concubine	Nia.
condemn	Calubo.
condense	Tuluqua.
condiment	Tabi.
condition	Sario.

confess	Orobo, yuchi.
confession	Orobo.
confessional	Orobo.
confinement	Eta.
confirm	Coto.
conform	Chala.
congregation	Ocora.
conjure	Itufa, ituhu.
conjurer	Itufa.
consecrate	Chie.
consent	Man, mo, pale.
consider	Areca, cume.
consort	Inihi.
consult	Ene.
consume	Core, pia.
contempt, hold in	Napura.
contempt, gesture	Piri.
contend	pera(mo), namere.
content	Isaco.
contented	Cume, orabo.
contentment	Orabo.
continually	Tuluqua, pira.
contradict	(Ta)qe.
contrary to	Aiman(ta).
contrition	Qilabo.
convalescence	Yabi.
cook	Gisano
cook fried cakes	Quiti.
cool	Hiamiauqa, ichicosa.
corn	Tapola, hola.
corn, the first	Hola.
corn crib	Abo pahama, pile, yache(ba).
corner	Oto.
corner, inside	Oyo.
corral	Apalu.
correct	Ma.
council	Orobo.

counsel	Areca, cume, orobisti.
counselor	Inihama, anacotima.
count	Yame.
counters	Iribo.
country	Uti.
courage	Yayi.
cousin	Ama, amita, aruqui, hiosa, niha, qie, yachi.
cover	Cuque, ucu, paca, naquilu.
cover (house)	Naquilu.
cover (plants)	Nacumono.
covet	Cura, cuna, man.
cowardly	Tapa, sipaca.
crackle (fire)	Isi.
cranberry (?)	Yucuta.
crane	Sicuri.
crazed	Echa, isu.
crazy	Mareheba.
create	Areca, chie, siqi.
creation	Areca.
creator	Areca, siqi.
criticize	Sara.
crop	Abara, baca, hola.
cross (noun)	Crusi.
cross (verb)	Abaca, basala.
crow (noun)	Caca.
crowd	Mocoro, tuquita.
crucify	Caco.
crush	Iparu, iqui.
cry	Iqua.
cry out	Yuchi.
cunning	Orobisti.
cup	Ucu.
cure	Ororbo, balu, hiomi, imo.
curse	Choya, hio, quiri, yaba.
custom	Cume.
cut	Cocho, cala, foro.

but open	Pali.
cutter	Cocho.

D

dally	Equete.
damage	Ate, ine, istico.
damsel	Aquita.
dance	Muqua.
dark	Chucu, laca.
daughter	Amita, ahono, chiri, pacano, piliqua, qie, ule, yuba.
daughter-in-law	Nubo, qiso, tafi, yame.
day	Ela, equela, nabucha.
dead	Nitimu, niroco, nihi, iqui.
death	Nihi.
debt	Ehe
decay	Upa.
decayed	Iqui.
deceased	Aiman(ta).
deceitful	Orobo.
deceive	Chala.
deception	Chala.
deck	Quanu.
declare	Aho, isi, tolobo.
decorate	Naquilu.
deed	Inino, ino, iso.
deep	Pata.
deer	Honoso.
defeat	Iqui.
defecate	Pala.
defend	Ebe.
delight	Nacupa, nula, pana, cobo.
delight oneself	Nimi.
delightful	Cachu, chico, isaco.

deliver	Huri, naca.
demon	Hiti.
demonstrate	Ene.
deny	Huri.
depreciate	Man.
deprivation	Hani.
depths	Machi.
descend into	Tapita.
descendant	Aruqui, hasomi.
descended from	Uqua.
desecrate	Maha, mele.
desire	Cume, mani, nacupa, qi, toco.
desire to drink	Neca.
despise	Caqui, chequa, hara, man, napura, noti, talama.
despised	Fara, femiti.
dessert	Core.
destroy	Iqui, yame.
devil	Hiti, miso.
devoted	Cume, hoba.
devotion, with	Melaba, noro.
dew	Iba, ibi.
diaphanous	Yala.
die	Iqui, nihi, tani.
dig	Pulu.
diligence	Eqe, hiri, qiti.
diligently	Qiti, soti, hiri, fere, hapetaqua.
diminished	Tuluqua.
diminution	Chichi.
direct	Ma.
directly	Tomo.
dirt	Chucu, qisa.
disable	Aneca.
disability	Aneca.
disagree	Haba.
disappear	Hura.
discharge	Ichu.

disciple	Discipulo, mochase, uqua.
discontinued	Isaco.
discord	Cai.
disemboweled	Icho.
disgrace	Chacaba.
disgrace, cause	Quiri.
disgust	Polon.
dish	Plato.
dishonor	Iquiti.
disinherit	Narutuqua.
disobey	Boyoti.
disorder, walk in	Sacasisota.
disordered	Tacuba.
disorderly	Cachhu.
dispose	Qeba(ni).
disposition	Cume.
dispute	Ica, siso.
disrespectful	Iqibi.
distance, at a	Nahi, colala.
distant	Bio.
distribute	Isaqi.
disturb	(Ta)qe.
disturbed	Choya.
disturbed in mind	Qili.
ditch	Pocha.
do	Areca, chie, ine, ino, isa, iso, inino, mo, quoso, yatacunachicosanco.
do quickly	Qiti.
doctor	Ituhu, orobo, isu.
doctrine	Ituhu.
dog	Efa.
doing	Iso.
door	Ucuchua.
double	Pacu.
doubt	Bayeti.
doubt, be in	Mucu, colahayo.
dove	Obe.

downcast	Enemi, quanimaca, nuba.
downward, to face	Nuba.
drag	Abota, qere, pili.
draw	Abota, qere.
draw out	Abota, qere.
drawing	Nibi.
dream	Hiqi.
dress	Quanu, abi.
drink	Ucu, ibi, mayu.
drink, desire to	Neca.
drive away	Hibi, ichu.
drop	Chola, chota, hocho.
drown	Mofa.
drum	Cane, sula, uli.
drunkard	Boco.
drunken, be	Boco.
dumpling	Chicolata, pilene.
dung	Asurupa.
dust	Api, qisa.
dwell	Hiba.
dwelling	Paha.
dyer	Chucu.

E

each	Reqe.
ear	Tiqi, metele (of an owl).
earnestly	Yame.
earth	Uti, iqe, iparu, acatala.
easy	Hiamiqua.
eat	He, ho, iparu, isotamale.
eat, have to	Cana.
eat something by grinding	Iparu.
eat with	Tabi.
eel	Caraca, sea, iyorona.

ENGLISH-TIMUCUA INDEX

effect	Iso, nahe.
efficacy	Iso.
eight	Piqinahu.
eject	Fa.
elder	Ecoya.
elevate	Acoro.
embarcation point	Yuque, cafa.
embark	Yale.
embrace	Tipari, habo, tara.
embroil	Naqi.
empty	Puchu.
emulate	Abo.
enamored	Cachu.
encounter	Nacaqui, caco.
end	Hiqui, hani, homa, ucutu.
endow	Ela.
enemy	Iri.
engender	Paca, siqi.
enjoy	Nacupa, orabo, pana.
enjoyment	Pana.
enlighten	Caro.
enough	Ha, naba, ona, quale, pita.
ensign	Hachinoroco.
enter	Echa, eca.
entertain	Coboso.
entirely	Ebele, coco.
entrust	Naca.
envy	Piqi.
equal	Eca, qua.
erase	Qere.
erect	Ete.
escape	Piqui.
especially	Qibe.
esteem	Ique, inocochie, nabo, naquo, eba, hituqua, quo.
eternal	Nanemi.
eternally	Nanemi.

evening	Ilaqe.
every	Acu, core, reqe, tooma.
everywhere	Paritima, reqe.
evil	Istico, chacaba, yati, iniba, maha.
exalt	Qua.
exaltation	Qua.
example	Orobo.
exchange	Chiqi, ichiqi, toi.
excrement	Ayahibanoma, asurupa.
exercise	Inino.
exert oneself	Abala.
exist	Areca.
exorcism	Ituhu.
expect	Behe.
expire	Nihi.
explain	Tolobo.
extinct	Niroco, nitimu.
extinguish	Timu.
extremity	Huru.
eye	Mucu.
eyebrow	Milisuru.

F

face	Mucu, nibi.
face downward	Nuba.
fail	Taima, tuba, chebe, hani, nahico.
fail to reach	Tuba.
faint	Mayu, nameya.
fair	Bapi, cachu.
faith	Behe, boho.
faithful	Nayuchami, boho, hacha.
fall	Biu, hocho, ete.
fall short	Nahico, tuba.
false	Tacuba.

ENGLISH-TIMUCUA INDEX

family	Hasomi.
famine	Cubita.
fancy (verb)	Cayo.
far	Bio, colala.
far away	Huri, haba.
farmer	Hulubo.
fast (verb)	Itori.
fat	Amara, neha.
father	Ite.
father-in-law	Nasi, nubo.
fathom	Pata.
fatigue	Pataqui.
fault	Chebe, iquimi.
favor	Namoqua, ara.
fear (exclamation)	Yo manta!, Qe!
fear	Paloco, neche.
fearless	Nayuchami.
feast	Coboso.
feather	Metele, tilo, cola.
feeble	Maca.
feebleness	Maca.
feel	Cume.
feelings	Yala.
female	Nia.
felt	Yata.
fence	Apalu.
ferret	Chiqua.
field	Eca, pile, abara.
fiesta	Fiesta.
fifth	Marua
fight	Ica, pera(mo), siso.
fight with	Putisi.
figure	Nibi.
file (verb)	Yari.
fill	Cumo.
filth	Asurupa.
filthy	Bara.

find	Yate.
finger ring	Epalu.
finish	Bara, hiqui, homa, pia, hani, pita.
finished	Atime.
fir	Taca.
fire-colored	Niho.
firm	Tari.
first	Yaha, qibe, mine.
firstborn	Yaha.
fish (noun)	Cuyu.
fish (as eaten)	Nataitema.
fish (verb)	Camapata, cuyu, quela.
fish basket	Puye.
fishhook	Yabi.
fish trap	Puye.
fish weir	Acatala, ichali.
fit	Chala.
five	Marua.
flagellation	Aboto.
flat	Queta.
flatness	Tapa.
flea	Ibi.
flee	Puru, putu.
flesh	Oco, soba.
flirt	Nula.
flood	Huque.
floor	Pecherereca.
flower	Chio.
fly	Arobotairibi, iribo, meya.
fly around	Parifo.
foam	Asisuqua.
fog	Licofaye.
food	Hono, soba.
fool	Nula.
foot	Ichiqi.
for	Beta, habeleta, habema, haleqe, iquimileqe.

forbid	Nahi.
force	Chocorino, eqe, yayi, tari.
forehead	Chito, sili.
forenoon	Uqua.
forest	Aya, huri.
forever	Nanemi.
forget	Paqe.
forgive	Man, paqe.
forgiveness	Man.
fort	Apalu.
fortitude	Yayi.
forward	Ecoyo.
four	Cheqeta.
fourth	Cheqeta.
fox	Habe.
fox (male)	Pufi.
fragments	Tiquire.
free	Huri.
freeze	Cala.
frequent	Fa, icacheti, cayo.
friend	Chico.
from	Ma, toco.
frost	Hutane, patu, torobo, yelo, yunco, epo, atimucu.
froth	Asisuqua.
fruit	Cala.
fry	Quiti.
fulfill	Iqui.

G

gain	Maha, mo.
gall	Atimucu.
gamble	Hapu.
game	Hapu.

ENGLISH-TIMUCUA INDEX

garrulous	Maracai.
gate	Ucuchua.
gather	Hebe.
generate	Ooboqi.
generations	Aruqui.
genitals (male)	Yuchino.
gentle	Cume.
gently	Cume, eani.
girl	Aquita, aruqui, chiri, siqi.
give	Huri, yaru, che, yate, quachi.
give nothing	Nate.
give oneself up to	Nate.
give quickly	Iso.
give spontaneously	Yaru.
give up	Hani.
gloomy	Niho.
glorify	Qua.
glorious	Chico.
glory	Iashio, isaco.
gnaw	Icaputa.
go	Aliho, abo, fa, ho, isaco, mi, nata, osobota, puen.
Go!	Into!
go apart	Ele.
go in	Echa, eca.
go in procession	Yari.
go out	Toco.
go quickly	Isapu.
go together	Nata.
go up to	Iqi.
god	Diosi.
godchild	Qiso.
goddaughter	Quilo, qiso.
godfather	Itora, qiso.
godmother	Quilo, nibira.
godson	Quilo.
gold	Hiyereba, nali.

ENGLISH-TIMUCUA INDEX

good Tera, isa, iniba.
good, to speak Iquito.
goodness Iniba.
gourd Chucu.
govern Ecoya.
governor Ecoya, itora.
grace Chico.
graceful Isa, tera.
gracious Sa.
granddaughter Quilo.
grandfather Itora.
grandmother Quilo, nibira.
grandson Qiso, quilo.
grant Chico.
grape (palmetto) Apu.
grape Bihi.
grasp Ebeta, huta.
grateful Quoso.
grave-digger Ebacalealeno.
gravy Neha.
grease Amara, neha, uque.
great Yayi, inibi, coco, mine, mora, noro, iyeno.
grt-grnddaughter Quilo.
grt-grndfather Itora, coesa, nariba.
grt-grndmother Yache, isa, quilo, nibira.
great-grandson Qiso, quilo.
greens Puya.
greet Hioco.
greyhound Efa.
grief Enemi, isticoco, yuchi, qilabo, ube, ufube, uhubi.
grieve Tuqui, man.
grind, with teeth Iparu.
groan Hachinarami.
ground (earth) Qisa.
grow Pocha.

grudge Qili.
guard Hoto, yale, epe.
guardian Nahi, yale.
guide Tomo.
guilt Iquimi.

H

habitation Paha.
hair Napona.
hair of the head Puchi.
hallow Abolo, qua.
hand Hue.
hands, with Penani.
handsome Sa, tera.
hang up Peqe.
hang upon Caco.
happen Iniqe.
happy Isaco, orabo.
hare Apichiara.
harm Ine, caluba.
harvest Abara, baca.
haste Bereta.
hasten Oso.
hastily Bereta, hapetaqua.
hat Chiqino.
hatch Chie.
hate Putu.
hateful Man.
have Hami, isote, nahi, ha-.
have, not to Cana.
have to eat Cana, nataitema.
haze Licofaye.
he Oqe, ma.
head Chito, cuna.

ENGLISH-TIMUCUA INDEX

heal	Aba, ebe, hiomi, hura, orobo.
health	Hima, hiomi.
heap together	Tuqui.
hear	Ocoto, tiqi.
heart	Cume.
heat	Heba, meta, niho.
heaven	Numa, nalimo.
heavy	Yamu.
heedless	Pacanihino.
hell	Ichira, hiti, infierno.
help	Ara, huta, ape, epa.
helper	Ara.
hen	Caya.
herb	Isu, nie, pole.
herbalist	Isu.
here	Ca, catoomohabela.
hide	Piqui, chiqe, pite.
highwayman	Fa.
hit	Eba, nequa.
hoe	Pesola, pulu.
hold	Iribo, man, nahi.
hole	Chua.
hollow out	Pulu.
honor	Aboqua, nabo, iquo, inocochie, quanu, nayele, quo, quoso.
hood	Iqi.
hook	Obo.
hope	Behe, bele.
horse	Caballo.
hot	Metaba, mela.
hour	Abi.
hour of	Nahomo.
house	Paha, anoti, elahiti.
how	Hacha.
how many	Chuca.
how often	Chuca.
however	Nacu.

howl	Bahuru, hachinacachi.
human	Ano.
humanity	Biro.
humble oneself	Polon.
humiliate	Ulechi.
humility	Ulechi.
hundred	Chupi.
hunger	Hono, cubita.
hungry	Hono.
hunt	Qe, bali, emi, iqui.
hunter	Bali, yahati.
hurricane	Huque.
hurry	Hete.
husband	Inihi.
husbandman	Hola.
hut	Pile.

I

I	Ho, honihe, na.
ice	Torobo, atimucu.
idol	Nibi.
if	Hana, heco, colahayo, na, tacu, una, cono, nacu.
ignominiously	Iquiti.
ignorant	Yaca, chaqueneti, mucu, choco.
Ilex vomitoria	Casino.
image	Nibi.
imitate	Iquente, cumen, ichiqe, naquero, nibi.
immediately	Aqio, naquana, qere, tomo.
impediment	Aneca.
important	Yayi.
impress	Cata, (ta)qe.
in	Eca, masi, paca, oyo, to.
in addition to	Uqua.

in company with	Uru.
in the air	Tola.
incite	Yutusu, tutu.
include	Homa.
increase	Yame.
increase beyond	Ita.
incur	Inino.
industry	Eqeta.
ineffective	Aneca.
infatuated with	Cachu.
infidel	Pira.
infinite	Homa.
inflame	Yutusu.
inflamed heart	Niho.
inform	Ma.
in front of	Emo.
injure	Paloco.
innocent	Qichi.
inquire	Iquito.
inside	Paca, naba, oyo.
inspiration	Cume.
instant	Abiti.
instant, in an	Abiti.
institute	Areca.
instruct	Eca, cume, nahiabo.
instruction	Cume.
instrument	Areca, chie, inoni, iso.
insult	Yuchi, iquiti.
intercede	Ebe.
intercessor	Ara.
interior	Oyo.
into	Echa, to.
inundation	Huque.
invisible	Ene.
invoke	Ituhu.
iron	Hiyereba, yafaraba.
irrigate	Nachiliqui.

is there not?	Toro.
it	Oqe, ma.

J

jest	Naquero.
join	Eca.
joined	Ocora, horo.
joy	Orabo, halaha, isaco, quo.
joy (expression of)	Hupep ie! Quale! A! Hachia!
joyous	Orabo.
judge	Areca, fara, sara, tacuba.
judgement	Sara.
jug	Saro.
just	Nasianele, tacuba, tera.

K

keep	Yale, ibatele.
kettle-drum	Cane, sula.
kill	Iqui, ilifo, nihi.
kind	Coesa, mo.
kindle a fire	Alata.
king	Rey.
kiss	Obacha.
kitchen	Hono.
knave	Istico.
kneel	Neqero.
knife	Picho, pali, pesa.
know	Isaco, nahiabo, tani, hi, nu, uqua.
knowledge	Man, nahiabo.

ENGLISH-TIMUCUA INDEX

L

labor	Isticoco, areca, tari.
laborer	Hulubo, ulubatari, tari.
lack	Chebe, hiri, intaribala, taima, tuba, hani.
ladle	Quiti.
lagoon	Ibi, camapata.
lake	Ibi, camapata.
lament	Mela.
lance	Ipunu.
land	Uti.
language	Heba.
large	Mine.
lascivious	Huta.
last	Homa, yuque, pira, tooma.
late	Fichi.
laugh	Iqibi, naqi.
laundress	Chara.
laurel	Naliqui, tola.
lavatory	Culafo.
law	Mani, cume.
lawless	Cachu.
lazily	Maca.
laziness	Beni, maca.
lazy	Alobo.
leading	Inibiti.
leaf, withered	Asileco.
leak	Epesoha.
lean	Tapa.
learn	Uqua, talaca.
leather	Hani, naha, to.
left	Eba.
left, to be	Inquenenela.
left, what is	Core.
lend	Hete.

lesser	Piri.
letter	Chara, nioco.
lewd	Beni.
lewdness	Beni.
liberate	Huri, epa, ibalu.
liberator	Huri.
lie (prevaricate)	Nura.
lie with	Ichu.
life	Balu.
light (noun)	Caro, taca, ea.
light (weight)	Afaba.
light a fire	Alata.
lighten	Mili.
lightly	Afa, inimi.
like	Chumosi, qua, quana, quene, quimo.
limited	Ita.
line	Qele.
lineage	Hasomi, qela.
lion	Hiyaraba, yaraha.
liquid	Ibi.
listen	Ocoto.
little	Chiri, inquenenela, huru, piri, qichi, mora, oroco, ule.
little by little	Eane.
live	Balu, hiba.
liver	Chofa.
load	Quoto, yale, iloco.
loan	Ehe, fete.
lock	Ataro.
long	Ihiriba.
long-established	Maquima.
look	Ene.
loosen	Chula, timoso.
lord	Ano, mine, hami.
lose	Benan, chebe, hocho, hani, melaba.
lose in gambling	Nihi.
loss	Chebe.

louse Hibe, iqe.
love Hoba, cume, huba, cachu, man, homa, cayo.
lover (male) Biro.
low Piri, flaco anorimati, chequama, faramiti, isinihimiti, pataquila, sipaca, tapa.
lower class Isticoco.
loyal Cobaqua.
loyalty Cobaqua.
lukewarm Yoso, maca, mero.
lungs Pielno.
lust Nacupa.
lust for Here, nacupa.

M

mad Mareheba.
maid Aquita.
mail Nioco.
maize Tapola.
majestic Yabo.
majesty Yabo.
make Areca, chie, iso, quoso.
make soup Quiti.
male Biro.
malice Maha.
malicious Orobo.
maliciousness Orobo.
man Biro, ano.
manner Iso, cume, mo.
manure Aururpa.
many Ara, puqua, inibi, inemi.
march in file Yari.
mark Qele, nibi.

marry	Hiba, inihi.
marsh	Hocha, yalu, machaba.
mass (religious)	Missa.
master	Ano.
master of	Yayi.
mean (unkind)	Anorimati, chequama, faramiti, isinihimiti, isi, pataquila, sipaca, tapa.
mean (verb)	Mo.
measure	Nahi, pata, pesanoma.
meat	Soba, picho.
meat store	Soba.
mediate	Ebe.
mediator	Ebe.
medicine	Meleni, niye.
medicine, to take	Ipo.
medicine man	Isu, isucu, yaba.
meditate	Mani.
meek	Cane.
meet	Nacaqui, namoyo.
melancholy	Niho.
melon	Meloni.
melon field	Melonipile.
melt	Quela, teyalo.
memory	Cume.
menstruate	Ibi.
merciful	Ebahio, cume, ma, melaba.
mercy	Cume, melaba, qilabo, hima, man.
merit	Yayi, inino, namoqua.
message	Nioco.
messenger	Nioco, chara.
midnight	Fichi.
milk	Iquine.
mind	Cume.
mingle	Chica.
miracle	Hiquo.
miraculous	Hiquo.

miraculously	Hiquo.
miserable	Sipaca, pataquila, isinihimiti, flaco.
misfortune	Chacaba, chequa, fara.
mist	Licofaye.
mistress	Nia.
mitigate	Nalepeti, naeye.
mix	Chica, ame, punu.
midday	Chito, iribo.
moccasin	Ichiqe.
mock	Beni, hio, nibi.
moderate	Hiamiqua, lepeti.
mollusk	Melo.
moment	Abi.
moment, in a	Abiti.
money	Hiyereba.
monk	Ite.
month	Acu.
moon	Acu.
more	Yayi, toca, toco, inibi, pira.
more than	Beta, yuba.
morning	Pilani, (na)bucha, becha.
morning, in the	Nayo, pilani.
mortal	Iquo.
most	Aco, ebele.
mother	Isa, nia, yanulema, yache, iquine.
mother-in-law	Nasi, nubo.
M-i-L of a chief	Iribo.
motive	Iniqe, uqua.
mountain	Aye.
mounted	Ehenta.
mouse	Nibilil.
mouth	Nipita.
move	Aro.
much	Ara, inibiti, intafayela, coco, ostobota, puqua, yayi.
mud	Iqe.
mulch	Nacume.

multiply	Ita, cato.
murky	Niho.
murmur	Iyobo, mo.

N

nail	Nachua.
name	Bisa, mo, ma, isi, heba.
near	Eqete, cabichi, qela, nahe, naheba.
neat	Isa.
necessities	Ucutu.
neck	Cuna.
need	Ucutu.
needs	Qe.
negate	Perefo.
neglect	Paca, hani.
negligent	Maca, pacanihino.
negligently	Maca.
neighbor	Mirica, ano.
nephew	Coni, ebo, ano, piliqua, ule.
nest	Chepa.
new	Chale, ele.
niece	Ebo, coni, piliqua, ule.
night	Ilaqe, pilani, nabucha.
nine	Peqecheqeta.
no	Ya, -ti, u.
no more	Ona.
noble	Itora, quo.
noon	Chito, iribo.
nose	Chini.
nostrils	Chini.
not	Ya, -ti.
nothing	Ya, -ti, ine, maha, toro.
nothing, to be	Yati.
novice	Mochase.

now	Aqio, heqe, cache, catoomahabela, leaqe, qete, hito.
now then	Into.

O

oak	Aha, tucu.
oar	Eba, cori, tola.
obedience	Boyoti, patafi.
obey	Uqua, boyoti, cobo.
obligation	Mo.
oblige	Nahi.
obscene	Coche.
obscure	Lacalaca, niho.
observe	Yale, ocoto.
obstinate	Namoro.
obstinately	Oyo.
occasion	Iniqe, uqua.
of	-si.
offence	Istico, caluba.
offend	Emo, yati, iquile, yurico, caluba, maha, mucu.
offensive	Iputu.
offer	Tacato, hio.
offering	Hio, taca.
Oh!	Á!, Aé!, Áe!, Cha!
Oh, if	Na.
Oh that	Inteca, cono, sicono.
oil	Uque.
old	Atafi, yache, iqui, yoloquala, maquima, pacha.
old man	Nariba, yache, (aon) miso.
old person	Nariba.
old woman	Yache.
omen	Yaba.

ENGLISH-TIMUCUA INDEX

omission Hani.
omit Hani.
on account of Iquimileqe, ube.
on the point of Naheme.
once Yaha.
one Yaha, mine, ocora, yo.
only Yaha, isimi, maha.
only-begotten Isimi.
open Chaba, ebe, fali, hayaro.
open (cut) Icho, palino.
opening Tolo.
openly Yalabaquana, nelacare.
opposite Neme.
oppress Tuqui.
or Yanacu.
ordain Areca.
order Isi, mo, ma.
order one's life Cume.
ordinarily Namono.
original sin Sulu.
orphan Piliqua.
other Eyo, toca.
ought Man.
out Huri.
out, to come Toco.
outside Haba, huri, uri.
overcome Faramiti, pataqui.
overturn Pilu.
owe Ehe.
owl Atofa, asacamaco, hitiqire, hororo.
own, one's Yaqequa.
own (verb) Hami, iso, nahi.
owner Hami.
oyster Sicali.

ENGLISH-TIMUCUA INDEX

P

paddle (noun)	Eba, tola, cori.
paddle (verb)	Abala.
paddle quickly	Isapu.
pagan	Istico.
pain	isticoco, uhubi.
paint	Nibi, quanu.
painter	Chara.
painting	Nibi.
pale	Mayu.
palm	Yapi.
palmetto	Yapi.
palmetto berry	Siapu.
panther	Hiyaraba, yaraha.
paper	Chara.
pardon	Chale, nate, chico, man.
parent	Ano.
part	Basala, yo, oco.
participate	Nasaqi.
particular	Naoqua, emo.
particularly	Namoqua, emo.
partridge	Caya.
party	Basala.
pass through/by	Qclc, basala, tasoro.
passion	Hachinara.
passion (Christian)	Habo, yaba.
past	Nanacu, pira, iqui, yuqua, mete.
path	Eye.
patience	Tari.
pay	Balua, chu, ehe.
pay attention	Cume.
pearl	Qereba.
pedigree	Hasomi.
penance	Balu.
penitence	Balu.

people	Ano.
perfect	Hana.
perform a ritual	Becha.
perhaps	Hana, colahayo.
perpetual	Nanomi.
persecution	Enemi, caqui.
persist	pera(mo).
person	Ano.
perspiration	Sile.
pertain	Taqua.
petition	Lapu.
picture	Nibi.
pierce	Icho, ihoto.
piety	Melaba, qilabo, hio.
pillow	Beqenino.
pious	Ebahio, cume, melaba.
pit	Chua.
pitch	Tiqui.
pity	Cume, melaba, qilabo, hio.
place	Tasi, to.
place, other	Yo.
plane (flat)	Queta.
plant	Isu, aso.
play	Mani, orabo, eqete.
play a game	Hapu.
please	Cobo.
pleasing	Isaco.
pleasure	Isaco.
plentiful	Bicota, ocorota.
plentifully	Bicota, ocorota.
plumage	Cola.
point out	Chano.
points	Iribo.
poke a fire	Yutusu.
pole	Aye, ema.
polish	Ique.
pollute	Pesa.

pond	Ibi, Tilono.
poor	Paqetosa.
port	Yuque, cafa.
portent	Ene.
possess	Hami, isote, nahi.
possessed	Echa.
possessed (demon)	Isu.
possessor	Hami.
post	Aye, ema, nioco.
postman	Chara.
pot	Uli.
pottage	Oco.
pottery	Uli.
pound up	Huya.
pour out	Toco.
poverty	Paqetosa.
power	Chocori, yayi, utina.
powerful	Aneca, yayi, nahi, noqua, utina.
powerless	Faramiti, sipaca.
praise	Iquo, inocochie, qunau, nabo, quo, quoso, nuba.
pray	Ituhu, tamalo.
prayer	Ituhu.
preach	Heba.
preceding	Mine.
precept	Heba.
precious	Quene.
pregnant	Ebo, eta.
prepare	Areca, beqelo, qeba(ni).
prescribe	Ma, mo.
present (verb)	Ape, hape.
presently	Aqio.
pretty	Bapi, sa, tera, cachu.
prevent	Aneca.
priest	Ite.
prince	Paracusi.
principal	Inibiti, qibe, mulu.

principally	Heqe, mulu, emo.
principle	Ichito.
prior (noun)	Mine.
privates (male)	Yuchino.
proceed	Toco.
process	Iso.
proclaim war	Iqua.
produce	Pocha.
promptly	Qiti, soti.
promptness	Hiri, qiti.
propagation	Isi.
property	Iso.
prostitute	Femitima, haraca, talama, noti, ubeta.
protect	Pata.
protestation	Tapo.
proudly	Soti.
provide	Qeba(ni), areca, nahio.
provoke	Man, tutu.
prune (noun)	Sibato.
publicly	Nela.
publish	Tolobo.
pull up	Iholo.
pulverize	Huya.
pumpkin	Chucu.
punish	Caluba.
punishment	Hachinara, caluba.
pupil	Uqua.
purchase	Mahaqua.
purgatory	Purgatorio.
purge	Nachiliqui.
purify	Chale, iqe.
purpose	Isamolacoco.
put	Tasi, to.
put into	Echa.
put on	Abi.

ENGLISH-TIMUCUA INDEX

Q

quagmire Hecha.
quarrel Ica, pera(mo), sare, siso, qili.
question Yechi.
quickly Bere, hapetaqua, hete, homo, yari, qiti, marema, ostanu, soti, mi, oso.
quickness Hiri.

R

rabbit Quelo.
raft Chique.
rain Huque, ibi, hiba.
rainbow Ibi.
raise Ete, acoro.
raise the eyes Maha.
rape Nu.
rascal Orobo.
rat Nibili.
ray of light Atulu.
reach Iquita.
reader Chara.
reason Iquimi.
reborn Eta.
receive Habo, uqua.
recognize Nahiabo, man.
red Pira.
redeem Huri.
refrigerate Ichicosa.
refuse Huri.
regale Coboso.
regard Uqua.
regenerate Balu.
regeneration Ele.

regret	Man.
regulation	Ibiri.
rejoice	Orabo, isaco.
related	Eta.
relation	Ano.
relationship	Ano, qela.
relative	Ano, miso.
relax	Chula.
relief	Afati.
relieved	Afati.
remain	Inquenenela, fa, hiba, iribo, nahi.
remedy	Haba, pichi.
renew	Ele.
renewal	Ele.
remove	Alabina.
renounce	Hani.
renovation	Ele.
repeat	Isi.
repeatedly	Tuluqua.
repent	Man.
replace	Ichiqe.
represent	Ene, nibi.
require	Lapu.
resident	Chiama.
resin	Tiqui.
resist	Iqili.
respect	Iquo, inocochie, qua.
respector	Quo.
resplendent	Caro, miya, mili, nahe.
responsible	Iqui.
rest	Isaco, machi, palucu.
resting place	Machi.
restore	Balu, fara, ipulu, canima, tuqui.
restrained	Cumemi.
resurrection	Balu, tuqui.
resuscitate	Balu.
retire	Quela.

return	Pilu, fare, toco, tuqui.
return something	Fari.
reveal	Caro, nahiabo.
revenge	Chiqi, ichiqi.
reverence	Cume, quoso, taca, utiti, nabo, nuba.
revive	Iqi, balu.
reward	Naho.
rich	Talaca.
ride	Ehenta.
ridicule	Hio.
right (correct)	Tomoti.
right (direction)	Fara.
ring	Epalu.
ripen	Bacara, nacume.
rise	Ete, iqi, iribo.
river	ibi.
road	Eye.
rock	Yobo.
rogue	Orobisti, istico.
roguish	Orobo.
roll about	Tipopili.
roof (noun)	Chito.
roof (verb)	Ucu.
rooster	Caya.
root	Ichaca, mulu.
rope	Amala, opomo.
rosin	Tiqui.
rot	Icho, upa.
round about	Pari.
row hard	Eba.
row quickly	Isapu.
rub	Napoti, pale.
rudeness	Beni.
ruin	Pataqui.
ruined	Isinihitimi, sipaca.
run	Abo, hitumo, yoho, isapu, oso, oco, oyo, toco.

run into problems	Oyo.
rupture	Apo.
rush	Hepo.

S

sackcloth	Amuna.
sacred person	Hio.
sacrifice	Hachi, tacato.
sacrament	Man.
sad	Enemi, istico, quanimaca, cume, niho, isaco.
sadden	Cume.
saint	Chico, santo.
sakiva	Halu.
salt	Api.
salutary	Tera, sa.
salute	Hioco.
salvation	Balu.
same	Yaqequa, qua, quanta, urunu.
same manner, in	Qele.
sanctify	Qua.
satisfaction	Ya, orabo, halaqua, quo, paqe.
satisfact., excl. of	Quale!, Á!, Hachia!
satisfied	Isaco, qere.
satisfy	Paqe.
save	Huri, balu, epa, ibalu.
savior	Epa, huri.
savor	Upaha.
saw (noun)	Seqe.
say	Abota, aho, asioqe, isi, mas, siso, tolo, heba, co, ma.
saying	Heba, isi.
scabby	Qepe.
scale a fish	Qeche.

ENGLISH-TIMUCUA INDEX

scalp	Napona.
scandal	Fara.
scandalize	Hiquo.
scarecrow	Aye.
scatter	Isaqi, tupi.
scorn	Napura, noti, mani, femiti, haraca.
scorpion	Silibacara.
scour	Ique.
scoundrel	Orobo.
scrape	Qere.
sea	Ibi, moca.
seal (verb)	Chie.
seamsttress	Amuna, chara, paru.
search	Hoto.
season	Ero.
second	Yucha.
second to	Pacano.
secretly	Lapa.
seduce	Huta.
see	Chano, ene.
seed	Asiquita.
seek	Qe.
seize	Huta.
seized	Ebe.
self	Isimi, coco, mache, qena, quana.
sell	Mahaqua.
send	Miso.
senile	Yoloqua.
senses	Sili.
sentence	Ma.
sentry box	Oqo.
separate	Eleta, haba, tupi.
sepulcher	Tuqua.
servant	Ate, cata, pequata, ino, cobo.
service	Ino, quoso.
set	Tasi.
set (sun)	Echa.

set up	Iribo, caqui.
settlement	Hica.
seven	Piqicha.
sew	Paru.
shady	Laca.
shake (cooking)	Quiti.
shake out	Puru.
share	Isaqi.
shatter	Pala.
shave	Cala.
she	Oqe, mine.
shed (noun)	Pile.
shed (verb)	Ipita, toco.
shell corn	Choho, puru.
shellfish	Esa, melo, honosta.
shine	Caro.
shining	Naheleco.
ship	Tico.
shoe	Ichiqe, sapato.
shoemaker	Paru, ichiqe.
shop	Mahaqua.
shoulder	Huqui, ocho.
shout	Iqua.
show	Ela, ene, tolobo.
shut	Maru.
sick	Iqilaba, sipaca, uhubi.
sickness	Iqilaba, qilabo.
side	Basala, oco.
side of	Uquale.
side, from side to	Basala.
sierra	Seqe.
sign	Hachinoroco, qele, nibi.
sign of the cross	Chie, qele.
signify	Isamolo, nibi.
silver	Hiyereba, nayo.
similar	Quene.
similar to	Qua.

simile	Quale.
sin	Intinino, iniheti, iquimi, ine, yati, istico, caluba.
since	Una.
sing	Elo, heba, nabucha, isi.
singer	Elo.
single	Yaha, pacano, maracai.
sir	Mine.
sister	Amita, hiosa, yacha, yachi, yuba, niha, niho, piliqua, poi.
sister-in-law	Tafi, yame, niquisa, tasi.
sit	Hiba.
six	Mareca.
skate	Echaca.
skin	Qechela, pequa.
sky	Numa, napula.
slave	Ate.
sleep	Hiqi, neca.
sleep with	Ichu.
sliver	Quara.
slothful	Maca.
slothfulness	Maca.
slowly	Beni.
slowness	Beni.
sly	Orobisti.
small	Chiri, uru, piri, qichi, ule.
smoke (noun)	Moco.
smoke (verb)	Ipopi, mayu.
snake	Elatubasa, iyola, yoroba.
snare	Uque.
sneeze	Atiqui, nahaqui.
snow	Nayo.
snuff up	Ipelo.
so	Qere, quene, eqe, iniqe, qua, quimo.
so, to be	Manan, nano.
so (Is that so?)	Chano?
sod	Asisi.

sodomite	Poranacu.
sodomy	Yuba.
softly	Eane.
soldier	Soldado.
sole	Yaha, isimi.
solely	Ita.
some	Yaha, maha.
something	Hachi, ine.
son	Chiri, qie, ahono, ule, yuba, pacano, piliqua, biro.
song	Elo.
son-in-law	Nasi, yame, qise, tafi.
soon	Marema, aquio.
sorcerer	Ituhu, isucu, yaba.
sorcery	Yala.
sort	Coesa, mo.
soul	Hiqiti.
spade	Pesola, pulu.
spatula	Quiti.
speak	Heba, ma, mo, isi.
speak, not to	Ate.
speak well	Qere.
speech	Heba, mo.
speed	Bereta.
spell (magic)	Yaba, oroba.
spill	Epesoha.
spinster	Pacano.
spirit	Atichicolo.
spirit, evil	Hiti.
spiritual relative	Hio.
spit	Tufa.
spittle	Halu.
splendor	Caro, naheleco.
splinters	Quara.
spoon	Quiti.
sport (verb)	Ura.
spouse	Hoto, inihi.

spot Qe.
spread Isaqi.
spy upon Paqe.
squash (vegetable) Chucu.
stale Atafi.
stand Ete, iribo.
stand up Iribo.
star Chubobo.
steal Nuque, uquale.
steer (verb) Foriso.
stench Upa.
step, at each Abiti.
stepfather Ite.
stepfather-in-law Quisoti.
stepmother Nibira.
stick Aye, ema.
stir Chica, quiti.
stir up the fire Yutusu.
stockade Apalu.
stone Yobo.
stop Hani, nanibeti.
storm Aqe, huque.
stoe Mahaqua.
storehouse Pile, abopaha.
straight Tomoti.
strangle Echa.
straw Echaca.
street Eye, paca.
strength Chocori, eqeta, yayi.
stretch Pata.
strife Cai.
strike Aboto.
strong Yayi, tari, chocori.
strongly Chocori.
stumble Aqui, ita.
stumbling Tiquemata.
subsequent Pacana.

subsequently	Qenele.
substance	Inino.
succeed in having	Nataite.
successor	Cobe.
succor	Ara, ebe, yobo.
such-&-such	Po.
suddenly	Hapetaque.
suffer	Hiyo, ino.
suffering	Hachinara, isticoco.
sufficient	Naqua.
suggest	Man.
suitable	Naeyanele.
sun	Ela.
supernatural	Hachitimo.
superstitious	Iqui.
supplicate	Tamalo.
surround	Patiro.
suspect	Caqui.
sustain	Esobo, he, iso, cobo, tari.
swamp	Hocha, machaba, yalu.
swan	Sicuri.
swear	Man, mo, tobo.
sweat	Sile.
sweep	Uri.
sweepings	Asurupa.
sweet	Yururuca.
sweetness	Oso.
swiftly	Afaquana.
swim	huba, uba.
sword-cutler	Mecalala.
symbol	Hachinoroco.

T

tail	Api.

tailor	Amuna, paru.
take	Huta.
take away	Nuquo, uqua.
take occasion to	Uqua.
take off	Ipita.
take with	Tabi.
taken	Ebeta.
talk	Mo.
tall	Ihiriba.
tamale	Chicolata pileno.
tambourine	Cane.
tar	Tiqui.
taste	Upaha.
teach	Eca, heba, natori, oho, uqua, isamolo, quachi.
teacher	Quachi.
tear (from eyes)	Ibi, mucu.
teat	Iquine.
tell	Mas, aho, heba, isi, ma, mo.
temper	Muti.
tempest	Napula.
temple	Diosi pahama.
tempt	Aho, hio, cume, tutu.
temptation	Hio, tutu.
ten	Tuma.
terminate	Hiqui.
termination	Hiqui.
terrify	Yoco.
terror	Yoco.
thank	Quoso.
That	Qe, ma, na, oohi, oca, oqe, oca, nano, eca, hami, yo, ca, maca, michu, mice, siqi, hachibono, catoomo.
that one	Hoqe, mistachicaqe, michu, mine.
that sort of thing	Po.
the	-ma, eca.
theft	Nuque.

then	Quene.
there	Heqe, qe, oqe, ona, ube.
these	Eca.
they	Oqecare.
thick from cold	Tuluqua.
thickly	Tuluqua.
thief	Nuque.
thin	Tapa.
thing	Hachi, apacha, ine, mo.
think	Cume, man, pali.
third	Hapu.
this	Ca, oca, ona, na.
thorn	Obo.
thou	Chi-, hochie, ya-.
though	Hacu.
thought	Man.
thoughtless	Pacanihino.
thousand	Chupi.
threaten	Yaba, nipati.
three	Hapu.
throat	Cuna.
through	Beta.
throw	Abota, fa, ecataqere.
throw away	Ichu.
throw down	Ichu, narutuquasota, nuba, peemo.
throw into	Ecataqere.
thunder	Ibora.
thunderbolt	Numa.
thus	Quene, qere, nano, quehasi, eqe.
tickle	Nula.
tie	Pile.
timber	Aye.
time	Abi, heqe, yuque.
time, it is	Cache.
tint	Naquilu.
tired	Pataquila, sipaca.
to	Emo, quimosi, -no.

ENGLISH-TIMUCUA INDEX

tobacco	Ipopi, hinino.
together	Ocora, tuqui, uquale, uru, horo, hoto, pasi.
together with	Uquale.
tomato	Sili.
tomb	Tuqua.
tomorrow	(Na)bucha, nayomoqe, pilani, becha.
tongue	Bali, ituqua, nipita.
torch	Siricale.
torment	Hachinara, isticoco, tuquita.
tornado	A̧qe.
torpor	Beni.
torture	Hachinara.
touch	Paqua, tuqui.
toward	Neme, beta, emo, ube.
town	Hica.
trade	Mahaqua.
trail	Eye.
transparency	Ea.
transparent	Ene, yala.
transplant	Iholo.
trap	Uque.
travel	Abo.
treat (by magic)	Oroba, orobo.
treatment	Iso.
tree	Aye.
tremble	Yaru, coyo.
tribulation	Hachinara.
tribute	Hachi.
trouble	Chuteo.
true	Nocomi, ona.
true, it is	Canola, nano.
truly	Quene, nocomi.
trust	Behe, bohe, naque, naca, naquo.
truth	Nocomi.
turf	Asisi.
turkey	Caya.

turn	Pilu.
turn about	Fori.
turn over	Tipopili.
turtle	Caramaba.
twin	Caru.
two	Yucha.

U

ultimately	Naho.
unable	Aneca, yate.
unchaste	Coche.
uncle	Ite, itora, nariba, neba.
unclean	Beni.
unction, extreme	Ibi.
under the earth	Acatala, naba.
understand	Mani, mucu, hituqua, nahiabo.
understanding	Nahiabo, orobo.
undertake	Ipitala.
ungrateful	Boyoti, cuyu.
unhonored	Nabo.
uninterruptedly	Naquana.
unite	Eca, hoto, huta.
unite with	Pata.
united	Ocora, tuqui, yaha.
unjustly	Tacuba.
unknown	Mucu.
unlearned	Nu.
unmarried	Pacano.
unwholesome	Beni.
up	Abo, tola.
uproot	Iholo.
upset	Pilu.
upward	Abo.
usage	Quoso.

use	Chie.
useful	Nahio.
utter	Heba, mo.

V

vacant	Puchu.
vacillate	Bayeti.
vainly	Maha.
vanish	Taima.
variegated	Nanareqe.
vassal	Cata, pequata.
vegetables	Puya.
vehemently	Soti.
venal	Iquo.
venerable	Quo.
venerate	Iquo, inocochie, qua, nabe, nariba, quo.
veneration	Qua.
venerator	Quo.
vengeance	Ichiqi.
very	Aco, ebele, yayi, coco, mora, pacha.
vexation	Chuteo, yurico.
vexed	Qere, chuteo.
vicar	Chiqi, ichiqi.
vile	Anorimati, chequama, faramiti, isinihimiti, pataquila, sipaca.
villain	Istico.
village	Hica.
violate	Nu.
viper	Iyola, yoroba, elatubasa.
virgin	Aquita.
virtue	Chocori, yayi, inino, iso, cume, tera.
viscosity	Ata.
visible	Ene.

vision	Ene.
voice	Cuna.
vomit	Hono, pilu.

W

wager	Qiruma.
waist	Eta.
wait for	Behe.
walk	Abi, aliho, hebetota, itinochiqequana.
walk apart	Eleta.
walk out	Toco.
walk quickly	Iso, qiti.
walk to and fro	Tipopili.
wander	Abo.
want	Is, man.
wanting	Ari.
war	Iri, putu.
war against	putisi.
war councilor	Heba, iri.
war cry	Iqua.
war prince	Paracusi.
warm	Metaba, mela.
warmth	Meta.
warrior	Iri.
wash	Chale, iqa, culafo, nachiliqui, samo.
wash one's hands	Coreso.
wash a wound	Queta.
watch	Hoto, behe, epe, yale, ibatele.
watch, to keep	Cabichi, nulufo.
water	Ibi.
watermelon	Sandia.
wave (water)	Ibi.
way	Coesa.

way, in that	Quene, quimo.
we	Heca.
weak	Fara, mayu, noqua.
weaken	Chula, mero.
weakened	Sipaca.
weakness	Maca.
weapons	Achitilo.
wearied	Pataquila.
weasel	Chiqua.
weave	Polo.
weaving stick	Polo.
weed	Isu.
weep	Ube.
weigh	Pesanoma, yamu.
weight	Pesanoma, yereba.
well (adverb)	Tera, balu, nela.
Well then!	Hito!
whale	Uchu.
wharf	Yuque, cafa.
what	Cha, quene, hacha, qe.
whatever	Hacha, qe, quene, reqe.
when	Haleqe, heqe, nahomo, qere.
whence	Cha, hacha.
where	Cha, hacha, qe.
which	Quene, michu.
while	Bete, qere.
whip	Aboto.
whistle	Elo.
white	Nayo.
whither	Cha, hacha.
whitish	Qepe.
who	Quene, chitaco, chonco, michu.
wholesome	Isa.
why	Hacha.
wicked	Anorimati, chequama.
wickedness	Iniba.
widow	Uba.

widower	Uba.
wide	Inihi.
will (noun)	Cume, man, mani.
win	Iqui.
wind	Aca, haca, aqe, ichira.
window	Tilipachua, fali.
wine	Ibi.
wine shop	Mahaqua.
winter	Ichira.
wisdom	Orobo.
wise	Orobo.
wish	Qi, man, cume, iso.
witch	Yaba.
with	Ocora, uquale, uru, quale, quana.
with pleasure	Halaqua.
withdraw	Quela, toco.
wither	Quela.
within	Oyo, naba.
without	Toro, hani, horo, cana.
witness	Yayi.
wizard	Itufa, miso, isucu, yaba.
wolf	Banehe.
woman	Nia.
woman, old	Yache.
womb	Eta.
wont	Hana, colahayo, hiba, fa, narutuquasota.
wood	Aye, ema.
woodpecker	Tinibo.
word	Heba, isi.
work	Ine, inino, iso, ino.
workman	Ulubatari.
world	Uti.
worm	Icho.
worship	Ete.
worth	Mo.
worthless	Sipaca, yati.

worthy	Namoqua, lehe, noti, iso.
worthy of being	Hemosi.
Would that!	Iteca!, Cono!, Sicono!, Hero!
wound	Qele, tasoro, eba, chipa, yube, qe, nacacha.
wound with words	Cato.
wrangle	Namoro, pera(mo).
wretched	Faramiti, sipaca, flaco.
wrinkles	Yuparala.
write	Chara.
writer	Chara.
writhe	Tipopili.

Y

yard (measure)	Ema.
year	Ero.
yellow	Nali.
yes	Yano, o, hana, canola.
yesterday	Qibo.
you	Chi-, hochie, -ya, -ye.
young	Chiri.
youth	Halifila.

5 INDEX OF AFFIXES & AFFIX COMBINATIONS

5 INDEX OF AFFIXES & AFFIX COMBINATIONS

1. PREFIXES

chi-	2nd person verbal subject (initial position); 2nd verbal object (second position).
ho-	1. *ho*[1]- lst person verbal subject (initial position); 1st person verbal object (second position). 2. *ho*[2]- pronoun designator in *honihe* 'I' and *hochie* 'you' only.
na-	Nominalizes the base to which it is attached (V>N).
ni-	lst person verbal subject (initial position); lst person verbal object (second position).

2. PREFIX COMBINATIONS

chiho-	'You' (subject) + 'me' (object) of verb.
chini-	'You' (subject) + 'me' (object) of verb.
hochi-	'I' (subject) + 'you' (object) of verb.
nichi-	'I' (subject) + 'you' (object) of verb.

3. SUFFIXES

-ba	lst or 2nd person plural verb subject (= 'we', 'you'). Verb designative suffix.
-be	Durative aspect indicator with verbs (= progressive tenses). Verb inflectional suffix.
-bi	Bounded action indicator with verbs (= past tenses). Verb inflectional suffix.

INDEX OF AFFIXES

-bo lst or 2nd person plural verb subject (= 'we', 'you'). Verb-designative suffix.

-ca Plural indicator with pronouns, nouns, verbs, and particles. Non-specific suffix.

-che Imperative mode indicator with verbs. Verb inflectional suffix.

-chu Perfective action indicator with verbs (= 'has', 'have', 'had'). Verb inflectional suffix.

-co Conditional action indicator with verbs (= 'may', 'might'). Verb-inflectional suffix.

-cu Subjunctive mode indicator with verbs (= 'if'). Verb-inflectional suffix.

-la Proximate time indicator with verbs (= 'now', regardless of tense). Verb inflectional suffix.

-le Proximate time indicator with verbs (= 'now', regardless of tense). Verb inflectional suffix.

-ma

1. *-ma*[1] Possession indicator with nouns (usually 'his', 'her', 'its', but may be used with any person). Noun inflectional suffix.
2. *-ma*[2] Definite goal-marker with nouns (= 'the'). Noun-designative suffix.
3. *-ma*[3] 3rd person plural verb subject (= 'they'). Verb-designative suffix.
4. *-ma*[4] Proximate time indicator with verbs (= 'now', regardless of tense). Verb inflectional suffix.

-mi

1. *-ma*[1] Possession indicator with nouns (usually = 'his', 'her', 'its', but may be used with any person). Noun inflectional suffix.
2. *-ma*[2] Definite goal-marker with nouns (= 'the'). Noun-designative suffix.

-mo

1. *-ma*[2] Definite goal-marker with nouns (= 'the'). Noun-designative suffix.
2. *-ma*[3] 3rd person plural verb subject (= 'they'). Verb-designative suffix.

-n

1. *-no*[1] 1 Active voice suffix with verbs. Verb-deriving suffix.

2. *-no*[2] Proximate time indicator with verbs (= 'now' regardless of tense). Verb inflectional suffix.

-na 1. *-na*[1] lst person possessive pronoun with nouns (= 'my', 'our'). Noun inflectional suffix. ALSO USED, rarely, at the end of finite verb forms to designate lst person singular verb subject, especially in questions.

2. *-na*[2] Durative aspect indicator with verbs (= progressive tenses). Verb inflectional suffix.

3. *-na*[3] Habitual/Iterative verbal action (= 'usually', 'again'). Verb inflectional suffix.

-ni 1. *-na*[1] lst person possessive pronoun with nouns (= 'my', 'our'). Noun inflectional suffix.

2. *-na*[3] Habitual/Iterative verbal action (= 'usually', 'again'). Verb inflectional suffix.

3. *-no*[1] Active voice suffix with verbs. Verb-deriving suffix.

-no 1. *-no*[1] Active voice suffix with verbs. Verb-deriving suffix.

2. *-no*[2] Proximate time indicator with verbs (= 'now', regardless of tense). Verb inflectional suffix.

-nu *-no*[1] Active voice suffix with verbs. Verb-deriving suffix. At the end of a lexeme usually = 'to' + verb base.

-o Punctual-Intensive emphasis with verbs. Verb inflectional suffix.

-qe Optative mode indicator with verbs (= 'may', 'might'). Verb inflectional suffix.

-qua Distant time indicator with verbs. Verb inflectional suffix.

-re Noun combining-form suffix (usually = plural). Noun-designative suffix.

-s *-so* Trans. verb indicator. Verb-deriving suffix.

-sa *-so* Trans. verb indicator. Verb-deriving suffix.

INDEX OF AFFIXES

-se 1. *-si*^{1} Reflexive/reciprocal goal-marker with nouns, verbs, and particles (= 'self'). Non-specific inflectional suffix.
2. *-so* Transitive verb indicator. Verb-deriving suffix.

-si 1. *-si*^{1} Reflexive/reciprocal goal-marker with nouns, verbs, and particles (= 'self'). Non-specific inflectional suffix.
2. *-si*^{2} Potential action aspect indicator with verbs (= 'perhaps', 'if'). Verb inflectional suffix.
3. *-so* Transitive verb indicator. Verb-deriving suffix.

-siba Frequent-action indicator, deriving nouns from verbs (= '-ative' as in 'talkative').

-so Transitive verb indicator. Verb-deriving suffix.

-su Transitive verb indicator. Verb-deriving suffix.

-ta Durative aspect indicator with verbs (= progressive tenses). Verb inflectional suffix.

-te Same as *-ta*.

-ta Same as *-te*, *-ta*.

-tiacu Proximate time indicator with verbs (= 'now'). Verb inflectional suffix.

-tooma Plural with nouns (= '-s'). Noun-designating suffix.

-ya 2nd person possessive pronoun with nouns (= 'your'). Noun inflectional suffix. ALSO USED, rarely, at the end of finite verb forms to designate 2nd person singular verb forms, especially in questions.

-ye Same as *-ya* with the same nominal and verbal uses.

4. FREQUENT SUFFIX COMBINATIONS

-belehanima 'Will always be . . . ' (Future Durative Proximate action).

INDEX OF AFFIXES

-bila	'Was . . .', '. . . was done' (Bounded Proximate action).
-bile	Same as *-bila.*
-bilehabela	'Shall have . . . ' (Future Bounded Durative Proximate action).
-bileqe	'If I were . . . ' (Bounded Proximate Optative action).
-bima	'Was . . . ' , '. . . was done' (Bounded Proximate action).
-bino	Same as *-bima.*
-care	Noun plural (= '-s').
-chica	2nd person plural subject with verbs (in questions).
-chunu	'Have always done . . ' (Perfective Habitual action).
-conacu	'If I may . . . ' (Conditional Habitual Subjunctive action).
-coqua	'Might have . . . ' (Conditional Distant action).
-habe	Imperative (Future Durative action).
-habela	'Shall be doing . . . ' (Future Durative Proximate action)
-habele	Same as *-habela.*
-hache	Imperative (Future Imperative action).
-hale	Imperative (Future Proximate action).
-hana	'Shall always do . . . ' (Future Habitual action).
-hanano	'Shall be doing . . . ' (Future Durative Proximate action).
-hanima	Same as *-hanano.*
-hano	Imperative (Future Proximate action).
-hateno	'Shall be doing . . . ' (Future Durative Proximate action).
-hela	'Can do . . . ' (Potential Proximate action).
-maqua	'In the . . . '
-mitila	'Their'.
-mitile	Same as *-mitila.*
-nica	1st person plural subject with verbs (in questions).

-nihero	'If I could . . . ' (Potential Durative action).
-noma	Instrument by which an action is performed.
-nte	'It is . . . '
-tele	Present tense (Durative Proximate action).
-tele	Same as *-tele.*
-tala	Same as *-tele, -tela.*
-tema	'The one who . . . '
-teno	Present tense (Durative Proximate action).
-tequa	Past tense (Durative Distant action).
-yaqe	2nd person plural subject with verbs (in questions).

5. ENCLITICS

-cho	Interrogative post-clitic.
-co	1. Interrogative post-clitic.
	2. Generalizing post-clitic (= 'the one who').
-có(co)	1. 'And'.
	2. Augmentative or intensive post-clitic.
-lechu	Vocative post-clitic.
-leqe	'And'.
-qi	1. Intensive post-clitic.
	2. Pointer (= 'that').
-qua	1. 'And'.
	2. Intensive post-clitic.
	3. Pointer (= 'that').
-qui	'And'.
-te	'And'.
-ti	Negative post-clitic.

6 FORMS CITED FROM OTHER LANGUAGES

6 FORMS CITED FROM OTHER LANGUAGES

GENERAL ALPHABETICAL LISTING

Only native American lexical forms are included in this alphabetical listing. Spanish forms are given in the second section of this index only.

A

a-	Warao	he, she, it
aba	Warao	put
aba	Chibcha	maize
abani	Warao	slow
ada	Lokono	tree
**abi*	Proto-Muskogean	kill
ahi	Warao	to cut
ahi	Hitchiti	tree
aiko	Matagalpa	moon
aiku	Cacaopera	moon
ak-	Alabama	he, this, that
aka·ka	Alabama	chicken
ak^{w}eru	Warao	border, coast
**ak^{w}i*	Proto-Muskogean	water
ale	Arekena	sun
-ali	Goajiro	sun
-ali	Piapoco	man
ampeki	Cuna	10
api	Piapoco	bone

FORMS CITED

araka	Warao	younger brother
arao	Warao	people
ari-	Warao	harvest
atabu	Warao	arrow
ataiihase	Warao	attack
atasa	Apalachee	war-club
atta	Cuna	hand
attale	Cuna	5
awa	Culino	tree
axo-nihino	Saixa (Chocó)	sun

B

ba-halo	Layaná	mouth
-bïta	Chacobo	with
-bo	Chacobo	noun plural
boe	Yaruro	star
bok	Choctaw	river
-buhu	Warao	can, be able

C

-ča	Cuna	perfect tense
časi	Alabama	maize
čayahli	Koasati	to walk
či	Choctaw	thou
čïkï	Chacobo	black
-čo	Chacobo	behind
čokpi	Ala., Koasati	100
čõ˙pi	Ala., Koasati	big, large
ču	Timote, Cuica	bird
č-u-pana	Carútana	liver

D

-dike	Lokono	ear
[*dokia*]	Warao	flame

FORMS CITED

[*duru-duru*]	Warao	alligator

E

(h)edexo	Chocó	moon
ehewere	Warao	sing, cradle song
eku-	Warao	enter
eku	Warao	in
emoera	Warao	to be soft
ena-	Genl. N. Maipuran	man
epa	Manare	maize
-eri	Taino	man
-eri	Tariana, Piapoco	moon
eri-	Amarizana	fire
eri	Achagua	sun, day

H

ha-	Warao	have
ha-	Warao	stop
hahinai	Warao	lose
haka	Warao	wind (noun)
hapi	Alabama, Koasati, Choctaw	salt
haši	Alabama	sun
háu	Island Carib	eat
-he	Achagua	hand
-he	Goajiro	future tense
-he	Choctaw	future tense
he	Waliperi	eat
(h)edexo	Chocó	moon
hepü	Canamarí	2
hi-	Warao	you (sg.)
hia-	Warao	you (sg .)
hiniha	Creek	councilman
(h)-ipe	Piapoco	earth
hiya	Baré	rain

FORMS CITED

ho-	Warao	eat
hoa	Warao	curse
hobi	Warao	drink
holahta	Apalachee	chief
hota	Warao	high land, mountain
hu	Xavante	jaguar
hua	Chocó	hand
hunu	Warao	shrimp
huya	Goajiro	rain
hynino	Taíno	tobacco

I

i-ba	Achagua, Goajiro, Piapoco	stone
ičina	Natchez	he
ifa	Koasati	dog
**ife*	Proto-Arawakan	capybara
i-ha	Achagua	eat
**ik . . .-a*	Proto-Muskogean	not
-ika	General Pre-Andine Maipuran	eat
i-ku-buti	Culino	kneel
i-lači-nu	Piro	night
ina-	Baré, Tariana, Baniva, Piapoco, Achagua	woman
ine	Warao	I
i-pa	Manao	stone
-ipá	Koasati	eat
-i-p/bi	Baré, Tariana, Arekena, Carútana	good
isa	Genl. N. Maipuran	good
isa	Marawa	blood
**iSo*	Proto-Tucano	alligator
iskí	Koasati	mother
itae	Chocó	mouth
iti	Catapolítani	blood

it^hi	Lokono	father
itopa	Choctaw	mouth
i-w-ita	Piapoco, Catapolítani	head
iya	Cuna	rain
**(iy)akare*	Proto-Arawakan	alligator

K

ka-	Warao	1 pl.
-ka	Warao	diminutive
-ka(ya)	Chacobo	here
**kač-*	Proto-Muskogean	cut
kači	General Pre-Andine Maipuran	cold
k-ači	Lokono	moon
kara-	Culino	strong
**kasero/katsero*	Proto-Tucanoan	skin, tree bark
k-e	Yavitero	moon
-ki	Chacobo	conditional
k-i	Baré	moon
-ko	Warao	optative
kobe	Warao	heart, breast, chest
-kore	Warao	simultaneous, conditional action
kore	Chocó	alligator
-ku	Warao	subjunctive
kukle	Cuna	7
kuku	Warao	cover
kulu·si	Koasati	bird
-kuna	Warao	subjunctive
kü-una	Manao	head
-k^wa	Brunca	tongue
k^wa	Manare	tongue
k^wa-	Cuna	1
k^wena	Cuna	1
k^wĩ mare	Chocó	5, 4

FORMS CITED

L

-la	Cuna	Present tense
lal	Mískito	head
la·na	Alabama, Koasati	yellow
la·ni	Creek	yellow
lel	Cuna	head
loča	Alabama, Koasati	dirty, black

M

ma-	Warao	1 sg.
-ma	Warao	goal-marker
-ma(la)	Cuna	plural
(k^{w}ĩ) mare	Chocó	5, 4
mata	Mískito	hand
matalal	Mískito	5
matasip	Mískito	5
m-axi	Yamamadí	sun
-mehere	Warao	desire
miłli	Apalachee	clean
miłł-n	Koasati	clean
misi	Warao	devil
-mo	Warao	plural agent
moi	Warao	to blow
mo·k	Atakapa	go
mon-uka	Warao	equal
mu	Warao	eye
muču·	Choctaw	wink

N

-na-	Chacobo	become
-na	Warao	V>N
-na	Cuna	present tense
na-	Warao	kill
naa-	Cuna	go
n-abi	Baré	bone
nahobo	Warao	know

naka	Warao	fall
nao-	Warao	come
-ne	Warao	gerundive
nea	Machiguenga	see
nerk^{w}*a*	Cuna	6
-ni~-ne~-n	Island Carib	1st singular
nibora	Warao	man
niha	Koasati	fat
ni-hara-baka	Warao	alligator
nihta	Alabama	day
niiskana	Cuna	stars
n-ika	Baré	bite
niła	Alabama	night
**niNaki*	Proto-Muskogean	night
nõhõ	Warao	hunger
noko	Warao	hear
-nollo	Chacobo	locative intrans.
-nollošọ	Chacobo	locative trans.
nu-	Baré	know
**nuči-*	Proto-Muskogean	sleep

O

obo	Warao	love
ohia	Warao	fox
oka	Campa	this
o-kera	Warao	light
okhiča	Alabama, Koasati	door
opahk-	Alabama, Koasati	swim
ora	Campa	that
óri	Lokono	snake
oriki	Warao	anger
orobo	Remokamekran	jaguar
oropa	Aponegikran	jaguar
ošta·ka	Alabama, Koasati	4

FORMS CITED

P

-pa	Gen'l Arawakan	number-designator
-(r)pa(a)	Cuna	noun plural
pa-	Gen'l E. Maipuran	house
pa(a)	Cuna	3
paak^{w}*a*	Cuna	third
paapakka	Cuna	8
-pak	Twahka (Paya)	noun plural
pakke	Cuna	5
pakkepakka	Cuna	9
pá'län ku-siä^{n}	Yuchi	village chief
pe-	Goajiro	house
pe	Chocó	maize
pi-	Apolista	house
-pi(i)	Cuna	plural
-p/bi	Gen'l N. Maipuran	hand
pičika	Shipibo-Conibo	5
pička	Quechua	5
pišika	Cavineña, Reyesano	5
p-k^{w}*a*	Chibcha	tongue
po-	Guahibo	house
po(o)	Cuna	2
**poa*	Proto-Tucanoan	hair
puru	Paumarí	black

R

ɼaku	Warao	uncle
r-ati	Baré	earth
-rau	Twahka (Paya)	noun plural
-re	Gen'l Arawakan	noun combining-form
rokia	Warao	flame
rop	Kayapó	jaguar
-(r)pa(a)	Cuna	noun plural
ru	Xavante	jaguar

ruru-ruru	Warao	alligator

S

-sebe	Warao	quantitative
-si	Warao	goal-marker
sina	Warao	who
sip	Miskito	complete
so	Warao	excrement
-ṣ̌o	Chacobo	transitive
soke	Cuna	say
so-poro	Terena	maize

T

-ta	Warao	occurrence-momentaneous
-tae	Cuna	habitual action
taera	Warao	strong
tak-	Gen'l Pre-Andine Maipuran	sun
tali	Baniva	mouth
-te	Campa	not
teki	Manao	ear
-ti	Warao	occurrence-durative
-ti	Cuna	V>N
-ti	Alabama, Koasati	not
t-i-ba	Baré	stone
tikba	Alabama, Koasati	fire
t-ike	Gen'l E. Maipuran	fire
tin	Ulua	hand
titi	Gen'l Pre-Andine Maipuran	fire
toma	Warao	meat
tó·tka	Creek	fire
tsi-iki	Culino	earth

*tsomi	Proto-Pre-Andine Maipuran	heart, breast, chest
tso-poro	Guaná	maize
tsu-huri	Culino	heart, breast, chest
ts-uma	Canamarí	back
tuke	Sumu, Ulua	tongue
tu-ulu	Chamicuro	heart, breast, chest
-tuma	Warao	noun plural

U

_-u_	Warao	intensive
uamala	Cuna	fish (noun pl.)
_u-be_	Yamamadí	house
uce	Cuna	hot
uku	Manao	eye
*ũkũ	Proto-Tucanoan	drink
ula	Natchez	snake
*umk^{w}a	Proto-Muskogean	rain
uni	Baré	water

W

_wa-_	Cuna	tongue
_wa-_	Baré, Apolista, Ipuriná	hand
_*wã_	Proto-Tucanoan	hand
waiku	Sumu	moon
waniku	Warao	moon
-wari	Warao	long
waro~waru	Yanomamo	man
wayli(n)	Apalachee	border, edge
_we-_	Piro, Lokono	hand
weni	Baniva, Yavitero, Maipuré	water
_-wi-_	Baniva, Piapoco	star

wi	Yaruro	water
wiri	Warao	to paddle
wivi	Esmeralda	water

X

*(x^{w}u/hu)pun-	Proto-Muskogean	go

Y

-ya	Cuna	present tense
yaba	Warao	to fish
y-ahe	Achagua	bone
-yana	Warao	not
yatu-	Warao	2d plural
yiwara	Warao	finish

Z

*zie	Proto-Tucanoan	blood

ALPHABETICAL LISTING BY LANGUAGE

Non-Timucua forms are arranged below alphabetically by language stock or family and, within each stock, by group.

1. ARAWAKAN

PROTO-ARAWAKAN

*ife	capybara
*(iy)akare	alligator

GENERAL ARAWAKAN

-pa	number-designator
-re	noun combining-form

FORMS CITED

NON-MAIPURAN ARAWAKAN

APOLISTA

	pi-	house
	wa-	hand

CHAMICURO

	tu-ulu	heart, breast, chest

CULINO

	awa	tree
	i-ki-buti	kneel
	kara-	strong
	tsu-huri	heart, breast, chest

PAUMARÍ

	puru	black

YAMAMADÍ

	m-axi	sun
	u-be	house

SOUTHERN MAIPURAN

GUANÁ

	tso-poro	maize

LAYANÁ

	ba-halo	mouth

TERENA

	so-poro	maize

PRE-ANDINE MAIPURAN

GENERAL

	-ika	eat
	kači	cold
	tak-	sun
	titi	fire

PROTO-

	**tsomi*	heart, breast, chest

FORMS CITED

CAMPA		
	oka	this
	ora	that
	-te	not
CANAMARÍ		
	hepü	2
	ts-uma	back
IPURINÁ		
	wa-	hand
MACHIGUENGA		
	nea	see
PIRO		
	i-lači-nu	night
EASTERN MAIPURAN		
GENERAL		
	pa-	house
	t-ike	fire
BANIVA		
	ina-	woman
	tali	mouth
	weni	water
	-wi-	star
YAVITERO		
	k-e	moon
	wenu	water
NORTHERN MAIPURAN		
GENERAL		
	ena-	man
	isa	good
	-p/bi	hand
ACHAGUA		
	eri	sun, day
	-he	hand
	i-ba	stone
	i-ha	eat
	ina-	woman

FORMS CITED

	y-ahe	bone
AMARIZANA		
	eri-	fire
AREKENA		
	ale	sun
	-i-p/bi	tail
BARÉ		
	hiya	rain
	ina-	woman
	-i-p/bi	tail
	k-i	moon
	n-abi	bone
	n-ika	bite
	nu-	know
	r-ati	earth
	t-i-ba	stone
	uni	water
	wa-	hand
CARÚTANA		
	č-u-pana	liver
	-i-p/bi	tail
CATAPOLÍTANI		
	iti	blood
	i-w-ita	head
GOAJIRO		
	-ali	sun
	-he	future tense
	huya	rain
	i-ba	stone
ISLAND CARIB		
	háu	eat
	-ni~-ne~-n	1st singular
LOKONO		
	ada	tree
	-dike	ear
	$it^{h}i$	father

	k-ači	moon
	óri	snake
MAIPURÉ		
	weni	water
MANAO		
	i-pa	stone
	kü-na	head
	teki	ear
	uku	eye
MARAWÁ		
	isa	blood
PIAPOCO		
	-ali	man
	api	bone
	-eri	moon
	(h)-ipe	earth
	i-ba	stone
	ina-	woman
	-i-w-ita	head
	-wi-	star
TAÍNO		
	-eri	man
	hynino	tobacco
TARIANA		
	-eri	moon
	ina-	woman
	-i-pb/i	tail
WALIPERI		
	he	eat

2. ATAKAPA

mo˙k	go

FORMS CITED

3. GÊ

APONEGIKRAN		
	oropa	jaguar
KAYAPÓ		
	rop	jaguar
REMOKAMEKRAN		
	orobo	jaguar
XAVANTE		
	hu~ru	jaguar

4. GUAHIBAN

GUAHIBO		
	po-	house

5. MACRO-CHIBCHAN

CHIBCHAN

BRUNCA		
	-k^{w}a	tongue
CHIBCHA		
	aba	maize
	p-k^{w}a	tongue
CUICA		
	ču	bird
CUNA		
	ampeki	10
	atta	hand
	attale	5
	-ča	perfect tense
	iya	rain
	kukle	7
	k^{w}a	1
	k^{w}ena	1
	-la	present tense
	lel	head
	-ma(la)	plural

FORMS CITED

	-na	present tense
	naa-	go
	nerk^{w}a	6
	niiskana	stars
	-(r)pa(a)	noun plural
	pa(a)	3
	paak^{w}a	third
	paapakka	8
	pakke	4
	pakkepakka	9
	-pi(i)	plural
	po(o)	2
	soke	say
	-tae	habitual action
	-ti	V>N
	uamala	fish (noun pl.)
	uce	hot
	wa-	tongue
	-ya	present tense
MANARE		
	epa	maize
	k^{w}a	tongue
TIMOTE		
	ču	bird
MISUMALPAN		
CACAOPERA		
	aiku	moon
MATAGALPA		
	aiko	moon
MÍSKITO		
	lal	head
	mata	hand
	matalal	5
	matasip	5
	sip	complete
SUMU		
	tuke	tongue

FORMS CITED

	waiku	moon
TWAHKA (PAYA)		
	-pak	noun plural
	-rau	noun plural
ULUA		
	tin	hand
	tuke	tongue
PAEZAN		
CHOCÓ		
	axo-nihino	sun
	(h)edexo	moon
	hua	hand
	itae	mouth
	kore	alligator
	k^{w}ĩ mare	5, 4
	pe	maize
WAROID		
WARAO		
	a-	he, she, it
	aba	put
	abani	slow
	ahi	to cut
	ak^{w}eru	border, coast
	araka	younger brother
	arao	people
	ari-	harvest
	atabu	arrow
	ataihase	attack
	-buhu	can, be able to
	[*dokia*]	flame
	[*duru-duru*]	alligator
	ehewere	sing, cradle song
	eku-	enter
	eku	in

FORMS CITED

emoera	be soft
ha-	have
ha-	stop
hahinai	lose
haka	wind (noun)
hi-	you (sg.)
hia-	you (sg.)
ho-	eat
hoa	curse
hobi	drink
hota	high land, mountain
hunu	shrimp
ine	I
ka-	1st plural
-ka	diminutive
-ko	optative
kobe	heart, breast, chest
-kore	simultaneous, conditional action
-ku	subjunctive
-kuna	subjunctive
ma-	1st singular
-ma	goal-marker
-mehere	desire
misi	devil
-mo	plural agent
moi	to blow
mon-uka	equal
mu	eye
-na	V>N
na-	kill
nahobo	know
naka	fall
nao-	come
-ne	gerundive
nibora	man
ni-hara-baka	alligator

	nõhõ	hunger
	noko	hear
	obo	love
	ohia	fox
	o-kera	light
	oriki	anger
	raku	uncle
	rokia	flame
	ruru-ruru	alligator
	-sebe	quantitative
	si	goal-marker
	sina	who
	so	excrement
	-ta	occurrence-momentaneous
	-ti	occurrence-durative
	toma	meat
	-tuma	noun plural
	-u	intensive
	waniku	moon
	-wari	long
	wiri	to paddle
	yaba	to fish
	-yana	not
	yatu-	2d plural
	yiwara	finish
YANOMAMA		
	waro~waru	man
YARURO		
ESMERALDA		
	wivi	water
YARURO		
	boe	star
	wi	water

FORMS CITED

6. MUSKOGEAN

PROTO-MUSKOGEAN

**abi*	kill
**ak*^{w}*i*	water
**ik . . . -a*	not
**kač-*	cut
**niNaki*	night
**nuči-*	sleep
**umk*^{w}*a*	rain
**(x*^{w}*u/hu)pun-*	go

EASTERN MUSKOGEAN

ALABAMA

ak-	he, this, that
aka·ka	chicken
čaši	maize
čokpi	100
čõ·pi	big, large
hapi	salt
haši	sun
la·na	yellow
loča	dirty, black
nihta	day
niła	night
okhiča	door
opahk-	swim
ošta·ka	4
-ti	not
tikba	fire

APALACHEE

atasa	war-club
holahta	chief
miłli	clean
wayli(n)	border, edge

CREEK

hiniha	councilman
la·ni	yellow

	tó·tka	fire
HITCHITI		
	ahi	tree
KOASATI		
	čayahli	to walk
	čokpi	100
	čõ·pi	big, large
	hapi	salt
	ifa	dog
	iskí	mother
	kulu·si	bird
	la·na	yellow
	loča	dirty, black
	miłł-n	clean
	niha	fat
	okhiča	door
	osta·ka	4
	-ti	not
	tikba	fire
WESTERN MUSKOGEAN		
CHOCTAW		
	bok	river
	či	thou
	hapi	salt
	-he	future tense
	itopa	mouth
	muču-	wink

7. NATCHEZ

	ula	snake

8. PANOAN

CHACOBO		
	-bïta	with
	-bo	noun plural

	čïkï	black
	-čo	behind
	-ka(ya)	here
	-ki	conditional
	-na-	become
	-noʔo	locative intransitive
	-noʔoṣo	locative transitive
	-ṣo	transitive
SHIPIBO-CONIBO		
	pičika	5

9. QUECHUA

QUECHUA		
	pička	5

10. TACANAN

CAVINEÑA		
	pišika	5
REYESANO		
	pišika	5

11. TUCANOAN

PROTO-TUCANOAN		
	**iSo(-ri)*	alligator
	**kasero*	skin, bark
	**katsero*	skin, bark
	**poa*	hair
	**ũkũ*	drink
	**wã*	hand
	**zie*	blood

12. TUPÍ

TUPINAMBÁ		
	yawar	jaguar

yakare	alligator

13. YUCHI

YUCHI

pá'län ku-siä^{n}	village chief

14. SPANISH

altar	altar
angel	angel
bizcocho	biscuit
canasta	basket
Christiano	Christian
discipulo	disciple
fiesta	fiesta
flaco	wretched
gato	cat
gisano	*guisar* cook (verb)
iglesia	church
infierno	hell
lucha	fight
missa	mass
melon	melon
pesa	weight
picu	arrow
plato	dish
purgatorio	purgatory
rey	king
sandia	watermelon
santo	saint
sapato	shoe
saro	jar
soldado	soldier
olla	pot
yelo (hielo)	frost

BIBLIOGRAPHY

BIBLIOGRAPHY

Adam, Lucien and **Julian Vinson, eds.**

1886 *Arte de la Lengva Timvquana, compvesto en 1614 por el Pe Francisco Pareja, y publicado conforme al ejemplar original único.* Bibliothèque Linguistique Américaine, t. xi, Maisonneuve Frères et Ch. Leclerc Éditeurs, Paris.

Archivo General de Indias (Sevilla)

1621 [Petition to the Spanish Crown] San Agustín, 1 setiembre 1621. 53-2-11.

1651 [Letter from Manuel, Cacique of Asile, Spanish by Fr. Alonso Escudero] San Agustín, 9 diciembre 1651. Escribanía de Cámara, Legajo 155, folios 380-383.

Barral, Basílio María de

1957 *Diccionario Guarao-Español, español-Guarao.* Monografías N°3, Sociedad de ciencias naturales La Salle, Editorial Sucre, Caracas.

Borhegyi, Stephen

1959 Pre-Columbian Cultural Connections between Meso-America and Ecuador. *Middle American Research Records*, vol. 2, no. 6, pp. 141-155.

Brinton, Daniel Garrison

1858 *Notes of the Floridian Peninsula.* Philadelphia.

Broadbent, Sylvia

1957 Rumsen I: Methods of Reconstitution. *International Journal of American Linguistics*, 23:275-280.

Bullen, Ripley P.

1972 The Orange Period of Peninsular Florida. *Fiber-Tempered Pottery in Southeastern United States and*

Northern Colombia: Its Origins, Context, and Significance, ed. by Ripley P. Bullen and James B. Stoltman. Florida Anthropological Society, *Publications 6*, pp. 9-33.

1978 Tocobaga Indians and Safety Harbor Culture. *Tacachale*, ed. by Jerald Milanich and Samuel Proctor, University Presses of Florida, Gainesville, pp. 50-58.

Campbell, Lyle

1979 Middle American Languages. *The Languages of Native America*, University of Texas Press, Austin, pp. 902-1000.

Claflin, William H.

1931 The Stallings Island Mound, Columbia County, Georgia. *Papers of the Peabody Museum of Archaeology and Ethnology*, Harvard University, Cambridge, vol. 14, no. 1, pp. 1-47.

Coe, Michael

1960 Archaeological Linkages with North and South America at La Victoria, Guatemala. *American Anthropologist*, vol. 62, pp. 363-393.

Conzemius, Éduard

1929 Notes on the Mískito and Sumu Languages of Eastern Nicaragua and Honduras. *International Journal of American Linguistics*, 5:57-115.

Crawford, James M.

1978 *The Mobilian Trade Language*. University of Tennessee Press, Knoxville.

1979 Timucua and Yuchi: Two Language Isolates of the Southeast. *The Languages of Native America*, ed. by Lyle Campbell and Marianne Mithun, University of Texas Press, Austin, pp. 327-354.

Deagan, Kathleen A.

1978 Cultures in Transition: Fusion and Assimilation among the Eastern Timucua. *Tacachale*, ed. by Jerald Milanich and Samuel Proctor, University Presses of Florida, Gainesville, pp. 89-119.

1985 The Archaeology of Sixteenth-Century St. Augustine. *Florida Anthropologist* 38:6-33.

1987 *Artifacts of the Spanish Colonies of Florida and the Caribbean, 1500-1800.* Vol. 1: *Ceramics, Glassware, and Beads.* Smithsonian Institution Press, Washington.

Edwards, Clinton R.

1965 Aboriginal Watercraft on the Pacific Coast of South America. *Ibero-America*, 47.

Entwistle, William J.

1942 *The Spanish Language.* Macmillan, New York.

Feldman, Robert A. and **Michael E. Moseley**

1978 The Northern Andes. *Ancient South America*, ed. by Jesse D. Jennings, W. H. Freeman and Company, San Francisco, pp. 139-177.

Ford, James A.

1969 *A Comparison of Formative Cultures in the Americas.* As *Smithsonian Contributions to Anthropology*, vol. 11, Smithsonian Institution Press, Washington.

Gatschet, Albert Samuel

1877*a* The Timucua Language. *Proceedings of the American Philosophical Society*, 16:626-642.

1877*b* Volk und Sprache der Timucua. *Zeitschrift für Ethnologie*, 9:245-260.

1878 The Timucua Language. *Proceedings of the American Philosophical Society*, 17:490-505.

1880 The Timucua Language. *Proceedings of the American Philosophical Society*, 18:465-502.

1881 Volk und Sprache der Timucua. *Zeitschrift für Ethnologie*, 13:189-200.

n.d. Atimoke (Texts, Linguistic and Historical Notes). Ms., 36 pp., United States National Museum, National Anthropological Archives, #2000, Washington.

Gatschet, Albert Samuel and **Raoul de la Grasserie**

1889 Textes en Langue Timucua. *Revue de Linguistique et de Philologie Comparée*, 22:320-346.

BIBLIOGRAPHY

Geiger, Fr. Maynard J. OFM

1937 *The Franciscan Conquest of Florida, 1573-1618.* As *Studies in Hispanic American History*, 1, The Catholic University of America, Washington.

1940 *Biographical Dictionary of the Franciscans in Spanish Florida and Cuba (1528-1841).* As *Franciscan Studies*, 21, Paterson, New Jersey.

Goggin, John M.

1953 An Introductory Outline of Timucua Archeology. Laboratory of Anthropology, University of Florida, Gainesville. Paper presented to the 1952 Southeastern Archeological Conference, Oct. 31-Nov. 1, Macon, Georgia, 16 pp.

Goeje, C.H. de

1930 The Inner Structure of the Warao Language of Guiana. *Journal de la Société des Américanistes de Paris*, n.s., 22:33-72.

Goodman, Morris

1971 The Strange Case of Mbugu. *Pidginization and Creolization of Languages*, ed. by Dell Hymes, Cambridge University Press, London, pp. 243-254.

Granberry, Julian

1956 Timucua I: Prosodics and Phonemics of the Mocama Dialect. *International Journal of American Linguistics*, 22:97-105.

1971 Final Collection of Texts, Vocabulary Lists, Grammar of Timucua (Penrose Fund Grant No. 4633, 1967). *Year Book of the American Philosophical Society*, 1970, Philadelphia, pp. 606-607.

1987 *A Grammar and Dictionary of the Timucua Language* [First Edition]. As *Anthropological Notes* No. 1, Horseshoe Beach, Florida.

1989 *A Grammar and Dictionary of the Timucua Language* [Second Edition]. As *Anthropological Notes, Island Archaeological Museum*, Horseshoe Beach, Florida.

1990 A Grammatical Sketch of Timucua. *International Journal of American Linguistics*, 56:60-101.

BIBLIOGRAPHY

1991 Amazonian Affiliation of the Timucua Language. *Language Change in South American Indian Languages*, ed. by Mary Ritchie Key, University of Pennsylvania Press, Philadelphia, pp. 195-242.

In press Antillean Languages and the Aboriginal Settlement of the Lucayan Islands: A Working Hypothesis. *Proceedings of the Bahamas 1492 Conference*, Freeport, Bahamas, November 1987.

MS*a* An Ethnohistoric Examination of the Timucua Concept of Time.

MS*b* Timucua Verbs.

MS*c* The Timucua Kin System.

MS*d* Timucua and Pano-Tacanan.

MS*e* **Eba** and **fara**: Ethnolinguistic Notes on Timucuan Handedness.

Grasserie, Raoul de la

1888*a* Esquisse d'une Grammaire du Timucua, Langue de la Floride. *Revue de Linguistique et de Philologie Comparée*, 21:209-234, 295-313.

1888*b* Textes Analysées et Vocabulaire de la Langue Timucua, *International Congress of Americanists, Proceedings*, 7:403-437.

1889 Vocabulaire Timucua. *Revue de Linguistique et de Philologie Comparée*, 22:168-183.

1892 *Vocabulaire Timucua.* Imp. Georges Jacob, Orléans.

Greenberg, Joseph H.

1960 The General Classification of Central and South American Languages. *Men and Cultures*, ed. by A. F. C. Wallace, University of Pennsylvania Press, Philadelphia, pp. 791-794.

Greenwell, Dale

1984 The Mississippi Gulf Coast. *Perspectives on Gulf Coast Prehistory*, ed. by Dave D. Davis, University Presses of Florida, Gainesville, pp. 124-155.

Haas, Mary R.

1940 Ablaut and its Function in Muskogee. *Language*, 18:141-150.

1941 The Classification of the Muskogean Languages. *Language, Culture, and Personality*, ed. by Leslie Spier, Menasha, Wisconsin, pp. 41-56.

1945 Dialects of the Muskogee Language. *International Journal of American Linguistics*, 11:69-74.

1946 A Proto-Muskogean Paradigm. *International Journal of American Linguistics*, 12:326-332.

1947 Development of Proto-Muskogean $*k^w$. *International Journal of American Linguistics*, 13:135-137.

1948 Classificatory Verbs in Muskogee. *International Journal of American Linguistics*, 14:244-246.

1949 The Position of Apalachee in the Muskogean Family. *International Journal of American Linguistics*, 15:121-127.

1950 On the Historical Development of Certain Long Vowels in Creek. *International Journal of American Linguistics*, 16:122-125.

1956 Natchez and the Muskogean Languages. *Language*, 32:61-72.

1960 Some Genetic Affiliations of Algonkin. *Culture in History*, Columbia University Press, New York, pp. 977-992.

1975 What is Mobilian? *Studies in Southeastern Indian Languages*, ed. by James M. Crawford, University of Georgia Press, Athens, pp. 257-261.

Hockett, Charles F.

1947 Problems of Morphemic Analysis. *Language*, 23:321-343 (reprinted 1957, *Readings in Linguistics*, ed. by Martin Joos, American Council of Learned Societies, pp. 229-242).

1958 *A Course in Modern Linguistics*. Macmillan, New York.

1961 Linguistic Elements and Their Relations. *Language*, 37:29-53.

Holmer, Nils Magnus

1946 Outline of Cuna Grammar. *International Journal of American Linguistics*, 12:185-197.

BIBLIOGRAPHY

Key, Mary Ritchie

1968 *Comparative Tacanan Phonology, with Cavineña Phonology and Notes on Pano-Tacanan Relationship.* Mouton, The Hague.

Kimball, Geoffrey

1987 A Grammatical Sketch of Apalachee. *International Journal of American Linguistics*, 53:136-174.

1988 An Apalachee Vocabulary. *International Journal of American Linguistics*, 54:387-398.

Lamb, Sydney

1966 *Outline of Stratificational Grammar.* Georgetown University Press, Washington.

Larson, Lewis H., Jr. SJ

1978 Historic Guale Indians of the Georgia Coast and the Impact of the Spanish Mission Effort. *Tacachale*, ed. by Jerald Milanich and Samuel Proctor, University Presses of Florida, Gainesville, pp. 120-140.

Lathrap, Donald W.

1970 *The Upper Amazon.* Praeger, New York.

1973 The Antiquity and Importance of Long-Distance Trade Relationships in the Moist Tropics of Pre-Columbian South America. *World Archaeology*, 5:170-186.

Lathrap, Donald W., Donald Collier, and **Helen Chandra**

1975 *Ancient Ecuador: Culture, Clay and Creativity 3000-300 B.C.* Field Museum of Natural History, Chicago.

Le Moyne, Jacques

1875 *Narrative of Le Moyne, an Artist Who Accompanied the French Expedition to Florida under Laudonnière, 1564.* Trans. from the Latin of De Bry. Osgood Company, Boston.

Loewen, Jacob A.

1963 Chocó II: Phonological Problems. *International Journal of American Linguistics*, 29:357-371.

Lorant, Stefan, ed.

1946 *The New World.* Duell, Sloan, and Pearce, New York.

BIBLIOGRAPHY

Loukotka, Čestmír

1968 *Classification of South American Indian Languages.* Ed. by Johannes Wilbert. *Latin American Center Reference Series*, vol. 7, University of California, Los Angeles.

Matteson, Esther

1972 Proto-Arawakan. *Comparative Studies in Amerindian Languages*, ed. by Esther Matteson, Alva Wheeler, Frances L. Jackson, Nathan Waltz, and Diana R. Christian, Mouton, The Hague, pp. 160-185.

McCorkle, Thomas

1981 The History of the Guayquerí: An Approach to the Anthropology of Northeastern Venezuela. *Kroeber Anthropological Society, Papers*, 6:60-87.

Meggers, Betty and **Clifford Evans**

1978 Lowland South America and the Antilles. *Ancient South America*, ed. by Jesse D. Jennings, W. H. Freeman and Company, San Francisco, pp. 287-335.

Migliazza, Ernest C.

1978 Some Evidences for Panoan-Yanomama Genetic Relationship. Paper presented at the Linguistic Society of America Summer Meeting, Urbana.

1985 Languages of the Orinoco-Amazon Region. *South American Indian Languages: Retrospect and Prospect*, ed. by Harriet W. Manelis Klein and Louisa R. Stark, University of Texas Press, Austin, pp. 17-139.

Milanich, Jerald T.

1971 *The Alachua Tradition of North-Central Florida.* As *Contributions of the Florida State Museum, Anthropology and History*, No. 17, Gainesville.

1973 The Southeastern Deptford Culture: A Preliminary Definition. Bureau of Historic Sites and Properties, *Bulletin No. 3*, Florida Department of State, Tallahassee, pp. 51-63.

1976 Georgia Origins of the Alachua Tradition. Bureau of Historic Sites and Properties, *Bulletin No. 5*, Florida

Department of State, Tallahassee, pp. 47-56.
1978 The Western Timucua: Patterns of Acculturation and Change. *Tacachale*, ed. by Jerald Milanich and Samuel Proctor, University Presses of Florida, Gainesville, pp. 59-88.

Milanich, Jerald T. and **Charles H. Fairbanks**
1980 *Florida Archaeology*. Academic Press, New York.

Milanich, Jerald T. and **William C. Sturtevant**
1972 *Francisco Pareja's 1613* Confessionario*: A Documentary Source for Timucuan Ethnography*. Division of Archives, History, and Records Management, Florida Department of State, Tallahassee.

Miller, James J.
1992 Effects of Environmental Change on Late Archaic People of Northeast Florida. *Florida Anthropologist*, 45:100-106.

Movilla, Fray Gregorio de
1635*a* *Forma Breve de administrar los Sacramentos a los Indios, y Españoles que viuen entre ellos*. Impresso en Mexico, Por Iuan Ruyz.
1635*b* *Explicacion de la Doctrina qve compvso el cardenal Belarmino, por mandado del Señor Papa Clemente 8. Tradvcida en Lengva Floridana: por el Padre Fr. Gregorio de Mouilla*. En Mexico. Impressa con Licencia en la Imprenta de Iuan Ruyz.

Newkumet, Phil J.
1940 Preliminary Report on Excavation of the Williams Mound, Leflore County, Oklahoma. *Oklahoma State Archaeological Society*, vol. 3, no. 2, pp. 1-9.

Noble, G. Kingsley
1965*a* *Proto-Arawakan and its Descendants*. As *International Journal of American Linguistics*, vol 3, no. 3, part II (also *Publication 38*, Indiana Research Center in Anthropology, Folklore and Linguistics, Bloomington).
1965*b* On the Genetic Affiliations of Timucua, An

Indigenous Language of Florida. *Journal de la Société des Américanistes de Paris*, 54(2):359-376.

Oré, Fr. Luis Gerónimo de OFM

1616 *The Martyrs of Florida (1513-1616)*. Trans. and ed. by Fr. Maynard Geiger OFM, *Franciscan Studies*, 18, Paterson, New Jersey, 1936.

Osborn, Henry

1967*a* Warao I: Phonology and Morphophonemics. *International Journal of American Linguistics*, 32:108-123.

1967*b* Warao II: Nouns, Relationals, and Demonstratives. *International Journal of American Linguistics*, 32:253-261.

1968 Warao III: Verbs and Suffixes. *International Journal of American Linguistics*, 33:46-64.

Pareja, Fray Francisco OFM

1612*a* *Cathecismo, en Lengua Castellana, y Timuquana.* En Mexico. En la Imprenta de la Viuda de Pedro Balli. Por C. Adriano Cesar.

1612*b* *Catechismo y Breve Exposicion de la Doctrina Christiana, Muy vtil y necessaria, asi para los Españoles, como para los Naturales, en Lengua Castellana, y Timuquana.* Con Licencia de los Svperiores, en Mexico, en casa de la viuda de Pedro Balli. Año de 1612. Por C. A. Cesar.

1613 *Confessionario En lengua Castellana, y Timuquana Con algunos consejos para animar al penitente.* Impresso con licencia en Mexico, en la Emprenta de la Viuda de Diego Lopez Daualos.

1614 *Arte y pronunciacion en Lengva Timvquana, y Castellana.* Impresso Con licencia en Meico. En la Emprenta de Ioan Ruyz. [Reprinted, 1886, by Adam and Vinson, which see].

1627 *Cathecismo, y Examen Para Los Que Comvlgan, En lengua Castellana, y Timuquana.* Con Privilegio En Mexico, en la Imprenta de Iuan Ruyz.

BIBLIOGRAPHY

Payne, David

1987 Some Morphological Elements of Maipuran Arawakan: Agreement Affixes and the Genitive Construction. *Languages Sciences*, 9:57-75.

1990 Some Widespread Grammatical Forms in South American Languages. *Amazonian Linguistics: Studies in Lowland South American Languages*, ed. by Doris L. Payne, University of Texas Press, Austin, pp. 75-87.

Phelps, Davis D.

1965 The Norwood Series of Fiber-Tempered Ceramics. *Southeastern Archaeological Conference Bulletin*, 2:65-69.

Prost, Gilbert R.

1962 Signaling of Transitive and Intransitive in Chacobo (Pano). *International Journal of American Linguistics*, 28:108-118.

Robertson, James Alexander, ed.

1933 *True Relation of the Hardships Suffered by Governor Fernando de Soto and Certain Portuguese Gentlemen During the Discovery of the Province of Florida, Now Newly Set Forth by a Gentleman of Elvas.* Trans. and ed. by James A. Robertson., 2 vols. Florida State Historical Society, Deland.

Rodrigues, Aryon dall'Igna

1985 Evidence for Tupí-Carib Relationships. *South American Indian Languages: Retrospect and Prospect*, ed. by Harriet Manelis Klein and Louisa R. Stark, University of Texas Press, Austin, pp. 371-404.

Roth, Walter E.

1924 An Introductory Study of the Arts, Crafts, and Customs of the Guiana Indians. *Thirty-Eighth Annual Report of the Bureau of American Ethnology, 1916-17*, Washington, pp. 26-745.

Rouse, Irving

1986 *Migrations in Prehistory: Inferring Population Movement from Cultural Remains.* Yale University

Press, New Haven.

Russo, Michael

1992 Chronologies and Cultures of the St. Marys Region of Northeast Florida and Southeast Georgia. *Florida Anthropologist*, 45:107-126.

Salomon, Frank

1977/78 Pochteca and Mindala: A Comparison of Long-Distance Traders in Ecuador and Mesoamerica. *Journal of the Steward Anthropological Society*, vol. 9, no. 1-2, pp. 231-246.

Schomburgk, Moritz Richard

1847 *Reisen in Britisch-Guiana in den Jahren 1840-44.* 3 vols. Verlagsbuchhandlung von J. J. Weber, Leipzig.

Sears, William H.

1964 The Southeastern United States. *Prehistoric Man in the New World*, ed. by Jesse D. Jennings and Edward Norbeck, University of Chicago Press, Chicago, pp. 259-287.

Shannon, George W., Jr.

1986 The Southeastern Fiber-Tempered Ceramic Tradition Reconsidered. *Ceramic Notes 3*, ed. by Prudence M. Rice, *Occasional Publications of the Ceramic Technology Laboratory*, Florida State Museum, Gainesville, pp. 47-79.

Smith, Buckingham

1858 The Timuquana Language. New York Historical Society, *The Historical Magazine*, 2(1):1-3.

1860*a* *Dos Cartas en Lengua Apalachino y Timuguana* [*sic*]. Privately printed (50 copies) by Buckingham Smith, New York.

1860*b* Books Printed in the Timuquana Language. New York Historical Society, *The Historical Magazine*, 4(2):39-40.

1860*c* Notes and Queries. New York Historical Society, *The Historical Magazine*, 4(8):180-181.

BIBLIOGRAPHY

Smith, Henry Lee, Jr.

1967 The Concept of the Morphophone. *Language*, 43:306-341.

Sorensen, Arthur P., Jr.

1967 Multilingualism in the Northwest Amazon. *American Anthropologist*, 69:670-684.

1985 An Emerging Tukanoan Linguistic Regionality: Policy Pressures. *South American Indian Languages*, ed. by Hariet Manelis Klein and Louisa R. Stark, University of Texas Press, Austin, pp. 140-156.

Spaulding, Robert K.

1948 *How Spanish Grew*. University of California Press, Berkeley.

Stimmel, Carole, Robert B. Heimann, and **R. G. V. Hancock**

1982 Indian Pottery from the Mississippi Valley: Coping with Bad Raw Materials. *Archaeological Ceramics*, ed. by Jacqueline S. Olin and Alan D. Franklin, Smithsonian Institution Press, Washington, pp. 219-228.

Swadesh, Morris

1964 Linguistic Overview. *Prehistoric Man in the New World*, ed. by Jesse D. Jennings and Edward Norbeck, University of Chicago Press, Chicago, pp. 527-556.

Swanton, John R.

1929 The Tawasa Language. *American Anthropologist*, 31:435-453.

1946 *The Indians of the Southeastern United States*. Bureau of American Ethnology, *Bulletin No. 137*, Washington.

n.d. *A Sketch of the Timucua Language*. Ms., 35 pp., United States National Museum, National Anthropological Archives, #2446g, Washington.

Taylor, Douglas M.

1977 *Languages of the West Indies*. The Johns Hopkins University Press, Baltimore.

BIBLIOGRAPHY

Taylor, Douglas M. and **Berendt Hoff**

1966 *Proto-Arawakan and its Descendants*, by G. Kingsley Noble: A Review. *International Journal of American Linguistics*, 32:303-308.

Trager, George L.

1963 *Linguistics is Linguistics*. As *Studies in Linguistics, Occasional Papers 10*, Buffalo.

Vinson, Julien

1883 Sur la Langue Timucua. *International Congress of Americanists, Proceedings*, 5:362-365.

Wallace, Alfred Russel

1889 *A Narrative of Travels on the Amazon and Rio Negro*. 2nd edition. Ward, Lock & Company, London.

Waltz, Nathan E. and **Alva Wheeler**

1972 Proto Tucanoan. *Comparative Studies in Amerindian Languages*, ed. by Esther Matteson, Alva Wheeler, Frances L. Jackson, Nathan Waltz, and Diana R. Christian, Mouton, The Hague, pp. 119-149.

Waring, Antonio J., Jr.

1968 Fiber-Tempered Pottery and its Cultural Affiliations on the Georgia-Carolina Coast. Originally published 1952. *Waring Papers: The Collected Works of Antonio J. Waring, Jr.*, ed. by Stephen Williams, *Papers of the Peabody Museum of Archaeology and Ethnology 58*, Harvard University, Cambridge, pp. 253-255.

Weisman, Brent R.

1992 *Excavations on the Franciscan Frontier: Archaeology at the Fig Springs Mission*. University Presses of Florida, Gainesville.

Wheeler, Alva

1972 Proto Chibchan. *Comparative Studies in Amerindian Languages*, ed. by Esther Matteson, Alva Wheeler, Frances L. Jackson, Nathan Waltz, and Diana R. Christian, Mouton, The Hague, pp. 93-108.

Wilbert, Johannes

1957 Prólogo. *Diccionario Guarao-Español, Español-*